Common Decency

Common Decency
Domestic Policies after Reagan

ALVIN L. SCHORR

with a contribution by James P. Comer

YALE UNIVERSITY PRESS
New Haven and London

Designed by Susan P. Fillion and set in
Baskerville type by Huron Valley Graphics, Inc.
Printed in the United States of America by
Vail-Ballou Press, Binghamton, N.Y.

Library of Congress Cataloging-in-Publication Data

Schorr, Alvin Louis, 1921–
    Common decency.

    Includes bibliographic references and index.
    1. United States—Social policy. I. Comer, James P.
II. Title.
HN65.S419 1986   361.6'1'0973 86–1615
ISBN 0–300–03603–5 (alk. paper)

*The paper in this book meets the guidelines for
permanence and durability of the Committee on
Production Guidelines for Book Longevity of the
Council on Library Resources.*

10   9   8   7   6   5   4   3   2   1

I grew up in a time and in circumstances that presented many practical difficulties and, much later, came to realize that I had moved among people who were naturally inclined to be helpful to anyone with whom they dealt.

One of these was a teacher of high school French, a subject in which I was not especially interested and far from proficient. She decided that I was not dressing properly for school and, after the briefest inquiry, that perhaps this was because I could not afford good clothing. After class one day she asked me to measure my trouser length, and some days later presented me with a pair of trousers and a mini-lecture on how to care for them. It seemed that her husband was a clothing manufacturer. I was embarrassed and bemused and she figured for a while in my adolescent fantasies.

Another was a dean of men at college who called me in to ask why, if I was majoring in English, I had registered for electives in psychology only. Interpreting this as another of life's bureaucratic hurdles, I produced a creative answer. He put a couple of questions to me about my goals and let me go. When nothing further happened, I understood that he thought I must be confused and wanted to start me thinking—nothing more.

This book is dedicated to these two and to the scores of other people, it seems to me now, who, casually and more than casually and without apparent self-interest, seemed by nature inclined to help me and, no doubt, others like me. Some were members of my family, many others not. They established for me an early faith in the innate decency of adults—in a climate that allows decency unfettered expression.

The French teacher was, or is, Grace Schaaf.
The dean of men was Morton Gottschall.

Contents

Acknowledgments

In preparing this book, I have had patient and thoughtful help from a number of experts. They have posed important queries and commented on drafts of chapters. Of course, none is responsible for errors that remain or for conclusions. With respect to the first two chapters, I wish to thank Mitchell I. Ginsberg and Robin Huws Jones; with respect to chapters 3 and 4, Robert M. Ball, Raymond Munts, and Bruno Stein; and with particular regard to the tax credit proposal, George Cooper and Deborah H. Schenk. I was first introduced to the idea of a "vanishing tax credit" by George Zeitlin. With respect to the chapter on housing, I want to thank Sol Ackerman, William G. Grigsby, Eric Hoddersen, Dennis Keating, Norman Krumholz, Henry B. Schechter, and Wendy Lauren Schorr; with respect to the chapter on education, Kenneth B. Clark, Gary Orfield, and William L. Taylor; and with respect to the chapter on health, Rashi Fein, Duncan Neuhauser, Arthur Newman, Jessica Lee Schorr Saxe, Lisbeth Bamberger Schorr, Samuel Whitman, and Allan Young.

Generous and painstaking secretarial help was provided by the late Josette Andrikanich and Theresa Brown. For sheer convenience, courtesy, and richness of collection, taken together, the Cleveland Public Library may be the best I have ever used.

I should acknowledge my debt to the family and other donors who established the Leonard W. Mayo Chair at the School of Applied Social Sciences, Case Western Reserve University. It provided essential time to pursue this work. Initial ideas were developed during one summer month at a legendary Rockefeller Foundation conference center.

A careful reader of these credits will detect that members of my family are expert in a number of the policy areas covered and lent their help. I should mention also my wife, Ann, my son, Kenneth, and my brother Daniel, whose advice and support were more general but unfailing. And I thank friends, in Cleveland especially, whose regular inquiries about progress sharpened my guilt at taking so long even as they assured me of at least a small circle of interest in the eventual product.

Introduction

Following an attempt by young offenders to escape detention in Paris some years ago, Jacques Prévert wrote a song:

Bandits, riff-raff, thieves, and scoundrels!
The pack that hunts down children
Is composed of decent people.

It is a paradox, perhaps most striking in our time, that citizens who are good neighbors and give time to charitable activities (seven billion hours a year in the United States) can also, in concert, behave brutally.

It appears that private and public behavior are separable in our minds. A possibly apocryphal story relates that President Ronald Reagan left a meeting about the national budget to be photographed for an Easter Seals poster. He was moved by the problem of the crippled child who joined him and said afterward that he would have done anything to help her. "Mr. President," someone remarked, "you have just cut from the budget $350 million for children like her." Again, as a one-time administrator of social services, I was often struck by how much more sympathy one feels for fellow employees whom one sees every day than for the clients or patients it is one's job to help. On occasion, I found it necessary to chide or dismiss someone who was not helpful in the way that was intended, earning resentment not only from the person involved but from others who thought the action hard (and no gratitude from clients, for how were they to know what they had been spared?).

So it is that we measure decency by our immediate experience and activity but often lack the imagination to project it into policies or administration—where decency or its absence has wider effect. That, in plain language, is the subject of this book: what decency requires of us outside the circle of our family and friends. Politicians, professionals, and technicians call this "policy." The circumstances of modern society, in which policy affects us as deeply as the good will of those who are nearby, require a more comprehensive view than is reflected in the words of William Blake: "He who would do good to another must do it in minute particulars; general good is the plea of the scoundrel, hypocrite, and flatterer." To be sure, the only reality of general good lies in minute particulars, but the person who rests solely on the good she does at first hand is ignorant, if not worse.

The post-World War II government policies that have been developed to do general good have come to be known as the welfare state. In recent years, these policies have been considerably reshaped. Here, my examination of decent policies starts from the basic structure of the welfare state, much of which remains in place, and attempts to think forward from it. Therefore, from time to time I refer to the kind of relationship between government and citizens at which this book aims as the "new" welfare state. Some of the ideas will be judged to be old and others new, but it is intended that their coherence should be new and instructive.

For some years now, I have taught university graduate students. Almost invariably, I ask them to examine their underlying objectives in attending social work school. They want to help their clients, they want to earn a living, and they want appropriate professional status; all this one takes for granted. But what do they seek for their community or country in seeking to help their clients in the particular way they have chosen? This turns out to be a difficult question, and some students never answer it for themselves. It is my contention that professionals who do not have a firm grasp on their own underlying objectives get lost in the maze of compromise that life and work require of anyone. They do not know how to distinguish a compromise that advances the interest of their clients from one that sells them out. They come to feel defeated or they become cynical; they burn out. So too for a society that does not understand its objectives or make them operational.

This book therefore begins with the objectives that decent people would pursue. We seek a social policy which, like functional architecture, shapes programs to reflect central purposes. One has only to look at the structure to know what is taking place inside. The second chapter names and makes an argument for five social objectives—fair shares, mainstreaming in program development, a drive toward full employment, selective decentralization of authority, and, with respect to color or ethnicity, integration. Some of these objectives have been closely examined by scholars—fair shares by philosophers like John Rawls and Michael Walzer, for example. Except as regards the handicapped, where the term has special meaning, mainstreaming has been little attended to. In any event, the heart of this book lies in tracking these objectives to the manner in which they would shape social security, welfare, and selected aspects of tax policy, and housing policy, health policy, and public education. The chapter on education was prepared by Dr. James P. Comer, an expert on the subject.

Naturally, I would be happy if readers were persuaded that the recommendations made here are sound. Even if not, however, I have worked at framing the issues in a way that makes it possible to examine alternative approaches to these social objectives and indeed to stage a reasonable discussion of the merits of the objectives themselves.

Economic questions may appear to be slighted. That is at least in part deliberate. In the past few years economics has so predominated in public discussion that the implication is that objectives such as civility, a sense of community, and minimizing physical and mental ill health must await "reindustrialization" or a steady rate of economic growth. Is that what we think? Conversely, do we believe that an increasingly wealthy society will automatically achieve such objectives? That is not our experience.

A healthy economy is the foundation of social policy. There is no question about that, but we need to agree on our social objectives and examine the course that will attain them. Some options in social policy are not central to economic objectives, one way or another. Moreover, we may conclude that achieving reduction in inter-group tensions, for example, is worth some trade-off in economic advancement. To understand the options and the trade-offs, however, one has to look at them bare.

Government programs are subject to change, rarely more so than recently; therefore the figures about government outlay or affected numbers of people available at this writing (1984–85) may quickly alter. However, the figures are used here not for accounting purposes but to indicate magnitudes and to illustrate a way of viewing programs. The welfare state—old or new, decent or not—is dynamic. It is not the program solution of the moment that counts in the long run but the principles it reflects and the direction of development. Still, the chapters that follow offer proposals with considerable specificity. For those who think them sound, they are a progam for the immediate future.

1

Struggle and Transition

We Americans are short-sighted and have short memories. We do not weigh the trouble that lies beyond our house and neighborhood. If last year's trouble appears to be fading, we do not think about it. We are not by any means free of anxiety, but we practice denial. Unemployment is a problem of other people, who are recognizable by their poor education or their skin color. Homelessness is an alien problem, afflicting sick people, vagrants, addicts. Denial or, more familiarly, optimism is a well-established characteristic of Americans. However, in recent years the test of the nation's welfare has been narrowing to one's self and one's immediate circle. Next to the discovery of sex and the invention of money, the Reagan administration will rank high in history as a force in the promotion of selfishness.

Still, a public anxiety that cannot be quelled generates such a phrase as "the new poor." What is the meaning of this interest in the new poor? Is it better to be "old poor"? We identify the new poor because they dramatize the truth that few of us are secure—a truth driven home in 1982 and 1983, when one family in three experienced involuntary unemployment. It was like a mugging on one's block. Of the current generation of children, one third will have been poor before they turn eighteen. All around us are social indicators of a disordered society—abuse of one family member by another, a high crime rate, apathetic minority groups that seem to have deserted public arenas. Something has gone wrong with our communal arrangements, but we do not connect a selfish society with a disordered society. We work at putting it out of mind; when we cannot, we call for a mandatory death sentence or more policeman on the streets and distract ourselves with the ensuing argument.

This uneasy self-interest, this anxious optimism are psychological background for sweeping changes in American social arrangements which, although under way for a decade or more, took clear shape in the 1980s. For years we had a growing government commitment to assure the basic needs of average Americans and of the disadvantaged. Distance in time from the circumstances that nourished that commitment—the Great Depression, World War II, the civil rights movement—and powerful social and economic forces have led to change. In this chapter, I name some of those forces.

Sources of Difficulty

One source of our difficulty lies deep in our ethos, which rotates around "liberty and the pursuit of happiness." By way of contrast, France's "equality and fraternity" are absent from our holiday rituals. Reflecting our founders' preoccupation with casting off tyranny, the United States Constitution assures its citizens little except freedom from interference (no small matter, to be sure). Ours is a libertarian constitution. The structure of the welfare state has had to be constructed, decade by decade, in judicial applications of eighteenth-century guarantees to twentieth-century industrial and urban reality. By contrast again, the French constitution says explicitly that whoever is in need, for physical, mental, or economic reasons, "has the right to obtain from the community the proper means of existence." The distinction that a commitment to fraternity creates in social institutions, not to say in civic attitudes, is profound.

Proceeding from what Americans would call a commitment to community, European countries have created a system of social insurance that embraces entire populations—all the aged, all the children, and so forth. They attempt to meet the needs of those who may be poor without asking them to perceive themselves as poor. Alone among Western industrial countries, the United States has a vast set of programs specifically for poor people—food stamps, Aid to Families with Dependent Children (AFDC), Supplemental Security Income (SSI), Medicaid. These programs are called "exceptionalist" by technicians because they deal with people defined as exceptions. Generally, they provide inadequate levels of benefits, operate in an atmosphere of public hostility, and are vulnerable to budget and other pressures.

This is not by any means to say that other Western countries do not have difficulty in realizing community—such difficulty is now epidemic—but only that the problem goes very deep for us. Our search for community is overlaid on the pursuit of happiness; under stress, it is subject to being shed. The problem can be detected in our Constitution and is a traceable thread in our institutions, as the broad use of exceptionalist programming illustrates. Very likely, irrepressible anxiety about status, a dynamic that has made us rich, is linked to rejection of too deep a brotherhood.

A more immediate source of changes in our welfare state lies in our "unsteady-state" economy. It has lately been argued that the success of Keynesian economics in the twenty-five or thirty years after World War II was a piece of luck. (Had we but known that we were lucky!) Markets for Western industry were vast. Government spending had years in which to expand without economic risk; only future generations would count the cost. As the birth rate had been low, for a time relatively few young people entered the labor force. High production and employment could be pursued without stimulating undue inflation. Regulatory mechanisms set in place during the Depression would deal with the transient economic problems that might arise.

That scene was not to survive. The countries that the United States was helping to renew, notably Germany and

Japan, revived very vigorously indeed. Our painful and expensive investment in Vietnam, though it moderated an incipient problem of unemployment, produced the first really alarming post-World War II inflation. Then, abruptly, higher oil prices were felt around the world, causing the American rate of inflation to soar and intensifying international competition. Poor management and poor labor productivity put American industry at a disadvantage in competing with other industrial countries. Inflation pushed up interest rates, making money for investment scarce precisely when it became obvious how badly it was needed.

It has become evident that our economy is troubled in fundamental ways. Poor management and poor productivity are not corrected by either government spending or restraint. Large sectors of industry appear to be obsolescent, nor is the issue simply how to secure investment and modernization. Shifts of technology and access to foreign labor forces may have moved some jobs abroad permanently. A changing occupational structure requires new qualifications in workers, and the grounding of skills may have to have been laid down in college or earlier. This is an anguishing personal problem for many who are sixty or fifty or even forty years old. The country staged a spectacular economic recovery in 1984, but the unemployment rate at its lowest point was still 7.2 percent, and widespread poverty persisted. An overwhelming budget deficit and a deficit in the balance of payments left planners anxious about the future of interest rates and the vulnerability of the American economy to foreign investment decisions. Some economists predicted another recession in about a year; others thought it would come later. However, its possibility or prospect is an ever-present reality.

This is all to say that the postwar welfare state, relying on a steady growth in wealth (and government revenue), and guided by Keynesian theory, was fated to end. The civil rights and anti-poverty struggles of the 1960s were carried on in the assumption that this wealthy country had enough for everyone. President Lyndon Johnson's call for equality "as a fact and a result" (not just a right and a theory)[1] faded quickly from public discourse (and from his own). At one time the economy could be counted on to produce more year by year, so people did not need to dwell upon whether the sum was divided fairly. This is no longer so. Indeed, real wages and salaries have been declining for a long time. (See chapter 4 for a discussion of the erosion of the family wage.) Viewed in terms of inequality over the past twenty years, only dramatically rising income transfers (Social Security, unemployment compensation, welfare) maintained a degree of stability in the distribution of income. Money earned in the free market—wages and salaries, interest, profits—was more unequally distributed and the tax system became less progressive; only income transfers tended to correct for an increase in inequality. Taking it all together, "the distribution of income *after* taxes and transfers was more unequal in 1985 than in 1966."[2] Even with recovery, in 1984 many families were living with lower incomes and expectations, and we saw, for example, the unprecedented development of two-worker families living in public shelters because they could not find affordable housing.

In 1977 Fred Hirsch, an American economist, published the prediction that class conflict would intensify, arriving at it by another chain of reasoning with a broader time perspective.[3] In barest outline, he argued that probably for the first time in history, because of industrialization, productive capacity could meet all needs that are basically required for survival or are private—needs like food and covering for the body, which may be satisfied without reference to what others have or value. Because that was new and represented progress, the question of shares, or relationship to what others had, temporarily faded from the view of the least privileged. It had truly been as Adam Smith said: The pursuit of private interest served the common good.

(It is curious now to reflect that, all the time that ideological battles were fought over welfare statism, we continued to operate broadly on free market principles. Criticism of the growth of government and overregulation could by no means be escaped, but fundamentally the search for private profit determined what was produced and consumed and how it was distributed.)

What became of that lovely passage in Western history? Now, Hirsch argued, we are largely concerned with needs created for us by others and satisfactions that are dependent on their relationship to what others have. The blacks who rioted in the Los Angeles ghetto in 1965 lived in housing that would have been regarded as adequate in many places in the United States, not to mention Latin America and Asia. It was not absolute deprivation that aroused them so much as how inferior their situation was to what they saw on their television screens. Apart from this, it becomes evident that democratized use may adulterate a service or product. This is a phenomenon that all but the comparatively young have experienced, in television programming, air travel, medical care. A service for the privileged becomes degraded by the changes in standards and bureaucratic processes that are applied when many can afford it. So one secures more income only to find that it does not buy "the good life." One feels one is running only to stay in place.

The paradox that increased productive capacity heightened the sense that there was not enough, Hirsch wrote, exposed the "distributional compulsion."[4] That is, when a society produces enough to meet survival needs, the struggle is more openly over shares.

In short, ours is a society more deeply devoted to individual freedom than to community. The problems that this preference casts up promise to be exacerbated as the distributional compulsion comes to the fore. Indeed, over the past two decades the relatively well-to-do have been getting an increasing share of all income from earnings and have been giving up a smaller share of taxes. This development went relatively unnoticed while attention focused on the rising cost of income transfers. In the past years, as they have felt the pain of living standards that were not rising and for many were falling, moderate- and middle-income people have supported cutbacks of income transfers in an effort to relieve the pressure on their own budgets. Cutting back unmasks the underlying inequities, and one might think that it adds to the likelihood that Hirsch's prediction of rising class conflict will be realized. However, the United States is perceived as a classless society and open conflict is absent at times when one most would expect it—in 1982 and 1983, for example. On the other hand, it sometimes flares up unexpectedly. But, with or without conflict, inequity is growing and it eats into our sense of community.

Instruments of Community

Simultaneously, there is a feeling of chaos in public arrangements. Rather different but psychologically reinforcing trends have come together. Rapid inflation is profoundly unsettling, altering the relationship of earnings and savings to expectations that people have thought were securely rooted. Rapid inflation was a temporary phenomenon, fortunately, but it has left its mark on attitudes. More material is a shift in occupational structures and in regional economies which, in turn, lead to relocation in search of work. Ours has always been a mobile culture, of course, but the feeling of moving toward opportunity is different from the feeling of being driven. Shifting family patterns—two-earner families, single-parent families, divorce and remarriage, companionate living together—are too well known to be dwelt upon here.

Liberationist developments may themselves have contributed to a feeling of dislocation. The affluence of the 1950s and 1960s freed people in a thousand ways. It provided space and time for political action and for a self-conscious search for identity. It provided money to support more than one household per family and so permitted or encouraged divorce. The desire for opportunity and freedom flowered—among blacks and Hispanics, among women, among poor people, among workers who perform the most menial tasks, among youth, among the handicapped, and so on.

With a few exceptions, these developments were not experienced as exhilarating, not by all those who might have felt themselves freed and certainly not by those who viewed one or another of these movements as hostile. It is well understood that all situations of rapid social change—sudden prosperity as well as sudden recession—tend to induce anomie.

All these rapidly moving changes in place and relationship

create a sense of loss of personal control and overlap with the reality of external or environmental disorder and the consequent multiplication of external controls. It may be simplest to introduce a point about this with an example. The *New York Times* uses tons of newsprint every day, which once came into New York on a spur of the Penn Central Railroad. Ultimately, in an effort to eliminate activities that were losing money, the railroad closed the spur. After that, the newsprint was trucked to the *Times* plant off Times Square, tearing up streets that had not been built for such a load. This externality, as economists call it, never entered the minds or calculations of Penn Central. Driving or crossing these streets, New Yorkers mutter about the city administration, or the work habits of maintenance employees, or the failure of New Yorkers to care. But this powerful cause of torn-up streets lies outside the reach of any of them. Like other problems we live with, this one has its source in disconnected decisions, many of them privately made, that we do not even identify. In the end, we impose constraints on individuals in a series of detailed measures because we failed to constrain our businesses and governmental units in the first place.

By 1980 the American public had turned against government controls. In doing so, they failed to distinguish between controls on individuals, which seemed increasingly onerous, and controls on major public and private activities and policies, which were often invisible. This is not an accidental oversight. In fact, we lack powerful instruments for expressing and effecting common purposes. Those we have are chiefly governmental; even they are frequently undermined and diluted. The most useful controls would be those of forward planning—consensus arrangements among industry, labor, and government; physical and development plans for cities and regions; a widely understood philosophy about what the government does; guidance and controls where the original decisions that produce externalities are made. An irony of Reagan administration-directed rebellion against controls is this: in giving even more freedom to those forces that are unseen and at variance with common or communal purpose, we add to chaos and the sense of impotence and so to the eventual multiplication of all controls—most painfully, controls upon individuals.

One reason that we lack instruments of common purpose may be that our political process demands extensive accommodation. The electoral process for the highest offices encourages blurring of what candidates intend. Ronald Reagan's attempt to do many of the things that he had advertised he would do was an astonishing feature of his first administration. *Campaign promise* is a term that everyone understands to mean "perishable." Particularly as their offices become the stage for the next campaign, office holders too state purposes in broad and ambiguous terms. The emphasis in legislation and programs shifts from year to year, if not from month to month, because of the shifting influence of competing interests. It is not unknown to find interest groups that seek greatly reduced and greatly increased spending, for example, engaged in supporting the same program. Each expects its interests to prevail when a bill is enacted. President Nixon's proposed welfare reform is an illustration. Administrative agencies, staffed over a different time period and in a different manner from elected offices, and which may also represent constituencies, apply their own judgments to implementation of law. In the end, ongoing programs reflect varied and even contradictory purposes.

This confused-sounding process may be unavoidable and even desirable for getting things done and for preserving stability in a diverse society. However, it does not facilitate common understanding of long-term, widely held objectives; nor does it facilitate the development of coherent programs. The increments of policy development on which much of our process depends do not move in a straight line. Rather, the policies that are implemented often appear to be vectors of opposing and unrelated forces, arriving where *no one* is pleased to see them arrive.

In order to have instruments of common purpose, we need to crystallize common purposes. The instruments would help to shape those underlying forces which give us so much trouble because they are out of communal sight and control; and the very understanding of common purposes would help to shape what the government itself does.

The Transitional Administration

The Reagan presidency marked a sharp change in the American view of the welfare state. It would be overly simple to suppose that the Reagan conception of limited government was new. In fact, public spending on social welfare had been leveling off since 1975, as rising citizen resistance was translated into government practice. In a sense, Reagan was chosen because he represented the electorate's conviction that government was too costly, too intrusive, and ineffective. Still, the first Reagan budget represented a breathtaking change—cutting the rate of growth of expenditures on income maintenance by half, for example. In 1981 demographic changes and a rising unemployment rate were unavoidably producing entitled beneficiaries; otherwise, even more dramatic spending reduction would have been demonstrated.

Much is, and is likely to remain, unsettled about what Americans intended in our welfare state. Textbooks discuss the term more often than they define it. It seems clear that it included, first, the sense that citizens are assured a measure of security "from the cradle to the grave;"* second, federal activism with respect to major social problems and vis-à-vis states and localities; and, third, a willingness to see government expenditures grow—especially as affluence appeared to increase revenue without undue pain. Three themes of the Reagan administration that represented changes in this view have been summarized as follows:

• A commitment to the idea that the public sector should be smaller and less intrusive, and that the private sector should be strengthened and made more influential.

*A term that both Franklin Roosevelt and Lord Beveridge have been credited with originating. See Frances Perkins, *The Roosevelt I Knew*, New York, Viking Press, 1946, p. 283. On the other hand, in Edward Bellamy's nineteenth-century utopian novel, *Looking Backward*, Dr. Leete instructs Julian West that "the nation guarantees the nurture, education, and comfortable maintenance of every citizen from the cradle to the grave." (Cambridge, Harvard University Press, 1967, p. 149.)

• A theory of federalism that involves reducing the role of the federal government by devolving federal responsibilities to state governments.

• A concept of programs to aid the poor that consists of providing adequate benefits to the "truly needy," and removing from welfare able-bodied persons who can make it on their own.[5]

Thus, federal aid to states and localities—which had risen steadily from $3 billion in 1955 to $95 billion in 1981—declined to $89 billion in 1982. Thus, in 1981 Congress combined fifty-four existing programs, which together were spending at a rate of $7 billion a year, into nine block grant programs, for which administrative responsibility was assigned to the states.

These objectives were explicit and deliberate. Other objectives became evident in the way administration proposals developed or in the statements of subordinate officials. Such latent policy may not always have been deliberate but rather may have been expressions of expediency or of inclinations that had not been sorted out. The objective of helping the "truly needy," with other euphemisms like "targeting benefits on the needy" and "focusing resources on those in need,"[6] turned out to mean cutting back on the so-called "means-tested" programs, the programs referred to earlier as exceptionalistic. "All means-tested programs," George Gilder put it flatly, "promote the value of being poor."[7] Food Stamps, Medicaid, and AFDC suffered far more in the early 1980s than Social Security or Medicare, for example. It is impossible to know whether this arose from administration and congressional preference or from a shrewd assessment of the political power of the constituencies involved. Probably both were factors.

A second latent objective became evident in the use of terms like "work disincentives and inequities."[8] The meaning was that people receiving government payments, if they also had income from work, should not have more altogether than comparable people who had only work. Prior administrations, Democratic and Republican, had popularized the same terms but with a different primary meaning. They wanted to insure that recipients would be better off if they worked than if they did not. This had been called "providing incentives," and the new administration was wiping these out.

It may be evident that the government cannot readily do everything at once. It cannot see to it that nonrecipients who work have the best incomes, recipients who work are somewhat worse off, and recipients who do not work at all are worst off (but have enough to live on). This would require exquisite management of which no government is capable, especially as low-income people tend to work one day and not the next. The Reagan administration's revisionist use of terms like *disincentives* and *inequities* (never whistle-blown, even by officialese-watcher William Safire) produced widespread confusion among those who had been taught that incentives were pro-work policy and who expected pro-work policy from the administration.

The so-called incentive systems had never been effective in getting people to work, however—a fact the new administration understood. (High unemployment is the powerful basic issue, and we have had it for many years now.) Therefore, wiping out incentive arrangements reduced welfare costs. In any case, the administration was playing a deeper game— relying on competition for available work to force people to take and hold jobs, and to discipline wages as well. (Every increase of 1 percent in the unemployment rate produces a perceptible depression in the wage trend about one year later.) For example, federal funding for state employment services was reduced, and the Comprehensive Employment and Training Program (CETA), a Nixon program intended to do exactly that, was wiped out despite record unemployment rates. As for welfare, people would be discouraged from seeing it as an alternative by new deterrents and, in any event, prevented from using it by narrowing eligibility.

A third latent objective of the Reagan administration was initiation of an extensive erosion of public and voluntary social services. That public services should decline was explicit, but ostensibly private social services were to be strengthened. However, business and philanthropic organizations said plaintively, repeatedly, and publicly, that voluntary funds could in no way replace withdrawn public funds. The Urban Institute estimated that the effect of first-round administration cuts would be a 50 percent reduction in the funding of voluntary social welfare agencies.[9] Funding cuts were replaced in part by increased contributions by corporations and increased charges to clients for services rendered.[10] From 1982 to 1985, according to another Urban Institute Study, social service organizations lost $9 billion, or more than 35 percent of their federal aid, and housing and neighborhood organizations lost 30 percent.[11] Extensive networks of public and voluntary services—including CETA, community action agencies, and health services such as infant and maternal care—were greatly reduced or wiped out. The anguish of struggling mental health clinics, day care centers for children, legal services for the poor, and organizations providing food and shelter was extensively reported.

Finally, the Reagan administration quickened the movement to increasingly unequal income shares. Its first budget, the Omnibus Budget and Reconciliation Act of 1981, is a striking illustration. The net effect of the act's tax and spending cuts was estimated as follows: If the act had been fully in effect in 1981, the poorest fifth of the population would have lost $1.2 billion while the richest fifth would have gained $36 billion.[12] Between 1983 and 1985, the Congressional Budget Office reported, that families earning less than $10,000 a year would lose $23 billion in income and government benefits while families earning more than $80,000 would gain $35 billion in after-tax income.[13] The Omnibus Budget and Reconciliation Act was, if not the largest, the most blatantly redistributive legislation of recent times.

In sum, the somewhat undefined American view of our welfare state was qualified by the administration in ways that had been proclaimed: the public sector made smaller—spending, especially, was reduced; devolution from federal to state government; and a narrowed conception of programs to aid the poor. The view of the welfare state was also altered in ways that were not originally clear or intended: exceptionalist or means-tested programs were cut more deeply than Social Security,

Medicare, and other mainstream programs; a policy of competition for scarce employment replaced incentive arrangements in income maintenance programs; voluntary social services were cut back; and the slow movement to an unequal distribution of income was given added impetus. Clearer in the carrying out of these latent objectives than in the early, explicit statements was a repudiation of cradle-to-grave security—a deliberate reintroduction of social insecurity.

A Glance Ahead

It is a view not limited to Democrats or liberals that more was changed during the Reagan presidency than a majority of the electorate intended. Public discontent was clear enough. What they did want was not so clear and was given shape by conservative economists and people with other kinds of right-of-center ideology. As these solutions fail to work, as the discomfort and pain of a large sector of the population break through denial and optimism, and especially when we come again into recession, the reaction may be severe. The American electorate is typically reactive, voting against as much as or more than voting for. Unless a great deal is done to clarify alternatives, the reaction may be against disorder, against the absence of planning, and against a lower standard of living. In the economic sphere, there have been any number of calls for more planning and more control, often in the interests of "reindustrialization."

Thus, the overriding danger is that the reaction, when it ignites, will move even further to the right. Kevin Phillips, not a fellow traveler by any means, warned in 1982 of such a development.[14] More recently, for exemplary purposes, he described how frustrated middle-class populism turned into fascism in Europe.[15] One recalls Sinclair Lewis's *It Can't Happen Here*.[16] To head that off, Phillips tried to steer the Reagan administration toward a broad coalition of government, business, and labor cohering around a strong nationalism. He recognized and warned that the result may be called a corporate state. Whether it would be benign, as in contemporary Sweden, or malignant, as in Mussolini's Italy, would depend on the balance of power and the electorate's grasp of the issues.

Thus, on one hand we face predictions of sharpened class conflict and on the other hand predictions of a move toward a corporate state—forecasts by no means unrelated. Much will depend on the thoughtfulness that in the immediate future goes into public debate of objectives other than the widely discussed goals of economic growth and lower unemployment. It seems important, then, to think through the shape of the next and new welfare state before the moment is upon us. The pre-Reagan welfare state developed by increments; some of the early increments are no longer functional and many parts of these programs are unrelated to one another. It would reflect poor imagination to try to return to the very programming that was swept away, nor in the real world is that likely to happen. In the pages that follow I will try to think through what might better be done.

First, I will take my own advice and offer a set of organizing objectives. These are not objectives that everyone will subscribe to, and it is a sign of the problem we have had about purposes that some of them may simply be unfamiliar. It has not been made apparent that such purposes, whether one supports or opposes them, have been at issue in domestic programs. In any event, these are the purposes around which succeeding chapters will outline the development of programs in a new welfare state. For those who do not share these objectives, setting them forth should at least help to frame the issues.

2

Five Principles
for Community

I t is important to move our society toward community. No one knows whether predictions of sharpened class conflict or a move toward corporatism will prove to be accurate. These are developments that most Americans would surely wish to avoid. But, even if they do not come to pass, it is important to undo the increasing fragmentation of our society (alienation and anomie, sociologists say) which is expressed in passivity, in violence turned inward—suicide and family abuse, for example—and in crime.

What Makes for a Sense of Community?

The appearance of a generation with a deep sense of fellow-feeling may arise from a social accident—the coincidence of a shared threat, common purpose, and victory against odds. Writing about the British "stalemate state" in the late 1950s, for example, Norman Mackenzie reflected that he continued to fight for reform because he was "old enough to remember and young enough to hope."[1] He was old enough to remember World War II and the blitz bombings of London—remember them as a time of struggle and hope rather than of destruction. In the United States, the

Depression of the 1930s seems to have left a similar mark, but the generation that was adult or approaching adulthood then is now absenting itself from public affairs.

The spirit of our own World War II generation, given center stage in the Kennedy years, seemed comradely and determined, but there was not as great a sense of struggle and sacrifice here as in the countries that were invaded or threatened with invasion. Or perhaps the spirit of Camelot was poisoned by the succession of the war in Vietnam and Watergate, with the mounting sense of moral inrectitude and no clear victory to celebrate. We do not yet know the long-term effects on morale of the war against poverty and the peace demonstrations. These movements were quickly repudiated, and the participants were denied acknowledgment even of the victories they had won. The war against poverty is said to have failed. The peace movement altered the plans of two presidents, but it was policy to deny its influence. The successes of the peace movement came in self-destructing bits— the phaseout of the draft with the escalation of bombing, and so forth. In the short run at least, many of the young men and women who participated came to sound cynical. The civil rights movement certainly seemed for a time to have had its successes. Whether its participants will continue to carry the sense of victory against odds in the face of subsequent disappointments remains to be seen.

The spirit of the several generations, overlapping, is powerful background. Foreground is what goes on today—the sense of fairness in social arrangements, the sense that all live by similar rules. A classic British study suggests two conditions that may, in particular, lead to a sense of "relative deprivation" or grievance. One is a person's position relative to others: How far removed does he perceive himself from others with whom he makes comparison? Second is a person's state of expectation: How does she judge the chance or likelihood of self-improvement?[2] A larger gap in relative positions and higher expectations tend to magnify a sense of grievance, a smaller gap or lower expectations to diminish it. American ideology leads to the most ambitious and hopeful comparisons, and so—with positions disparate and relatively fixed—

the sense of grievance is great. The National Commission on the Causes and Prevention of Violence saw this problem as one of the major causes of a high crime rate.[3]

The issue of relative deprivation fixes attention on psychological or social-psychological issues but also on the real world. The former focus concerns the way in which public perception is structured. The perennial "is the glass half-full or half-empty" metaphor, applied to civil rights, unemployment rates, inflation, or whatever, arises from arguments about satisfactory progress made after the fact. However, it is possible to arrange domestic programming so that its very structure expresses a drive for fairness and community. The nature of our political system makes that peculiarly important to do. That is, our political parties overlap in point of view and in program much more than the political parties of Europe or Canada. Many voters fail to see their aspirations represented vigorously and continuously—even by a party out of power.

As for the real world, citizens now widely feel that the rhetoric of leaders is meaningless and that they are manipulated by manipulators of the media. Cynical and distrustful, when they do not lapse into romanticism (not an uncommon partner of cynicism), citizens look for real movement—a gain in purchasing power, in occupational security, better housing and neighborhood, and so forth. What is happening to and around us comes to the fore in attempts to avoid a sense of grievance or to enhance a sense of community.

In short, it may be difficult for a nation to create the conditions that weld a generation together in a sense of common purpose and achievement; nations do not bring times of trial upon themselves simply to develop character. However, we can choose to do these things that will enhance community: we can shape instruments that express national purpose. The trappings of a welfare state—its educational system, Social Security, health programming, the control of the design of cities and availability of housing—are prominent among such instruments. We will always have such programs, of course, but their structure is significant as a statement for or against community. Apart from programs, we can exercise control over private and governmental activities that have serious undesirable consequences or that lead to an unbearable sense of chaos. And we can seek to do this at the level of the Penn Central decision to eliminate its spur into New York instead of fruitlessly trying to preserve the streets afterward. Finally, for the large majority of the population, we can seek to reduce the sense of irreducible disadvantage—to facilitate a perception that their efforts will be rewarded in the real world.

In the remainder of this chapter, five closely related principles that provide structure to these purposes will be offered to guide domestic social programming. The principles are fair shares, or a nearer approach to equality; mainstreaming in social insurance and social services; full employment; selective decentralization of authority; and integration with respect to color or ethnicity.

Fair Shares

We are accustomed to think of income in terms of established relationships—an engineer's salary, so much rent for a piece of land, so much interest on our savings—as if these were intrinsic values. Viewed differently, however, wages, rent, and interest simply serve to divide up the nation's goods and services. The validity of this view becomes plain in inflationary times, when money seems to lose absolute meaning and becomes meaningful only in relation to other sums of money.

The division that results always seems imperfect. In the end, we apply correctives like preferences and graduated rates to the tax system and pay out money through cash transfers such as Social Security. The tax and transfer systems have other purposes as well, but leveling out or increasing disparities is one purpose. Nor is government activity the only or even the initial redistributive mechanism. Income (or what it will buy) is redistributed when businesses charge less to a large customer than to a small one, when an airline gives a bonus to a passenger (especially as his employer may be paying the bill), when the same token buys a subway ride from the Bronx to Manhattan or to Brooklyn. The motive may be competitive, or simplicity in doing business, or, as with reduced prices for children or the aged, sympathy with the plight of others.

Redistribution is implicit when a woman earns less for specified work than a man and a youth less than an adult, and when a lower hourly rate is paid for the same work performed part-time rather than full-time. Our system of prices, wages, and return on capital is riddled with preferences that favor some and injure others. So too is our tax and transfer system. It would be naive or utopian to investigate whether there should be preferences at all. A more practical question is to what ends preferences ought to operate. Two answers, which need not be pursued here, concern competition and efficiency. A third has to do with the power of some interests (large consumers, organized rural purchasers, organized labor) to compel preferential treatment, the incapacity of others to resist invidious treatment, and the social desirability of discrimination one way or another. This third set of answers involves issues of socially sanctioned redistribution.

The question whether a welfare state by definition seeks fair shares has, like the Loch Ness monster, long lain beneath the surface of public debate, surfaced occasionally, and never been nailed down. By 1950, conservative Europeans were already arguing that it was not essential to a welfare state that it redistribute income; that would destroy creativity, promote uniformity, and enhance the power of the state.[4] On the other hand a classic study, this one American, took as a premise that a welfare state aims at reducing inequality, but concluded that this objective would surely be subverted.[5] (One should pause to give credit to its authors, Harold Wilensky and Charles Lebeaux; this was a fearless and accurate forecast.) On both sides of the Atlantic, the adversaries came together on a lowest-common-denominator agreement that dominated the public objective: assured provision of minimum levels of food, housing, health care, and so forth. Egalitarians carped and muttered without serious effect.

Nevertheless, the average standard of living of disadvantaged Americans rose steadily from 1950 to perhaps 1975. Then why should the new welfare state take fair shares as an underlying principle? The question has roots in religion and

ethics. The Old Testament year of Jubilee was a time for free-
ing slaves and returning property to owners who had lost it.
Moving right along from biblical times, we note Irving Kristol's
rueful report in the midst of the war against poverty. It was
widely accepted, he said, "that the existence of inequality is a
legitimate provocation to social criticism. Every inequality is on
the defensive, must prove itself against the imputation of injustice and unnaturalness."[6] John Rawls's formulation is widely
cited: "All goods are to be distributed equally unless an unequal distribution of any or all of these goods is to the advantage of the least favored."[7]

The contemporary counterargument relies on the need of
an industrial society for hierarchy and graded rewards. In
economists' terms, social justice is pitted against efficiency—
that is against the capacity of self-interest and the private market to provide the most production when least interfered with.
"For over a century [this presumption] has survived on theo-
retical speculation rather than sound empirical evidence";[8] nevertheless the presumption holds sway among economists. It is a
difficulty that arguments from social justice and from efficiency do not meet, and there is no way of settling how much
equality or how much efficiency is desirable. In the end economists and everyone else find a pragmatic position somewhere
between the implicit extremes. A compromise position on inequality is worked out in the public arena, where it is a shifting
(but in its result not far shifting) vector of conscience, unrest,
and economic and political power.

But framing a welfare state precipitates more specific reasons for moving toward equality. One reason has more or less
been foreshadowed by the discussion so far; we will return to
it in a moment. Another reason has to do with poverty.

It is a premise that a true welfare state will eliminate or at
least greatly reduce poverty, and in discussions of this objective the argument about fair shares takes on the most heat.
For example:

> Conservatives accept the proposition that the federal government
> has a role to play in setting national goals, such as reducing pov-
> erty. We are not even arguing with liberal objectives in many

instances. But we disagree about the means of achieving them. In our view, the primary responsibility for extricating the able-bodied poor from poverty rests with the poor themselves. The function of government is to help them do so.

This does not preclude federal activism in insuring opportunity. But such activism should be directed at empowering the poor to make choices. . . .

The liberal welfare state has shortchanged the poor for one paramount reason: It has strayed from its original goal of eliminating the dole to one of income redistribution for its own sake.[9]

We set aside the implication that an attempt to move income from the less wealthy to the more wealthy, as the Reagan administration did, is not redistribution. We note the power of the appeal in these sentences to taking responsibility for one's self—a view that strikes a chord in the American ethos. (Difficulties with this view are explored in chapter 4 in a brief discussion of the income development of poor families.) However, a fundamental problem of this view concerns the assumption that poverty is an objectively defined level of living related to basic bodily needs and social decency. Viewed across countries or across time in our own country, it is evident that poverty is defined in relation to average family income. Victor Fuchs, who explored definitions of poverty over an extended period of time, concluded that "any family [is poor] whose income is less than one-half the median family income."[10] By that definition, a more or less stable 20 percent of the population has been poor since 1947. One can press the point over a longer period of time. By the current government definition of poverty (upwards of $10,000 for a family of four), at the turn of the century almost everyone should have been called poor. But assessing the situation eighty years ago, Robert Hunter, in a book called *Poverty,* offered the estimate that 12 to 24 percent of the population was poor.[11] Hunter's method was less sophisticated that Fuchs's; nevertheless, in a much less affluent time, his estimate also straddled 20 percent.

Our relatively recent experience, embracing the civil rights movement and the war against poverty, also illustrates the point. With poverty defined by technicians in relation to presumed minimum need and adjusted only for inflation, the government reported smaller numbers of poor people year by year. But it was not the public sense that there were fewer poor people. The figures that were used to define poverty (about $3,000 for a family of four in 1964, $5,000 in 1974) came to strain credulity. As general income went up, unconsciously the perception of what minimally is needed went up also. Mollie Orshansky, who had devised the government's definition, by 1978 publicly recommended a more generous one. In 1980 a Labor Department panel of experts proposed a definition based on half of what average families would spend in any given year. Such a level would float upward as average real income and expenditures moved upward.[12]

More instructive than the definition of poverty is the *proportion* of the population that is regarded as poor—that stable 20 percent. The share of national income of the poorest 20 percent of the population has averaged around 5 percent since the Great Depression. Full employment and government controls during World War II brought it up modestly; after the war it fell back. The civil rights movement and the war against poverty produced a blip upward, now gone from the screen. A moment's reflection may suggest that the two stable percentages—20 percent and 5 percent—are linked. If we perceive as poor those families that have less than half of the median income, as Fuchs suggests, with exquisite management the poorest fifth of the population might be kept from poverty with about one tenth of national income—that is, with half of their strictly proportional share. But if their share is only one twentieth the task is hopeless. In other words, reducing poverty in any consequential way requires a less unequal distribution of income.

Following this reasoning, a 1977 study examined what might be required to increase the share of the poorest fifth of the population to 10 percent of national income.[13] A total of $55–$60 billion would have had to be shifted from the 40 percent of the population with most income to the 40 percent with least, the largest part of the shifted money going to the lowest 20 percent. Although such a shift seemed formidable, we have since far exceeded that magnitude—in the opposite direction. The 1981 Budget Act referred to in chapter 1 produced in a single year a decline of 0.2 percent in the income share of the poorest fifth of the population and an increase of 0.9 percent for the richest fifth.[14]

Apart from the question of reducing poverty, the distribution of income is a broad indication of the fate of various disadvantaged groups. For many years, the median income of black families was 50–55 percent of the income of white families. With the civil rights movement, it climbed to 61 percent—only to start a steady decline in 1971. Women earn less than men on the average; youths earn less than older people. All these discrepancies represent average differences in training and experience, but they also represent simple discrimination. Other special groups, including families headed by women, the aged, and Hispanics, also consistently occupy the lower reaches of income distribution. That is, disadvantage attaches to color, primary language, sex, and age, characteristics over which individuals have little control. In such a circumstance, if it continues for long, disadvantage is experienced as an issue of caste rather than class. To put the matter modestly, it goes against community.

To sum up, a welfare state would take fair (or fairer) shares as a program principle because it is the only way substantially to reduce poverty, as the citizenry perceives poverty. And, second, a welfare state seeks national community, and fair shares is a surrogate for or general indicator of improvement for all or most historically aggrieved groups.

Mainstreaming Income Maintenance and Social Services

Mainstreaming is the opposite of means-testing or exceptionalism in welfare state policy. With means-testing, a person or family wishing to qualify for a benefit must demonstrate having less than a certain specified income. Upon that demonstration, the program fills the income deficit or provides a relevant service such as medical care. There may be additional requirements, of course, such as age or veteran status. That a beneficiary is exceptional—that is, shamefully different and needy—may be established in other ways, but in our society means-testing is the most common. *Mainstream* defines programs that, whatever the primary criteria for entitlement, are not means-tested.

The issue of mainstreaming versus means-testing has long woven in and out of welfare state and fair shares debate. Programming in the United States was dominated by social insurance ideology from 1935 to perhaps 1960. We identified major risks to income—old age, disability, widowhood, orphanhood, unemployment—and framed a program that would guard against each risk. Based on criteria of entitlement that might be expected to affect anyone rather than on low income, these were and are mainstream programs. Means-tested public assistance or welfare was to be a relatively small device for people with special, temporary needs. If large numbers required welfare for a long time, that would highlight the need to improve or expand social insurance and so minimize welfare. American emphasis on mainstream programs emerged from the Great Depression and underlies the program expansion that followed World War II—periods, I have suggested, that forged a sense of community.

However, discontent with mainstreaming was voiced almost from the beginning. "Why," asked a 1949 British critique, "should any social service be provided *without* a test of need?"[15] Underlying such questions was the view that programs ought to benefit those who had paid taxes for them; benefits to those who had not contributed should be provided only when strictly necessary. This view pointed at a policy that would maintain inequality—necessary and justifiable inequality, it was held. The issue was prominent during the struggle in the United States to enact health insurance. Under pressure to offer some alternative, opponents of an insurance approach argued that demonstrated need should be the basic criterion of a new national program. At some risk of getting nothing at all, old people rejected the idea. Wilbur J. Cohen explained in 1960: "We need a system which creates no invidious distinctions based on income—one where an individual is entitled to receive benefits on the basis of his general contribution to society."[16] The eventual outcome was a compromise—mainstream Medicare for the aged and means-tested Medicaid for all others.

By then, a substantial reversal of mainstreaming was underway in Western countries. Freshly arrived at here, a view fundamentally like the 1949 British critique was increasingly expressed: Social Security ought to be more like private insurance.[17] People would get what their taxes had paid for, and poverty would be dealt with in a redesigned means-tested program (variously called negative income tax, guaranteed income, and so forth). For a variety of reasons, there was a growing feeling in all Western countries that welfare state spending was getting out of hand. Means-testing was seen as a way to limit spending, at least on the poor. Paradoxically, at the same time some argued that it was a way to assure *more* money for the poor. That is, a sum could be set aside for them and not wasted on people who were not poor. This argument, framed during the early raptures of cost-benefit analysts, was sincere if ingenuous.

In any event, from the mid-1960s on Social Security benefits tended to be improved by across-the-board percentage increases and therefore went disproportionately to beneficiaries in the upper salaried brackets. New mainstream programs were not devised for new risks that assumed importance, notably the burden of child support in large two-parent families and in single-parent families. For those reasons and because of a generally rising standard of living, apparent need grew, and so public assistance and the food stamp program flourished. Thus, between 1968 and 1973 the annual cost of social insurance increased by 77 percent but the cost of means-tested programs increased by 130 percent. The Reagan transition abruptly reversed a fifteen-year trend toward means-testing. The Administration's motives were perhaps pragmatic (means-tested programs were politically vulnerable) or perhaps uncaring, but in one sense they were preparing the ground for sounder policies. Two gauges of means-testing as grand policy—its effect on the income of the poor and its effect on feelings of community—may make this clear.

A simple observation as to the first gauge is that, even at

peak growth, means-tested programs are a small fraction of total payments. In 1982, for example, the major means-tested programs (for example, AFDC and food stamps) cost $34 billion annually and the mainstream programs (chiefly Social Security and civil service retirement) $188 billion. Bear in mind that social insurance makes payments to poor people that are disproportionate to their contribution. (That is what the "social" in social insurance means and precisely what critics have complained about.) Then the effect of reshaping these programs to resemble private insurance would be to reduce poor people's share in payments that would be far larger than those of the programs that would, in return, be conserved for them.

The loss to the poor is worse than simple arithmetic may indicate. The level of expenditure and the quality of administration of government programs are not fixed by initial legislation but are a continuous function of the interest and power of the programs' constituencies. The constituency of means-tested programs by definition comprises the most powerless people in the country. Similarly, sociologists have pointed out that programs with low-status beneficiaries tend to have low-status staffs, and vice versa. That is, the bureaucracies of means-tested programs themselves carry little weight. Thus, the promise to do well with means-tested programs, whatever the immediate national impulse, is in the long run never carried out. Mainstream programs are another matter. Thus, in 1966 the poorest fifth of the population received 57 percent of all government cash-maintenance payments. A decade later, with all programs growing and means-tested ones growing by far the fastest, the share of the poorest fifth dropped to 36 percent.[18]

This is all to say that, broadly regarded, extensive means-testing proves to be a rationing device. It may be so not by concerted design, but because political forces and program dynamics (to which we will come in a moment) combine to restrain quality and growth while mainstream programs flourish. Invidious rationing for the poor does not seem a sound principle for a welfare state.

The other gauge of means-testing as policy is its effect on feelings of community. No one who has applied for both AFDC and survivors' insurance under Social Security, or received medical attention in a public clinic for the poor and also as a private patient, or lived in public and in private housing fails to understand the radical difference in treatment. The difference is an effect of stigma—the feeling that means-testing is associated with failure and being deviant. Officials widely reflect their distaste for their clients in their treatment of them, and needy people are reluctant to apply for benefits. In 1975, for example, a study by the Joint Economic Committee of Congress found that only about a third of the people thought to be entitled to food stamps were receiving them. Stigma and—not unrelated—a complex and difficult application process were thought to be major reasons.[19] As the policy balance in the United States shifts heavily toward means-tested food, housing, medical care, and higher education, we move toward a duplex society. One portion of the population lives with a free market while an underclass lives in a world of welfare, Medicaid, and housing administrators.

It is not simply that the world of the poor is Dickensian. As the programs grow they become difficult to administer. Suspicion of dishonesty translates into the multiplication of verifications and regulations, some unreasonable and others impossible to administer. On the other side of the table the suspicion grows that this is all a subterfuge for denial. With program deterioration, the staff who are potentially best find other work, exacerbating the difficulties. The poor and the officials with whom they deal become trapped in a partnership that is increasingly hostile. There was a time when a welfare worker's small black notebook, carried in the hand, assured safe passage in any ghetto in the country. Now many welfare workers decline to visit recipients at all (compounding administrative problems, of course), and many offices post armed guards. This is not a design for community. The means-tested population lives in a mean and passively or actively angry world, closed off from the rest of the citizenry, who do not meet them even in government offices.

Thus, means-testing may appear to set aside sums of

money that are efficiently used for the poor, but the appearance is misleading.* Seen in its true relation to political processes or over the long term, means-testing sets aside comparatively small sums and leaves even those sums vulnerable to reduction. Moreover, means-testing tends to segregate and stigmatize. Under strong budgetary pressures, as we have seen in these last years, common sense has seemed to suggest that means-testing would protect the poor. Experience suggests that this is so only in the very short run. In any event, some means-tested programs will presumably always be needed. It is not reasonable to expect to design mainstream programs that will deal with every contingency. The question is one of balance. Until recently, the balance has been going in the wrong direction, and the United States relies on means-testing far more than any other industrial country.

It is obvious that adherence to the broad principle of mainstreaming would not end political struggles about shares. Instead of focusing on a division of resources between the poor and everyone else (that is, between means-tested and mainstream programs), the struggle would focus on the design of the mainstream programs themselves. Attention would have to be paid to the interests of the poor, but what was won for them would have some promise of stability. That poor people received over half of what was paid out in cash income maintenance in 1966 is an indication that mainstreaming can work to their relative advantage. But there may be circumstances, especially in the short run, when it seems simpler to redistribute by means-testing. Although such appearances may be

---

*Moreover, means-tested programs are not necessarily effective in limiting payments to those who are poor. Particularly when they deal with people who may have income from work, they must make provision for necessary expenses. Frequently they are designed to allow extra income or incentive, and so many are included who are not poor.

For example, in 1969 a President's Commission on Income Maintenance Programs recommended a negative income tax that, when fully in effect, would have had two-thirds of its cost going to people above the poverty level. The same commission, considering an increase in the minimum social security benefit, found that only one-third of the cost would go to people above the poverty level.[20] Careful exploration makes it plain that only at very low payment levels do means-tested programs tend to be efficient in this sense.[21]

deceptive, they are not always so. Thus, at the very start of discussing principles, we see that any two or more of them may be in conflict. Arriving at desirable policies will require thoughtful balancing and trading off.

Full Employment

Just within the past few years, the unemployment rate has fluctuated between 3.5 percent (1969) and 10.6 percent (1983). In the same period the number of people employed, a statistic that incumbent administrations have lately preferred, increased steadily from almost 80 million to 110 million. Unemployment rates carry with them a bleak penumbra—those partially employed, those employed below their skill level, and those who have decided that it is futile to look for work. Statisticians debate these definitions but a generalization is clear: a higher unemployment rate casts a longer and deeper shadow. The unemployment rate reflects a single point in time, of course. In 1969, when it registered a low 3.5 percent, 12.5 percent of the population at some time during the year experienced unemployment. The national objective, made law in 1946 and again in 1978, has been to keep the unemployment rate below roughly 4 percent. By 1978, however, most planners and interest groups regarded a 4-percent goal as purely rhetorical.

The argument about full employment—what the objective ought to be, at what cost it ought to be met, and whether indeed it still makes sense to talk about it—is central among political and economic issues. In chapter 1, I noted that intransigent technical problems must be unraveled if we are to achieve goals that include full employment. Furthermore, interest groups are in conflict at every stage of judgment. For example, economists believe that a so-called natural rate of unemployment—once 5 percent, now perhaps 6 percent—is the minimum rate consistent with stable prices. Thus, policies that push the unemployment rate down will benefit those who want jobs and will hurt those who lose from inflation. The country will not embark on such a course without a struggle.

Finally, changes in the labor force and in the welfare state itself have moderated the impact of unemployment and may have changed the argument. On the one hand, the mass entry of married women into the labor market has meant that with one family member unemployed another may yet be employed; thus families suffering unemployment are not necessarily deprived of all income. At the same time, Unemployment Insurance (UI) relieves the financial impact of unemployment. Thus, during the 1970s the national cost of UI fluctuated between $1 billion and $18 billion a year, indicating the magnitude of the financial cushion that was applied when unemployment increased. Figures such as these are more comforting in the aggregate than in particular cases. For example, single parents (mostly women) and their children constitute a large and growing underclass in terms of income and employment, and, for various reasons, they are least likely to be entitled to UI. Pointing out the relative financial stability of two-worker families can serve only to embitter single parents.

How to reach full employment, whose interests to serve, and what the personal financial consequences of unemployment are are difficult issues. Facing the question of employment goals, one may also become embroiled in a more difficult because somewhat futuristic argument about the continuing economic necessity for work. A series of pamphlets from the Fund for the Republic (described by its officials as "a wholly disowned subsidiary of the Ford Foundation") and a 1963 book by Robert Theobald set forth a thesis that was popular for a while.[22] It held that cybernation is moving so fast that wages no longer provide a reasonable method of distributing the nation's income. Therefore, we must find other ways than wages and salaries to get money to people. (Theobald was an early proponent of a guaranteed income.) The daily news about computers and robotics overlaps with this old dream (or nightmare—it is hard to know which). It leaves a layer of anxiety in people's minds that high unemployment is neither temporary nor the result of ignorance about how to manage the economy but an augury of the inescapable future.

Theobald's thesis sounds quaint now. Since he wrote, the size of the labor force has expanded much beyond what anyone imagined, and the proportion of the population at work has increased. And still unsatisfied material need is evident in the widespread decay of public facilities and in deprivation of housing and other consumer goods. Computerization, the decline of manual labor, and the simultaneous growth of service employment appear mainly to portend a shift of jobs from some fields to others. That is a disaster for people who, for one reason or another, cannot compete for new jobs, but it is not the end of work. The focus of concern has lately moved to whether Americans can be fully competitive in production rather than whether goods will produce themselves. It is that the United States wants a large piece of the action, not that the action is at an end. The title of a book reviewing the evidence in this matter sums it up—*Work Is Here to Stay, Alas.*[23]

Obviously, economic issues with respect to full employment cannot be resolved in these brief comments. Setting those aside for expert discussion elsewhere, it may nevertheless be evident that a new welfare state must take as a premise the nearest approximation of full employment that is possible. That is so for distributive reasons, in order to promote community, and for practical reasons of program design.

It is a commonplace observation that blacks and women are the last hired and first fired. The unemployment rate of blacks tends to be almost twice or, more recently, more than twice the white rate. The unemployment rate of women has at times been lower than that of men. On looking into that statistic, however, one finds that almost two-thirds of the so-called discouraged workers (not working but not counted as unemployed) are women and that many women report themselves as working part-time because they cannot find full-time work. Youths are a third group that suffers unemployment disproportionately. The further we fall short of full employment, the wider is the gap between whites and blacks,[24] men and women, adults and youths. It has been estimated that for every one-point decrease in the unemployment rate among men aged 35–44, the employment rate among young people goes up by 4.5 percent and among black youths by 6.3 percent.[25]

The distributive implications of these relationships are obvious. Wages and salaries account for about three-fourths of all income. It goes without saying that the relatively low income of blacks, women, youths, Hispanics, the aged, and other disadvantaged groups reflect unemployment trends. Thus the disadvantage in income shares already noted, and thus the reversal of the modest 1960s trend toward equalization. One can argue that compensatory education and equal opportunity should be able to reduce income inequality, whatever the overall unemployment rate. That may be so in the very long run, but considerable national energy has been invested in such strategies, at least briefly, and they have not had lasting effects of that sort. Without an approximation of full employment, it is entirely likely that we shall continue to have more than acceptable inequality in income.

The implication of income inequality for community has already been indicated and need not be dwelt on, but unemployment has a more direct link to community and its converse, alienation. Sigmund Freud once observed that the two central drives are for love and work (*Liebe und Arbeit*), a psychological truth that is widely appreciated. It is well understood that work roots a person in society and (if the word can be used without invidious loading) tends to discipline him or her. In a review of the substantial literature on this subject that developed after 1930, Marie Jahoda identifies five elements of rootedness or discipline that are disturbed or destroyed by unemployment. They are "the experience [or structuring] of time, the reduction of social contacts, the lack of participation in collective purposes, the absence of an acceptable status and its consequences for personal identity, and the absence of regular activity."[26]

That is a dense black hole of a quotation. In all these matters, the unemployed feel disorganized and deprived. One need not wonder at the fact that the single most disabling quality in terms of capacity to work is extended unemployment. Similar psychological effects—despair and depression—and behavioral manifestations such as child abuse were widely reported in the United States in 1982 and 1983. Dr. M. Harvey Brenner, of Johns Hopkins University, established a quantitative connection between the unemployment rate and, six years later, rates of suicide, homicide, and admission to mental hospitals.[27] Scholarly controversy erupted about the time periods and precise ratios involved, but that there is some connection was not disputed.

It is not clear in what circumstances such unrootedness turns into unruly anti-government activity. Reading the evidence rather more from Europe than the United States, Jahoda concluded that "mass unemployment led to resignation in personal lives and in social matters, not to revolution."[28] Still, she noted that widespread unemployment can lead people to welcome doubtful saviors—Hitler by the Austrians, for example. An interesting English study of school dropouts in 1981 went a step further than tracing the path from unemployment to apathy and resignation, observing that the youths retained a considerable sense of targetless hostility.[29] The study was especially interesting because it was completed in Birmingham well before the extensive rioting by youths there. Perhaps it helps to explain the conclusion of a British commission that the widespread urban rioting in 1981 arose from urban decay and unemployment.[30]

Experience teaches that unemployed youths and young adults are especially volatile socially. We bear in mind that the unemployment rate of youths in the United States has always been relatively high and, depending on the severity of overall unemployment, has sometimes exceeded 30–40 percent. At times, more than half of all black teenagers have been unemployed.

Turning from the question of community, considerations of policy design also require us to accept full employment as an assumption. To begin with, our social insurances link entitlement to a work record and levels of benefits to earnings levels. That is, those who have worked little or not at all are not entitled to Social Security or UI. Those who have earned more get more when they retire or become disabled or otherwise qualify. Thus, unemployment means low unemployment and retirement insurance benefits in the future, a problem which, presumably, a welfare state will have to find some other way to address. Second, substantial unemployment causes program costs to rise uncontrollably at the very moment when the government budget is likely to be under the greatest pressure. The effect of unemployment on the demand for UI and welfare is obvious. Beyond that, people who are unemployed suffer more illnesses and so need more medical care (but may not seek it—another set of problems). It is a fact, not difficult to understand, that people who have lost their jobs apply in larger numbers for disability insurance and elect early retirement under Social Security.

Third, the program judgments that must be made in a climate of high unemployment are complex and painful. Is the person really sick? Is there really no work available? Regulations proliferate and officials and citizens become engaged in extended and tortured applications and reviews. Pressed by the very budget problems that unemployment creates, experts and legislators attempt to design programs that will create incentive to work and that will distinguish between the truly and falsely needy. If we have learned anything from the experience of the 1960s and 1970s, surely it is that we do not know how successfully to fine-tune large government programs to evaluate and deal with people in trouble case by case.

In short, the significance of full employment for a welfare state is, first, its capacity to create a more egalitarian division of income and, second, its direct impact on the citizen's sense of participation in society. Whether the absence of such a sense is reflected in upheaval or apathy may not be the critical question. Our society could quite well go down not with a bang but a whimper. And, finally, extensive unemployment can create dilemmas of policy that are difficult or impossible to solve.

I do not propose a specific figure to designate full employment. Absent a better understanding of the economic processes involved and technical agreement on what is possible, the objective is a direction more than a number. However, the direction of a new welfare state in this matter cannot be in doubt. Therefore, the policies discussed in the chapters that follow are based on the assumption of a government commitment to full employment and are shaped to facilitate full employment.

Selective Decentralization

Like imprinted DNA, choices that were made in 1935—strictly federal Social Security, shared state and federal public assistance, state-administered Unemployment Insurance, local and state administration of social services—shape the power relations of the several jurisdictions fifty years later. A revolution in communications and in the dissemination of news in this half century has made us geographically one country. For this reason and because of the very growth of federal spending, federal power has muscled in on state and local power. The formal relationships survive but at the same time public assistance, for example, answers to extensive federal regulation.

Anxiety and doubt about the flow of power to the center reach back many years. The Hoover Commission was established in 1948 to study the growing complexity and inefficiency of the federal government. People were already concerned about federal growth and coordination but not yet explicitly about state and local weakness. That came in 1959 with the creation of the Advisory Commission on Intergovernmental Relations. The tendency of presidents and congresses to be prescriptive with respect to states was by then reinforced by the conviction that state governments were incompetent. Such a view led Lyndon Johnson's administration, launching the war against poverty, to eliminate the middleman and deal directly with localities. (That cities more than states were controlled by the Democratic party was not overlooked.) Naturally, the Nixon administration turned back to the states, proclaiming the original "new federalism." Profiting from experience, however, it then launched a variety of efforts to enhance the management capacity of states. The Reagan administration brought new federalism to a new peak, proposing more than Congress would enact but even so bringing off substantial decentralization, particularly in social and health services.

Movement of power and authority from the periphery to the center or from the base to the top was paralleled by trends within states and localities. A strong populist tradition tended

to be somewhat eroded as state governments organized to provide welfare state services. As immigrant populations were assimilated and moved out of urban ghettoes, the social service
agencies that had begun life to serve them tended also to move
outward. As suburbanization contributed to the deterioration
and deficits of central cities, welfare departments, counseling
agencies, health departments, and schools centralized their activities in the interest of efficiency and coordination. By the
1950s, urban core areas vied with rural areas for the distinction
of being the most underserved in the nation. Less compact
suburban and rural areas tended to be served by regional organizations and thus did not incorporate the ethnic traditions
of neighborhood organization. Professionals observed that social support groups (a term given currency later) and neighborhood organizations were being undermined.

The tide began visibly to move in the opposite direction by
the 1960s. Urban renewal legislation already required citizen
participation in the planning of cleared areas. President Kennedy's Community Health Centers Act (1963) shifted the site
of treatment for mental illness to communities and specified
community involvement in planning. The war against poverty
was based on "maximum feasible involvement" of the poor—
involvement that came to fuller fruition with "model cities"
legislation intended to rebuild neighborhoods. Sharp struggles were fought, most notably in New York City, to turn
school systems back to neighborhoods. London and Paris,
long organized from the neighborhood up, were touted as
examples for American cities. In the aftermath of the war
against poverty, open conflict declined but organizers toiled
assiduously at the grass roots. Community organizers spoke in
new acronyms like ACORN, CHD, and PUSH.[31]

In 1977, President Carter appointed a National Commission on Neighborhoods; its recommendations were aimed at
supporting neighborhood economies and citizen organizations. At about the same time, the American Enterprise Institute proferred a conservative ideological framework for this
well-established movement. They argued in a report that "mediating structures"—the family, the church, the neighborhood, and voluntary organizations—should stand between in-

dividuals and the large institutions of public life. Government should stop trying to provide service or financing directly and, wherever possible, use mediating structures for social purposes.[32] Whether all these developments meant that the people were gaining power at the expense of state and local governments is uncertain, but it became obligatory in public discussion to echo an old populism or the new conservatism or both.

One can cite instances in which neighborhood organizations were successful—even spectacularly so—in achieving local objectives, but it is hard to weigh them in the overall balance. A difficulty in assessing their relative effect may be illustrated by our national experience with deinstitutionalization of the aged and mentally ill. The movement began with the technological revolution known as tranquilizers. The development of new drugs meant that patients could be turned loose from hospitals with less danger. Soon professionals pressed for deinstitutionalization as more humane and cost-effective. On the heels of that came the accident that Medicaid was organized to pay for outpatient care and care in general hospitals but not in state mental hospitals.* This meant that turning people loose shifted the costs of their care from the states to the federal government.

In the end, only a third of the planned mental health centers materialized, and little else was done to serve released patients. Half of those released from mental hospitals are readmitted within a year.[33] Well before economic difficulties exacerbated the problem, therefore, inner-city and other neighborhoods struggled with populations of homeless people drifting through their streets. Neighborhood groups may try to push such people onto other neighborhoods, and they may resist halfway houses and emergency shelters being located within their boundaries. However, they have no way to tackle the fundamental issues of Medicaid financing and so-

---

*Organizing Medicaid in this fashion was intended to avoid federal assumption of the costs of mental hospitals, which states had long been paying. No one realized, or pointed out, that states would use deinstitutionalization to the same effect.

cial service provision, partly because the connection is obscure. Moreover, the problem is likely to affect and arouse neighborhood groups long after the fundamental issues have been settled.

/ Thus, it is fruitless—worse than fruitless, it is a deception—to promote decentralization and neighborhood organization in relation to issues too broad or remote to be influenced. On the other hand, Americans desire and from time to time demand to be heard on the issues that concern them, in a manner that is personal and immediate. Thus a fundamental problem in promoting decentralization is relating local involvement to issues concerning which local groups are or can be relevant.

Considering this problem, the Committee for Economic Development (CED) argued that centralization and decentralization might be embraced at once. It is not functions, they said, that should be divided among levels of government, but "power over functions." In other words, advice might be solicited on a neighborhood level for transportation, sewage disposal, and other services that are perforce administered regionally.[34] This is an attractive concept if applied with integrity. But many of the advisory groups incorporating representatives of the poor have declined into purely nominal, "front office" functions, and activist grass-roots groups are barely aware of them. That is a potential unsound outcome of the distinction CED offered, and it would have to be guarded against. Beyond that, it is possible for neighborhood groups to combine in state and national organizations that have the weight and professional capacity to bring influence to bear on state and national issues. Organizations such as ACORN have tried to do that, and Jesse Jackson campaigned for the presidential nomination from a base in PUSH. Third, it is possible to distinguish functions over which power can be and ought to be exercised at neighborhood or local levels. For example, the boroughs of inner London exercise authority over personal social services, housing, and environmental health, but education and health are functions of larger authorities.

Decentralization has been used in this discussion to refer to levels of government as well as to the role of citizens. Both meanings are intended. Relevant constituencies that may not always be addressed in terms of neighborhood—ethnic and client groups, for example—are also implied. In considering the new welfare state, we opt for selective decentralization for the familiar reason of community: local community under-girds national community. We are persuaded also that home rule and "power to the people" are so ingrained in our traditions that they will find an outlet. It is better to plan for them than to subvert or become locked in opposing neighborhood influence and authority. This means in particular the avoidance of hypocrisy about the relationship of a neighborhood purview to centralized administration and decisions; conversely, it means timely (that is, sufficiently early) consultation by government units and the translation of neighborhood views into government policy.[35]

Integration

The distinction between desegregation and integration resides partly in posture (proper versus activist) and partly in objective. The objective of integration is not satisfied with a legal, neutral result. It implies contact and communication between ethnic groups, though not necessarily between all members of such groups, and movement toward equality of outcome.[36] Early debate surrounding the Supreme Court's desegregation cases barely referred to integration. It was as if a grammatical principle about double negatives were governing: if one could negate segregation—that is, wipe out the legal and administrative basis for discrimination—then affirmative integration would follow. There was an occasional passing thought, quickly dismissed, that "the result might simply be a change from one form of segregation to another."[37] Within ten years, however, Justice Hugo Black would observe with some asperity that the situation reflected "entirely too much deliberation and not enough speed."[38] Once again, the "dominant white majority in each historical period pulled back from the point of extensive reform."[39]

By 1964, Milton Gordon painstakingly argued that it is neither "the responsibility nor the prerogative of the government to attempt to impose integration." Especially, the government should not attempt to impose desegregation "in an institutional area where such segregation is not a function of racial discrimination directly but results from discrimination operating in another institutional area."[40] It was as if he understood precisely the manner in which desegregation and discrimination would be perpetuated—that is, with employment and residential patterns and low income serving as proxies for open segregation. In the more than two decades that have passed, the attitudes of the white population toward blacks have shifted substantially, even to increased tolerance of intermarriage. But the practice of separation has changed much less, and resistance to government activism against segregation continues to be powerful. In short, for much of the population "segregation is illegal but desegregation is not mandatory."[41]

Thus, a preference for integration over desegregation derives from a recognition that segregation and discrimination have a deep and complex root pattern, of which law and legally regulated practices constitute only one chief system. If we seek integration, we must pursue it actively. Another kind of reason to prefer integration may be offered in the words of W. E. B. DuBois:

> The human contact of human beings must be increased; the policy which brings into sympathetic touch and understanding, men and women, rich and poor, capitalist and laborer, Asiatic and European, must bring into closer contact and mutual knowledge the white and black people of this land. It is a most frightful indictment . . . that ten million people are coming to believe that all white people are liars and thieves, and the whites in turn believe that the chief industry of Negroes is raping white women.[42]

That was said seventy years ago, and DuBois is remembered as a militant, but obviously he understood that form without content is a poor thing.

Differences in the reasons for endorsing integration take shape in attitudes toward affirmative action, enforcement of civil rights laws, and the impact of broad government policy. An executive order issued by President Kennedy in 1961 for-

mulated a government policy "to encourage by positive measures equal opportunity" in government service and contracts.
The Civil Rights Act of 1964, prohibiting discrimination in
employment, was interpreted by administrative agencies and
courts to authorize affirmative action. The term came to be
understood to mean "the conscious use of race and sex as a
remedial device in allocating jobs or educational opportunities."[43] Whether affirmative action does or should include
establishing minimum quotas of minority placements has provoked sharp controversy. Some think that quotas are racist,
others that effective affirmative action requires quotas. This
issue apart, a wide range of affirmative actions are possible,
including minority-conscious recruitment, bias-free assessment of qualifications, remedial preparatory programs, and
monitoring of employment and enrollment patterns.

Enforcement of civil rights law fluctuates with the spirit of
the times. Early in its history, the Federal Housing Administration actively encouraged the use of restrictive covenants,
and other federal housing agencies tacitly or openly collabo-
rated in discrimination. In time, Congress, the courts, and
administrative agencies provided grounds for actively preventing discrimination. Nevertheless, the Commission on Civil
Rights reported in 1961 that the Federal Housing Administration, the Public Housing Administration, and the Urban
Renewal Administration had not effectively used the tools
given to them to assure equal opportunity.[44] Enforcement
tightened with the civil rights awakening and slackened in the
late 1960s and 1970s. A survey in 1985 found that "most of
the nearly 10 million residents of federally financed housing
are segregated by race, with whites faring much better than
black and Hispanic people."[45] Yet *Twenty Years After Brown*
listed eleven separate recommendations, almost all under existing authority and most of them requiring no new money
but only deliberate use of existing programs. At bottom, it is
objective and will that were and are at issue.[46]

So too with discrimination in education and employment.
The introduction to an evaluation of federal employment policies in 1969 concludes with this cool, "pragmatic" formulation
of the government's aims: ". . . to make progress towards

equality at a rate which balances value considerations of justice and equal opportunity and the interests of certain groups which have long resisted changes in personnel patterns and practices, the outcome frequently being a greater emphasis on voluntary action to achieve positive results than on the use of sanctions to force compliance."[47] In 1983, the U.S. Department of Justice tried to persuade the federal courts that individuals, not groups of people, are injured by discrimination and that the department should therefore not be expected to pursue class-action suits. In a thousand ways a government can strengthen or, as in this case, weaken civil rights enforcement.

It would be as futile to argue that a government can enforce sanctions against discrimination at considerable remove from the wishes of the citizenry as to suppose that it can successfully conduct foreign wars that the public opposes. However, interest groups are not necessarily the citizenry, and governments sometimes confuse the two. In any event, it is an assumption here that in the new welfare state laws against discrimination would be vigorously enforced.

In *An American Dilemma,* Gunnar Myrdal forecast that "social engineering will increasingly be demanded. Many things that for a long period have been predominantly a matter of individual adjustment will become more and more determined by political decision and public regulations."[48] He can hardly have imagined in 1944 the extent to which public decisions would shape the relations of blacks and whites, most deeply in ways not understood or at any rate not confronted. The 1977 report of the Civil Rights Commission put the matter as follows: "Because of the extensive nature of its involvement in housing and community development, the Federal government has been the single most influential entity in creating and maintaining urban residential segregation."[49] Federal subsidy, mortgage guarantees, highway and community facility programs created the suburbs in their present shape and style. The issue in this matter is not enforcement but, even more important, grasping the effect of government programming with respect to integration. Government-created forces that produced segregation can, if systematically understood and used, move us in the opposite direction.

To sum up, the principle of integration is necessary to the new welfare state because racism is extensive and deeply rooted in the United States. Unless a new affirmative result is sought, racism will survive and flourish; that much is confirmed by history. Moreover, community is not achieved without communication, and it is community we seek—not "salt and pepper" schools, not a showplace Shaker Heights on the plain above Hough and Glenville, not black physicians in Black Medical Associations. Major instruments of integration are affirmative action, enforcement of civil rights laws, and an appreciation of the long-term impact on integration of the most powerful programs and policies over which the government presides. The most important of these may not, at first sight, appear directly related to segregation or integration. It is a long and difficult road the nation should traverse, but the alternative of apartheid by proxy is not acceptable.

In this chapter, I have dealt with five principles of a new welfare state—fair shares, mainstreaming, full employment, decentralization, and integration. With these as guidance, I go on to consider major areas of domestic social policy. These are Social Security and welfare, housing, health, and education.

On the whole, the society that decent people would shape is likely to require more rather than less government spending. However, this book is more about *how* than about *how much*. To make this plain, programs in the chapters that follow will be developed as if the question is how to spend the same amount of money that would otherwise be spent. Where additional expenditures may be required, balancing savings will be suggested or the magnitude of additional spending—in no case very large—will be suggested.

3

Income Security:
The Social Insurances

Our system of providing income security has developed mainly in two ways—through the social insurances and means-tested programs. (Veterans' benefits may be regarded as a third category, combining service-connected and means-tested benefits.) The social insurances flourished for perhaps three decades before facing serious criticism. Despite initial opposition which resurfaced from time to time, the effects of public support could be seen in rising benefit levels and in the addition of new programs for the widowed, orphaned, and disabled. Later, a shift in tide could be seen in technical constrictions of entitlement and in an increasing reliance on means-testing to address new needs. Support and resistance coexisted in the 1960s; the Medicare-Medicaid compromise was perhaps a striking illustration.

By 1980 the basic commitment of the American people to the social insurances was under severe test. To complaints that middle-income people were not getting their full share was added the well-publicized threat that Social Security was in danger of bankruptcy. The 1979 Advisory Council on Social Security took pains to deny "that this commitment is waning" or that financial difficulties were serious.[1] The steep rises in unemployment that followed almost immediately cut into Social Security revenues and presented a financial crisis after all. President Reagan appointed a National Commission on Social Security Reform to work out the problem, and, in a 1983 report, they recommended the following:

> The Congress, in its deliberations in financing proposals, should not alter the fundamental structure of the Social Security program or undermine its fundamental principles. The National Commission considered, but rejected, proposals to make the Social Security program a voluntary one, or to transform it into a program under which benefits are a product exclusively of the contributions paid, or to convert it into a fully funded program, or to change it to a program under which benefits are conditioned on the showing of financial need.[2]

Thus, although social insurance principles were severely tested and some provisions were modified to meet criticism, the principles were in the end affirmed. Those principles are (1) income is a matter of right or entitlement; (2) benefits are based on a record of work and are related to the level of contributions; and (3) at the same time, benefit formulas are devised in a manner that favors those with the lowest incomes. In this chapter, I accept the same general premises. In that sense, my strategy here is incremental. The modifications proposed would chiefly strengthen mainstreaming and the programs' egalitarian effect. Means-tested programs such as ssi and AFDC will be considered in the next chapter as ways to help people whom mainstream programs cannot readily reach. It will be seen that social change requires the introduction of one major new mainstream program.

Before dealing with specific programs, I address two potent problems that the social insurances face. They are the relationship of social insurance to private insurance and tax benefits and the prospect or possibility of intergenerational conflict.

Social Security and Private Retirement

Social Security developed alongside a number of preexisting programs—civil service retirement, military retirement, railroad retirement, and programs for employees of state and local governments. States and localities had the option of participating in Social Security or not, and for a while a few localities that had originally chosen to participate withdrew. They were under financial pressure and, as they had their own retirement programs, Social Security seemed a good place to save money. These parallel programs created difficulties for Social Security. Federal employees not covered by Social Security could qualify with comparatively little private employment and small contributions, drawing off Social Security funds that could not be spared. The nonparticipation and, worse, prospective withdrawal of states and other localities would reduce overall contributions to Social Security. Powerful political forces supported existing arrangements. In the climate of crisis that led to the Commission on Reform, Congress required that new federal employees be covered under Social Security, and states and localities were no longer permitted to withdraw from the system. Despite opposition to these changes, they were sound moves in strengthening the financing of Social Security and completing it as a universal system.

At the same time, private pensions developed momentum that may in the long run undermine Social Security. A few private enterprises had provided pension plans for many years, but real growth got under way during World War II. With wages frozen by the government and industry extensively unionized, collective bargaining focused on fringe benefits such as pension plans. Coverage expanded rapidly in union and nonunion plants, moving decade by decade from 10 million workers in 1950 to 19 million, 26 million, and 36 million. After 1980, coverage seemed to stabilize. In many plans it was difficult to achieve vesting; as workers lost or changed jobs, they found that they had lost the right to benefits. The 1950s saw some scandals involving poorly administered plans and outright embezzlement. In the 1960s, it became clear that a number of plans were inadequately funded, and some were not able to meet pension obligations.

Out of these dissatisfactions, in 1974 Congress enacted a complex regulatory bill that came to be known by its acronym,

ERISA (Employee Retirement Income Security Act). Simply understanding ERISA became a new industry, and it was charged for a time that its complexity drove businesses to give up pension plans. However, one explicit objective was to force businesses that wanted to cover favored executives to cover all employees. Private pension plans did not markedly contract and those that closed may have been worth closing.[3] Total assets grew to $900 billion by 1983. Recent crisis-induced limitations on Social Security benefits have sharpened interest in accumulating private pension rights. At the same time, extensive tax advantages have been provided for funds invested privately for retirement purposes—so-called IRAs and Keogh accounts. By 1983, 20 percent of the population had IRAs; $35 billion was transferred to IRA accounts in that single year and again in 1984.

A clear public theory about the desirable relationship of private and public arrangements for retirement cannot be discerned. Put more bluntly, IRA and Keogh accounts are encouraged out of what is said to be a national need for investment (though experience indicates that they chiefly represent money shifted from other types of savings). Private pension policy arises from collective bargaining strategy and as a fallout from tax policy. Workers and the rest of the public make decisions as consumers, turning to private pensions for improved protection when they perceive public programs to be inadequate. That is, investment policy, collective bargaining policy, and tax policy may substantially conflict with retirement policy. Currently, half of the work force is not covered by a private pension plan, and only half of those covered have vested benefits.[4] Workers not covered and workers without vested benefits are concentrated in smaller companies with lower wage scales. Therefore, a turning to private pensions is likely to work well for those with higher incomes and to the disadvantage of the less well paid. As business, industry, and labor move to improve private pensions, however, they occupy territory that Social Security may then find easier to abandon.

This prospect is not a vagrant, alarmed fantasy. Discrete judgments and advantages have come together in a tidal

movement toward private pensions. Indeed some, insensitive
to irony, have argued that private enterprise should be required to provide private pension plans. A special committee
of Congress proposed that "Congress should emphasize pension policies that provide a *balance* between sources of retirement income."[5] Carefully examined, the implication is a system of private pensions providing levels of retirement income
that people can afford to buy, Social Security to provide the
minimum necessary retirement income, and ssi enlarged to
meet the needs of those who remain needy. Thus, provision
for the income security of the aged would substantially be
divided in three, and two of its parts would suffer from the
difficulties of programs important mainly to the poorer portion of the population. It is this sort of eventuality that the
Commission on Reform forthrightly rejected, but the practical
situation will in time preempt any argument about principles.

The alternative is, of course, the sort of universal Social
Security we think we have assured. This does not require
preventing individuals and businesses from investing in pension plans—they may purchase security as they purchase any
consumer or business item. However, it is poor public policy
to provide government incentives and subsidies for such pur-
chases. For example, in 1985 special tax provisions for employer pension plans and IRAs, taken together, cost the government $66 billion in forgone revenue. Such incentives have
adverse effects apart from tending to undermine a universal
system of Social Security. Particularly for middle-income and
poor people, they give an entirely misleading impression of
long-term security. For example, for the average employee,
vesting requires ten years of service. Employees with less service—over half of all covered employees—may gain no right
to proceeds from retirement contributions on their behalf.
Indeed, one effect of ERISA has been to widen the gap in
vested rights between high- and low-salaried employees.[6] Moreover, few if any private plans are able to adjust for inflation.
It has been estimated that by the year 2000 this failure may
shrink the real value of benefits by more than half.[7]

And finally, like all tax shelters, these incentives return the
most income to the rich and the least to the poor. This is so

when an individual's money is invested in a retirement plan, both because those in the higher tax brackets are forgiven more in taxes and because they can afford to contribute more. It is so because, in effect, they then use the government's money (that is, the taxes that have been deferred) to earn more income. When they retire, they pay lower taxes on reduced income. While at work, one third of the tax benefits of employer pension plans and two thirds of the tax benefits of individual plans go to the 5 percent of employees who are most highly paid (those who earned over $30,000 a year in 1977).[8] In retirement, private pensions represent 1 percent of the income of the poorest fifth of the aged population but 9 percent of the income of the richest fifth.[9] All in all, it can be argued that the wages of the less well paid wind up lower because payments are being made to pension plans that will benefit the more highly paid. In any case, the effect of government-subsidized private pensions, earlier and later, is to widen the gap between rich and poor.

To put all this affirmatively in program terms, a new welfare state would remove or substantially reduce the employee's tax exemption for funds withdrawn from income for retirement purposes. Similarly, payments by employers into retirement plans would (at least in part) be regarded as income to the person on whose behalf the payment was made. On the other hand, no tax would be due on principal when it is withdrawn for retirement income. This is a very substantial shift in conception and surely subject to resistance from those who have the most to lose—insurance and other business interests that have formed around these funds and people who would resent government interference with their personal finances. (There would, of course, be no interference with anything they choose to do without tax advantage.) Perhaps the immediate objective would be to stop adding to government incentives for private insurance. For the longer term, just as these incentives have slowly been built up, they should slowly be reduced. One possible gradualist device is a dollar limitation on the tax-free sum that could go into an individual's retirement arrangements. Such a limit would decline in real value over the years as inflation proceeds.

Intergenerational Conflict

One problem that has arisen in the recent controversy about Social Security may be expressed in a simple ratio: By the year 2020, the ratio of workers to retirees is expected to decline from the 1980 rate of about three to one to about two to one. That is, as the number of elderly increases, supporting them will weigh more heavily on proportionately fewer workers. This forecast is not certain. It assumes continuation of a low birth rate, and more dubiously it assumes low immigration. Also, it fails to capture the important related fact that fewer children will be dependent on workers. In any event, the total number of dependent people will not shift very much: there will be more elderly but fewer children dependent on the working-age population.

Nevertheless, the public perception is that the elderly are becoming a larger burden than they were, and, as it happens, qualitative changes exacerbate the problem of numbers. The proportion of elderly who are over seventy-five has been increasing faster than the total; these "old old" are now 40 percent of the total. That is to say, more care and services will be needed as well as income. Further, the movement of women into the labor force poses the possibility that family care, which has been by far the preponderant resource for old people, will become less available. Presumably the aged and their families will turn to organized resources for help. Simultaneously, medical care represents an almost uncontrollable demand on national resources, and medical care of the elderly is a very large portion of that cost. All these trends come together to mean that the aged will seek and will appear to be seeking more in public resources.

Because of their numbers and the quality of their political activity, the aged have been comparatively successful in pressing their needs in the national arena. Twenty years ago the median income of the aged was about 40 percent of the income of younger adults; it is now well over 50 percent. In that period, the share of the gross national product that the aged receive through social insurance has increased from 2 percent to over 5 percent. Concurrently, despite high unemployment,

Congress has moved in various ways to discourage the aged from retiring. As the number of the aged swell even more and especially if the sense of scarce public resources persists, the aged may find themselves pitted against younger people in a naked struggle for jobs and government funds. Thus, speaking of the foremost congressional activist for the aged, the director of a policy institute said with some heat, "Young scholars without jobs would like to lynch Claude Pepper."[10]

Some who have seen the problem on the horizon have sought to plan ahead for all groups and have counseled restraint in pressing the needs of the aged. A few advocacy organizations representing the aged, on one hand, and children, on the other—the Gray Panthers and the Children's Defense Fund, as examples—have tried to cross generational lines in framing their programs. In doing this, they are closer to their constituents than more partisan advocates. Old people and their children and grandchildren, who together are most of the population, care more about one another than is commonly acknowledged. Despite the appearances created by interest groups, the aged are often more interested in their children and grandchildren than in themselves.

A type of national leadership is needed, both in and out of government, that aims at mutual accommodation of such groups. One aid to accommodation is to frame programs that are not limited to a single age group or risk. In fact, Social Security is such a set of programs—one third of its beneficiaries are the disabled or the widowed or children. In a sense the aged, because they are potent politically, have carried the struggle for adequate Social Security on behalf of these other eleven million. Another aid to accommodation would be to see that significant needy groups are not left behind in a general movement toward security. I shall return to these prescriptions.

I approach programming from a social insurance point of view—that is, with the assumption that those groups of the population that are seriously at risk in terms of income or security can be identified and that mainstream programs can be devised that will substantially protect them. The name by which Social Security goes in legislation—Old Age, Survivors, and Disability Insurance (OASDI)—is itself a phylogeny of such risks or populations: first retirement, or the aged; then survivorship, or widows and orphans; and finally disability. Unemployment is a risk that was identified early and was accorded an independent program—Unemployment Insurance (UI) or Unemployment Compensation. Other identified risks are injury while working (covered by Workers' Compensation) and the loss of income while ill.

The terms in which newer major risks are formulated overlap: (1) children in large families and in single-parent families; (2) women, especially those who are heads of single-parent families, and those who are aged and divorced or separated, thus not adequately provided for by Social Security; and (3) the unemployed and underemployed—in particular the groups that are hard hit by a new economic environment, such as the young, who so extensively suffer unemployment, and men and women in middle age whose experience and skills are no longer salable.

In one way or another, program development in the new welfare state would improve existing provision and address these newer risks. The basic correction for underemployment and unemployment is adequate wages and the provision of jobs; that goes without saying. Here we consider only the social insurances that fill in at the margins of economic policy or where it fails.

Old Age, Survivors, and Disability Insurance

One may assess the fairness and effectiveness of the OASDI system in a variety of ways. The proportion of beneficiaries who are poor is one measure. For example, the proportion of the aged in poverty declined from 35 percent in 1959 to 15 percent in 1979 (at which point it stabilized), an improvement due in large measure to Social Security. The portion of prior income that is replaced is another measure. A widely cited rule of thumb is that "retirement money income of from 65 percent to 80 percent of previous wage income" would allow the aged in good health to maintain prior standards of living.[11] The so-called replacement rate of Social Security—

that is, the portion of prior wages that the benefit provides—varies from 53 percent for low-paid workers to 28 percent for the highest-paid workers. Thus, the low-paid workers fall short of the desired 65 percent; with income from private pensions and assets, highly paid workers approximate that objective. The most significant measure, in the present context, is the degree to which a program tends to diminish inequality. That effect has lately been declining; inequality among the aged is far greater here than in other Western countries. It is to this that I shall primarily attend.[12]

If we are to be free of cant about redistribution, it is important to understand the source of funds. Although the worker's Social Security tax ultimately determines his benefits, these benefits are not paid out of his own money. Beneficiaries are paid with the contributions of current workers, who will in turn receive benefits out of the contributions of future workers. The transfer thus takes place between generations. One reason that benefits can keep pace with inflation and with a rising standard of living as well is that current workers are (in general) producing and earning more. Thus, from the point of view of commercial insurance, beneficiaries receive more than they have paid for. By one calculation, an average person retiring in 1980 received a benefit worth (in constant dollars) something over twice her contributions. Calculated differently, the average low-paid man retiring in 1982 received a benefit of $371 a month, of which his contributions had paid for $105; thus he received a subsidy of $266. An average highly paid man received monthly benefits of $705, of which his contributions had paid for $284; thus he received a subsidy of $421. Calculations for a woman who was retiring or for a worker with a dependent spouse produced different numbers, but with a similar relationship.[13]* Therefore, every

---

*Such calculations are extensively debatable on technical grounds. For example, they can only with great difficulty take into account the financial benefit from having been insured against death and disability prior to retirement. However, these exercises serve to suggest how much every retiree gains from the system and that the system benefits the poorer proportionately more but the richer more in absolute terms.

beneficiary is substantially subsidized, by current workers or by the government, as one prefers—and the highest-paid worker is subsidized more. If more than half of what is paid out is subsidy, as these calculations indicate, the objectives of the subsidy are surely open to discussion. At the very least, the lowest paid should receive the same subsidy as the highest paid.

Proposed improvements in Social Security may seem essentially technical and, taken singly, minor in impact. Taken together, however, the possibilities influence the payment of many billions of dollars. The reports of the 1979 Advisory Council on Social Security canvass scores of these issues.[14] Several are selected for discussion to indicate the direction change would take, given the principles offered earlier.

Retirement Age and Retirement Test

The manner in which baby busts and baby booms have worked out and the movement of women into work combine to produce this effect: "In the upcoming decades, 'older workers' will be competing against the largest cohort of middle-aged workers in our country's history."[15] There will be far fewer workers under thirty-five years of age and slightly fewer over sixty. These trends have led some to argue that it will not be possible to fill jobs unless the aged work in increased numbers. On the other hand, economic changes suggest the possibility of substantial unemployment among middle-aged workers and, therefore, public pressure on older workers to retire or work part-time. In fact, older people who work now typically work part-time.

The substantial entry of women into the work force has been widely recorded. Not so widely understood and in a way baffling is that in the same period—that is, during the past three decades—men's participation in the labor force has been declining. The decline has been greater among men in their late fifties than among younger men, and greatest among men at or approaching retirement age. In 1960, 81 percent of men aged sixty to sixty-four were in the labor force; by 1980, this had fallen to 61 percent. The employment of older women, too, has been falling off somewhat. Over the years, life expectancy has of course been increasing. The period of retirement is thus stretching in two directions at once, beginning earlier and ending later. Although the development is complex and subject to argument, it seems clear that a substantial portion of the withdrawal from work around the age of sixty-five is accounted for by failing health and the difficulty of finding jobs.[16] Poor health and difficulty in finding work interact, of course. The man who thinks work is unavailable is likely to regard a condition from which he has long suffered as more disabling. It is no surprise that those who are not very employable tend to have low incomes and assets.[17] Overwhelmingly, they apply for early retirement under Social Security, thus accepting a reduced retirement benefit as well.

Against this background, in 1983 Congress raised the age at which full Social Security retirement benefits could be claimed to sixty-six and, later, to sixty-seven, step-ups to take effect in the next century. For the public, this issue is somewhat confused with a feeling that old people should not be forced to retire—a quite different matter. The availability of full benefits at the age of sixty-five does not force anyone to apply for them. For Congress, the precipitating issue was simpler: delayed retirement was part of a package that would save money and so balance income and outgo. A one-year delay in retirement age is effectively a 7-percent cut in benefits, a two-year delay is a 13-percent cut. These cuts, it seems plain, will fall on the aged who are least able to sustain them— that is, those who will by then not have been working anyway and whose incomes will be lowest.

One cannot quarrel with the need for prudent financing, but at the same time Congress has been moving to allow those who work to draw virtually full retirement benefits. Approximately 15 percent of aged people now work. Until recently, they gave up $1 in benefits for every $2 earned over $7,320 a year. (This figure goes up automatically each year.) This was itself a considerable liberalization of the original test of retirement, a condition of entitlement satisfied only if people had no income from work. The aged will now give up $1 for every $3 earned in excess of $7,320 a year. A moment's reflection on these numbers will suggest what is in fact the case: that these 15 percent of working elderly have by far higher incomes than the rest of the aged. Yet this change creates an immediate increased cost cancelling the future saving from a one-year delay in retirement age.*

In sum, while old men and old women show a long-term tendency to withdraw from working, voting with the seat of their pants, so to speak, Social Security policy appears to be trying to induce them, if not force them, to work longer. Because these Social Security policies do not create jobs or reduce the number of middle-aged people competing for jobs or move private pensions to similar policies, the number of aged who work is not likely to be affected very much after all.[18] But meanwhile Social Security funds will have been redirected to precisely the wrong people, and many will be more needy or needy longer.

Within current costs, Social Security should rather reestablish sixty-five as the appropriate age for retirement. Annual earnings that are free of reductions should be held at $7,320 a year (with modest inflation, they will play a smaller role), and it would be well to return to a $1 for $2 reduction in benefits. The funds so freed should be used to improve benefit levels for those who retire at sixty-two—the age that is in fact, though not in principle, the preferred time for retirement. Current benefit reductions for those retiring at sixty-two have cut into benefit levels for the poorer among the retired and so have assured penury for the balance of their days. The moves proposed here would permit those of the aged who wish to work to do so, but with less in the way of Social Security supplementation. It would redirect benefit payments to the poorer among the aged. More broadly, it would moderate the desperation with which aged people com-

---

*The added cost for a small proportion of relatively well-off aged was compounded by another provision. People between sixty-five and seventy years of age have received a 3-percent increase in delayed benefits for each year they did not draw benefits. That sweetening is gradually to be increased to 8 percent a year, virtually a 50-percent increase in benefits for those who, chances are, would in any case be working for salaries that would have led them to forgo benefits during the specified years.

pete with younger people for jobs when not enough jobs are available for all.

Upgraded Benefits for the Old Old

In modern times, a critical problem of aging lies in feelings about losing command over one's self and surroundings.[19] The issue has to do with changes in bodily functioning, with the loss of power once exercised through position or work, and with the loss of power in relation to family and friends. Some of these changes are inevitable, but modern American practices enforce an abrupt transition, once uncommon, from power to powerlessness. Yesterday one worked; today one draws a pension. Yesterday others needed something from an aged person; today she disposes of no product, no promotions, and has turned over her home and savings to her children in order to qualify for government benefits. To put the point directly, the day-to-day arrangements between old people and their families are a complex blend of economic exchange and services in which it is often unclear who is the net beneficiary. Sentiment and responsibility play large roles, but they interact with true power to dispose of money and property.

If it is plausible that the design of Social Security ought to support rather than undermine the aged person's sense of control over himself and his own resources, a number of issues may come to mind. Among them is the issue, in any case complex, of how to deal with the needs of increasing numbers of frail or "functionally dependent" old people. In general, the issue has been approached as a Medicare, Medicaid, or social services matter. That is, how does one alter the rules of these programs to pay for the necessary care, or how do we deploy professional services to provide it? Proposed solutions are expensive, in part because they tend to establish new agencies or coordinating devices. Because they are expensive, they invent and incorporate devices for determining whether aged people qualify for help—medical teams, careful evaluations of income, and so forth—which replace the old person's judgment with the government's or the community's.

It may be more workable to treat the cost of home care

through a so-called constant-attendance allowance. As the name suggests, this is an allowance that pays in whole or in part for an attendant. In many countries such allowances were developed initially out of disability programs. They have provoked interest here primarily out of anxiety about the cost of institutional care and the movement of women into paid work. In some countries, payments are made automatically at retirement age to those who have been receiving disability benefits. In other countries, payments are based on proven medical need. Payment is made whether home help is purchased or provided by the family or not provided at all; the choice belongs to the beneficiary. As it happens, in the United States the Veterans Administration provides such a benefit—means-tested, not mainstream—to aged veterans. Within a decade, more than half the aged men in the United States will be veterans. A Social Security attendance allowance, not related to veteran status, would eliminate the need for a veterans' benefit that will otherwise assume large proportions.

Generally speaking, a plausible argument can be made for reworking benefit levels to pay less at sixty-five, more at seventy-five, and even more at the age of eighty-five.[20] (It is a quirk of the development of Social Security that the system now works in the opposite direction—that is, the benefits of sixty-five-year-olds now average about 15 percent more than benefits of the oldest.) With advancing age, needs tend to increase and resources to be depleted. Benefit levels may reasonably, if roughly, be adjusted. If this were done, an attendance allowance for the aged would simply fold into the benefit formula. The government would deal with the cost issues as an income strategy—a strategy that it administers with relative efficiency and simplicity.

For example, in 1979 an average decrease of $30 a month in the benefit of the younger retired would, without net cost to the system, have made it possible to increase the average benefits at age seventy-five by $45 a month and at eighty-five by $50 a month *more*. Instead of declining with age, as benefits did in 1979, they would have averaged $276 a month for those from sixty-five to seventy-four years old, $332 a month for those up to eighty-four years of age, and $359 a month for those over eighty-five. The changeover would not be made by actually reducing anyone's benefit, of course. In the end, funds will have to be allocated somewhere to deal with growing needs for at-home care. If additional Social Security funds are not available, however, such a changeover could be achieved over time by differentially redirecting cost-of-living increases. The "young old" should not be outraged at the change, as they themselves may hope in time to benefit.

With respect to an attendance allowance for younger people who are disabled, it is harder to provide simple, rough justice. As disability beneficiaries are, by definition, very severely disabled, it may be appropriate to accord them one of the higher benefit levels available to the aged. Thus, the implicit assumption would be that they all need at least some part-time attendance. However, the definition of disability goes to occupational capacity, not capacity to care for one's self. Moreover, particularly if other changes liberalized the benefit, families might find themselves with Social Security considerably in excess of the beneficiary's earning capacity. That is, there might be a problem about incentive to return to work. It is possible to be obsessive about this issue (as some academic doctoral departments have demonstrated) but it cannot be ignored. It may be preferable, therefore, to begin with a determination of the need for constant attendance by the same physician who certifies physical disability, and the provision of an additional allowance to such beneficiaries.

The changes involved in an attendance allowance would tend to redirect funds from those among the aged who are better off to those who are poorer. It would place some control in the hands of the aged and disabled needing care, rather than with family members or outside agencies. And it would be a step toward the mainstream solution of a problem already larger on the horizon than the shadow of a man's outstretched palm.

Family Benefits

Age and benefits at retirement concern chiefly the aged, naturally. Other issues are of more moment to younger adults and children. For example, although the Social Security benefit is in principle based on one's earnings and contributions, this could mean an average of lifetime earnings or, by contrast, an average of the highest three or five years of earnings. One can readily see the opposing arguments about fairness: The first approach is more like private insurance, paying out in relation to all that was paid in, while a "high three" or "high five" formula enables people to maintain the style of life they have achieved. Social Security adopts a third approach, using earnings from the age of twenty-one to sixty-two but dropping from the calculation the five years of lowest earnings. It then updates the benefit in terms of the level of current wages.

Just how high benefits should be is not really the issue—that is determined by other elements in the calculation. The issue is rather how different kinds of beneficiaries will share in total benefits. For example, after some years of uncertainty and back-and-forthing, Congress wiped out the minimum benefit in 1981. (Unaffected was a special minimum benefit for those who had worked a long time at very low wages.) The general minimum benefit had assured $122 a month to those to whom the regular benefit calculation would have given less. A study of who would lose from the change revealed that 80 percent were housewives with an average of about eight years of paid employment before retirement.[21] Obviously, the regular benefit calculation would also work out better for such people if more than five years were disregarded. These particular women are an example, extreme to be sure, of women in general. Because of housework or child care, women tend to be employed for fewer years than men. A higher drop-out formula would benefit women relative to men (except for couples, in which case gain and loss might cancel out).

A similar issue arises with respect to disability and survivors insurance. With the existing provision for five drop-out years, if a thirty-year-old worker dies or becomes disabled, benefits may be based on only five or six years of work. It has therefore been proposed (without avail, fortunately) that drop-out years should be scaled to age, disregarding no more than one year of earnings for each six years after the age of twenty-two.[22] Such a provision would take aim precisely at young families with children, reducing their benefits relative to other beneficiaries. On the other hand, it may be reasonable to provide more drop-out years to those who have been at work for forty years; and a ratio of one-for-six represents only a very small improvement. Robert Ball has proposed movement over some years toward a calculation based on the highest-paid thirty years of employment.[23] At retirement, many years from now, such a formula would tend to favor women, for reasons already indicated, and also men who have been unemployed for an extended period. That young adults who are currently unemployed for long periods should not find themselves penalized at retirement may appeal to one's sense of justice.

The calculation of a beneficiary's payment apart, his dependents are also entitled to benefits—50, 75, or 100 percent of his benefit, depending on circumstance. Among dependents benefited in this manner in 1981 were 4.4 million children, some of them college students and disabled older children, the large majority under eighteen. From the program's beginning, there has been concern that the family of a worker who has died or become disabled should not wind up with more in benefits than was being earned. Therefore a maximum is imposed on the amount a family may receive, varying from 150 to 188 percent of the basic benefit. The main effect, it may seem obvious, is to reduce benefits to families with more than one child. Thus, in 1979 children in one-child families were receiving their proper 50 percent of a parent's benefit, but children in three-child families were, after a pro-rated reduction, getting an average of about 25 percent of a parent's benefit. Studies have found that 4 percent of the cases receiving AFDC also receive social insurance—a plain indication that the Social Security benefit level is far too low for them. (Overlap also means unnecessary duplication of administration.) More broadly, a third of families receiving survivors insurance are nevertheless poor.[24]

To sum up with respect to family benefits, it would be well in a calculation of benefit levels to disregard at least five years of low earnings and to consider no more than the worker's best thirty years. It would be reasonable to reinstitute a general minimum benefit. Prominent in the reasons why Congress wiped it out was the feeling that federal workers collect the minimum Social Security benefit in addition to generous civil service retirement. Congress subsequently disposed of that anxiety, requiring civil servants to be covered under Social Security. A modest minimum benefit would mainly provide income to people who would otherwise turn to ssi anyway. Finally, the maximum family benefit should be liberalized to provide better support levels for dependent children. Although it is appropriate to limit family benefits somehow, it may at the same time be specified that the effect should not be to reduce the prorated benefit of any particular entitled child below, say, $150 a month.

Women under Social Security

Congress and the courts have steadily been correcting gender-based inequities in Social Security. For example, a woman who was divorced after a long marriage would once have found herself cut off from benefits based on her ex-husband's earnings. Now she is entitled to those benefits if she was married for at least ten years. Equal treatment provides a payoff for men as well. Now a widowed father who chooses to stay at home with his children can receive benefits just as a widowed mother can. The 1979 Advisory Council counted nine remaining essentially technical distinctions in Social Security law based on gender; Congress has been whittling away at them.

The substantial issue is now more exactly autonomy than equity. If marriage is a partnership of equals, benefits for a woman should be based solely on her own earnings. Currently, the majority of women receive benefits based on their husband's earnings. Because in general women have worked shorter periods at lower wages, a benefit as a wife—50 percent of the husband's benefit—often turns out to be larger than a benefit based on her own earnings. That is itself a grievance. Her own work adds nothing to her benefit; thus she has contributed taxes and receives nothing for them. To be sure, this is because the now-offensive assumption that she will be dependent entitles her to a benefit even though she makes no Social Security contribution at all.

Many solutions have been offered. A government task force has proposed giving Social Security credit to women for housework at home, giving recognition where it seems appropriate and building up women's own retirement credits. But defining housework for this purpose would be a daunting problem. What woman or, for that matter, man could be excluded from the definition? And who would pay the tax—the woman? her husband? the government? A solution called *earnings-sharing* has produced more public support. In each year, half the total earnings of a married couple would be credited to each person, regardless of who earned more or whether, indeed, both worked. If they divorced, each would from that time earn retirement credit solely from his or her own income.* Such a plan provides autonomy and additional benefits when a second partner works and is equitable in the face of divorce.

Earnings-sharing also raises thorny technical problems that could not be resolved without substantial increased cost or with lower levels of benefits to some kinds of families—one-earner couples, for example. Moreover, women, though they gain autonomy, may in the event turn out to have lost in level of benefits. That is, under such a plan, their benefits as wives would end and women's benefits would depend much more heavily than now on their own earnings. Then what are women's own earnings likely to be? For many years to come women will receive Social Security who reached adulthood at a time when comparatively few women worked. Statisticians estimate that even women born in 1970 will average only twenty-three years of paid work. Women are more likely than men to work part-time. And the average earnings of women seem to be stuck at a point well under two-thirds those of men. We

*A somewhat more radical scheme called a double-decker plan is offered to achieve equity for women and fairer distribution of benefits as well. See Martha N. Ozawa, *Social Security: Toward a More Equitable and Rational System*, St. Louis, Washington University, October 1982; Martha N. Ozawa, "Social Insurance and Redistribution," in Alvin L. Schorr, ed., *Jubilee for Our Times*, New York, Columbia University Press, 1977; 1979 Advisory Council on Social Security, op. cit.; and "Men and Women: Changing Roles and Social Security," *Social Security Bulletin*, v. 42, no. 5, May 1979.

hope for improvement, but that is meanwhile the fact. By retirement, in short, women will have worked fewer years, fewer hours, for lower wages. In terms of earnings, many will be counted poor. Unrelieved by the option of taking a wife's benefit, their benefit will reflect lifelong disadvantage.

The autonomy issue is a persuasive argument for earnings-sharing, but its limitations for women suggest a cautious approach to transition. Such a changeover should be staged to take effect many years in the future, when the women who are affected will be retiring from a world of work in which they may reasonably be expected to have participated. Other protections for women would be provided in ways we have been discussing. A list of recommended changes may indicate their relevance for women.

• maintaining retirement age at sixty-five and improving benefits at sixty-two (financed by giving less in benefits to those who are able to work after sixty-five).

• upgrading benefits for the old old (achieved by reallocating cost-of-living increases to develop three levels of benefits).

• liberalizing maximum payments for families.

• restoring a general minimum benefit.

• disregarding more years of low earnings at retirement for those approaching sixty-two or sixty-five.

Such provisions will turn out to benefit women in particular. That should not be surprising. Women are prominent among the poor; policies that help the poor will help women, and vice versa. In particular, the very aged poor are predominantly women; it is women who raise the children affected by rigorous maximum payments; and women raising children and doing housework naturally have interrupted work histories.

These are selected examples of a variety of technical issues that arise in a complex system. The effects of such changes, it may be perceived, would be to redirect program funds to the least affluent, to substitute mainstream Social Security for ssi and afdc, and to address the needs of women and children more effectively.

Unemployment Insurance

As with Social Security, issues concerning UI may sound technical, but in current economic circumstances they have large effects. An encyclopedic report by the National Commission on Unemployment Compensation[25] canvasses these issues; a few are selected here for discussion. It would be fruitless to go very far without noting the financial difficulties of the UI system.

In contrast with Social Security, UI is administered by states, in conformity with federal law. The tax on employers that finances UI is established by the individual states, but with great sensitivity to federal provisions. The federal government taxes the first $7,000 of wages paid to each employee at 3.5 percent but forgives as much as 2.7 percent if paid as a state UI tax. In effect, the specified wage ceiling and forgiveness of federal taxes establish state minimum taxes. About a third of the states tax wages above $7,000; all but one have tax rates higher than 2.7 percent.

During the 1970s, UI faced unprecedented demands. High unemployment brought more applications for benefits; and initial benefit payments almost doubled between 1974 and 1975. The duration of unemployment lengthened, increasing the average period over which payments were made. But the ceiling on taxable wages covers less than half of all wages. (At $3,000 in 1940, the ceiling included 98 percent of all wages.) That is, rising wage levels were not reflected in payroll tax collections to nearly the extent necessary to balance expenditures. State trust funds were exhausted; by 1983, nineteen states had had to borrow a total of $8 billion from the federal government.

Facing a problem of inadequate revenue that became acute with widespread unemployment, the National Commission recommended raising the taxable ceiling in accordance with a formula based on the national average wage. The ceiling would start at 50 percent of the average wage in covered employment and rise in stages to 65 percent.[26] However, Congress has taken an alternative route, raising the federal tax rate effective in 1985 to 6.2 percent (and raising the federal forgiveness for payments as state taxes to 5.4 percent). The effect is to place the largest burden of the increase on low-wage employers. It almost doubles the tax on salaries up to $7,000 but taxes salaries above that level not at all. Presumably, the burden of the tax increase will constrain the wages of low-wage employees in these enterprises or tend to eliminate their jobs. A nation concerned about full employment or fairer income shares or both will substitute the higher ceiling recommended by the National Commission for the higher tax rate that was enacted.

Taxing Benefits

State UI benefits were free of taxation until, in 1979, half of the benefits became subject to taxation for couples with income over $25,000 and for individuals with incomes over $20,000. Because few unemployed people had incomes that were much higher, the revenue produced was (in federal terms) negligible—less than half a billion dollars. There was nevertheless extensive resentment; the policy issue is an important one for a welfare state.

Although families of unemployed workers may be in considerable difficulty, many others have adequate incomes. They may have income from assets, or other members of the family may be working, or a person may be unemployed for a few weeks but earn decent income the rest of the year. An analysis for 1970 indicates that about half of UI benefits were received by families with incomes higher than the median.[27] Although they are probably an overstatement in current terms, the 1970 figures indicate the broad income span over which UI benefits may be spread. For upper-income families a tax-free UI benefit is a windfall when compared with wages. Conversely, it is frivolous to argue that a tax on incomes over $20,000 or $25,000 is a tax on the poor. Whether one thinks taxing UI is really an approach to a fairer tax structure and to fairer income shares may depend on the standard of comparison. If UI income is to be taxed but various corporate and upper-income escapes from taxes go untouched, middle-income families will suffer in comparison with upper-income families. But if a new welfare state sets out to improve fairness throughout the tax structure, as it should, then UI should play its part. In short, it seems appropriate that UI benefits should be taxed as ordinary income, and it would be reasonable to pair such a policy with a comparable change in some egregious upper-income tax loopholes.

Some have said that taxing UI benefits (and Social Security benefits, for that matter) is means-testing. This position fails to define means-testing precisely. Unemployment Insurance is a mainstream program because benefits are available on the basis of a work record and the fact of being involuntarily unemployed—without regard to income. There is no test of means, nor is the income tax such a test. To cast the matter differently, means-testing may be seen as the application of a *special* tax to a government benefit. That is, an AFDC recipient may lose a dollar in benefits for every dollar earned or, in special circumstances, a dollar for every two dollars earned, but either way she would not be liable for income tax. In the unlikely event that AFDC levels were high enough to make her liable for income tax, she would pay at a 12- or 14-percent rate. Thus AFDC imposes an *additional* tax of 100, 50, or almost 40 percent; that is means-testing. To extend the concept of means-testing to include any application of the progressive income tax is to suggest, for example, that all wages are means-tested and to extinguish the distinction between means-testing and mainstreaming.

Benefits

The heart of the question for beneficiaries is what they receive. In general, the objective has been to replace half of one's prior earnings. A few states liberalize their payment formulas to provide additional sums for dependents or for low-wage earners. On the other hand, all states place a maximum on benefits, designed to avoid very high (and expensive) UI payments. Few states have raised the maximum nearly in concert with rising wage levels, so that the average benefit paid (about $127 a week in early 1985) is now rather a third than a half of average prior earnings. Among a variety of possible devices for improving this record, the National Commission recommended requiring each state to adopt a maximum that would be no less than two-thirds of the state's average wages. This would require all but a half dozen states to raise the maximum immediately; all would then rise regularly with wage levels. The commission was not so firm with respect to allowances for dependents, only gently urging such benefits upon states. The issue is quite the same as in Survivors Insurance. On one hand, substantial dependents' benefits may increase a UI payment so that it exceeds prior wages. On the other hand, as the National Commission itself found, UI is "least adequate for household heads . . . and especially inadequate for single earners with large families."[28] A resolution should be sought that provides some increased benefit for each child (or other dependent) without creating dramatic situations of overpayment relative to prior wages. If a federal requirement in this matter may seem to infringe on the state-federal relationship in UI the same result might be achieved with generous federal sharing of the cost.

Quite as serious for many who are unemployed is how long they may expect to receive benefits. Regular state programs provide benefits for about six months, but in recent times one-quarter of those who are unemployed have been out of work longer. In the absence of UI, most of these families would not be eligible for any means-tested benefit other than food stamps, and poverty among them would increase dramatically.[29] Nevertheless, somewhat limited studies (but better studies are not available) indicate that three months after UI benefits are exhausted, fewer than a third of the long-term unemployed have found work.[30] For such reasons, over the years Congress has devised a series of extended benefit programs, financed with state and federal UI funds, which added thirteen weeks to the potential duration of benefits. Eight to fourteen weeks more were added to duration in 1982 by a temporary program financed out of federal general revenues. The temporary program was discontinued in 1985. In implicit, stubborn adherence to the view that long-term unemployment is an oddity, these special programs incorporated a "trigger." That is, a striking increase in unemployment level in a particular state is required to establish the need for extended benefits and to trigger the program. There have been bizarre effects. At one point, extended benefits triggered *off* in Ohio and Indiana when their unemployment rate was 13 percent.

We should not fail to note that about 10 percent of the labor force is not covered by UI, even in principle. More to the point, fewer than half of those who are unemployed held "insured" employment. Many have not worked long enough for coverage, and, conspicuously, the uninsured include domestic workers, certain types of agricultural workers, and young adults seeking work for the first time. The first groups are inevitably the lowest paid and most vulnerable workers, and it seems important that coverage be worked out for them in the basic system. Young adults present a separate problem for which, to be sure, some solution must also be envisioned.

The halting and clumsy development of extended benefit programs, with one set thought to be permanent and another temporary, is not simply a result of confusion and lack of concern. A series of unrelated social changes have altered the context in which UI operates. First, it was devised as a state-administered program, largely financed by a state tax on employers. As unemployment and the average duration of unemployment increased, states' finances suffered as well, and they became less able to carry or even share the costs. Thus, the temporary nature of the program financed out of general revenues expressed the federal government's reluctant engagement. Second, in many cases those who are now unemployed will not work again with the skills they have. These include young people: the nation has not come to terms with how to get them into UI. To be sure, it is distressing to think that youths should emerge from school into UI benefit payments. Included on the other hand are the adult long-term unemployed—those out of work six months or more. They move from regular to extended benefits, if they can, coming in time to concentrate on survival techniques: which other family member can work? sell the house? apply for food stamps or welfare? The idea of identifying and preparing for a new occupation may come late or not seem practical.

Third, older middle-aged people turn to thoughts of early retirement. *Discouraged worker* describes a person not working but not seeking work—and therefore not counted as unemployed. In the same sense, many of these early retirement people are permanently discouraged workers. In contrast with trends for other age groups, as noted earlier, both men and women in their late fifties and early sixties appear increasingly to opt out of work. Social Security statistics clearly reflect the program pressure they create for earlier retirement; and they need more nearly adequate benefits at retirement.[31] This is not a development envisioned in the design of Social Security. It complicates the task of finding an objective test of retirement because whether benefits are being sought mainly because work seems unavailable is uncertain. Similarly, it adds to the difficulty of testing entitlement for disability insurance. Applicants cannot find work and feel disabled— perhaps in some ways they are; it is a close judgment to say they are not. At the same time there is, of course, considerable pressure to move in the opposite program direction—that is, to delay retirement age. The permanent and temporary extended benefit UI programs are fragmentary attempts to meet the human problems that are a consequence of these changes—fragmentary because the changes have not been assimilated.

It may be evident that a program solution is required that deals with all three issues. Proposals that surface from time to time envision a program based on the assumption that anyone who has sought work unsuccessfully for six months is likely to require special help in finding work, if not training or retraining. In one way or another, the proposals combine an additional period of benefit payments with training and evaluation of job skills and potential. As an option, the program may be made available to people who have not exhausted regular UI, but who conclude that such a program suits their needs. The National Commission recommended such a plan, carefully limited as to services and to the ages of beneficiaries (sixty to sixty-four), and mentioned without recommendation a more ambitious expert plan prepared for them.[32] The latter, in part means-tested, would have added about $1.5 billion to the cost of UI. Such a program would replace both the permanent and temporary extended benefit programs.

A program of insurance or assistance for the unemployed that is combined with well-considered job training offers an opportunity to young adults who have not been able to settle into work. Federally financed, it accepts continuing financial responsibility. And it offers an alternative to middle-aged or pre-retirement adults, releasing Social Security to deal with genuine retirement and genuine disability. Under conditions of high unemployment, such a program involves a large federal outlay. On the other hand, it seems unsound to move forward with so many people both young and old floundering in employment and survival terms. All that floundering also carries a calculable cost.

In regard to UI, then, a program is envisioned for the long-term (six months or more) unemployed that would replace the existing programs. Congress has already provided for a large part of the increased cost, although I propose to substitute a more egalitarian tax formula. Benefits for dependents would also contribute to fairer income shares. Moving in the directions indicated would improve mainstreaming at least marginally. Support for a reformed extended benefits program is aimed at rationalizing the UI program and simplifying its relationship to Social Security. Most important, the new program would be equipped to meet the retraining and job-finding needs as well as the basic income needs of its beneficiaries. It would establish federal responsibility in an area that arises, after all, out of national management and circumstances. And the program would serve the common needs of young adults, the middle-aged, and those approaching retirement.

Workers' Compensation and Temporary Illness

Workers' Compensation protects the income of workers in the event of on-the-job injury or illness and provides medical and rehabilitation services. Major development of the programs occurred in the decade after 1908, but it was not fully organized across the country until 1949. Now every state provides coverage, and 87 percent of the workers across the country are covered. An entitled worker earning an average wage receives as a benefit about 60 percent of prior earnings.[33] Benefits may also be provided to survivors of entitled workers.

Issues in this program are similar to those in Social Security and UI.[34] The objective in terms of wage replacement is 66 percent of prior wages. A shortfall occurs because states require a waiting period for benefits, apply a maximum to payment levels, and, especially, fail to adjust payments upward to take account of the number of dependents. The question of including so-far-uncovered workers, about 13 percent of those who work for wages and salaries, is another major issue. An issue peculiar to Workers' Compensation is the level of contentiousness engendered in its administration. A large proportion of cases—including as many as a third to a half of serious cases—are contested. Growing concern about environmental issues and workplace safety can only serve to exacerbate the already excessive levels of conflict in the administration of this program. The problem may lie in inadequate definition of the illnesses that are covered or in poor methods of determining the level of disability and therefore of payment.[35]

A final major area of income loss and protection has to do with temporary illness. Sick leave in government service and in private enterprise provides the largest share of protection— $9.7 billion in 1981. Other major types of protection include individually carried insurance and payments under insurance provided by employers ($3.5 billion in 1981).[36] Six states, including populous California and New York, and Puerto Rico, by law require employers to provide so-called Temporary Disability Insurance. These protections have not matured to the same extent as other social insurance, so that nationally a little less than two thirds of workers are protected, and wage replacement is only 38 percent (1981).[37] In addition to other familiar issues, a significant question would be whether and how to establish a national system of income protection for workers who are ill.

I forbear to go into the issues connected with Workers' Compensation and protection in the event of illness. In principle, the discussion and the resolution of the problems would follow earlier sections. The major question that would have to be worked out is whether protection in the event of illness may be left to private enterprise and collective bargaining, where it chiefly lodges now, or whether states should mandate protection. Undoubtedly, the poorest workers are now the most poorly protected.

In this chapter, I have surveyed issues in Social Security and Unemployment Insurance that lend themselves to discussion in terms of the objectives of a new welfare state. It has simply been noted that Workers' Compensation and protection in the event of temporary illness contain similar issues. In general, the issues have been treated as if very little additional government funding is likely to be available. Indeed, with respect to some recommendations (taxing benefits and disregarding income from work), additional program income or savings would be realized that could be channeled to the increased cost of other recommendations. If additional government funding were available, the task of realizing changes would of course be easier, but the emphasis here is on the distribution of benefits rather than on their level.

We have paid attention to the effect of these recommendations on women; attention is also required to their effect on blacks and other minority groups. Black men and women have a shorter life expectancy than whites; consequently they do not in the same proportions collect retirement insurance. On the other hand, they are overrepresented among those who collect survivors insurance and disability insurance. These are unfortunate consequences that also flow from a shortened life expectancy as well as higher rates of poverty and unemployment. The story for Hispanics is similar. Because blacks and Hispanics are more likely to be poor, they would benefit to a greater extent from policies designed to reach the poor—the policies pursued here. Yet these policies are, in a bureaucratic sense, color-blind. No civil servant or application form need ask color or ethnicity. Because the disadvantage of minorities is so largely a class disadvantage, policies designed to achieve fairer shares will benefit them as long as substantial minority disadvantage persists.

The policies that are indicated in this chapter do not confront at least one major set of risks to income; that is perhaps obvious. Struggling with that problem is the task of the next chapter.

4

Women and Children
Last (But Their
Time Has Come)

s improvements in the social insurances will
come in increments, one way or another, it is
difficult to know where the greatest shortfalls
will occur. Much will depend on the health of
the economy and the mood of the country regarding public funds. One thing is clear: the instruments of
social insurance that we have, even if enriched and improved,
cannot deal adequately with the income problem of families
and children. We begin by trying to grasp the magnitude and
nature of that problem.

Of all the poor in the United States, 40 percent are children. The poverty rate for children declined to a low of 14
percent during the 1960s and has since steadily gone up again
to over 20 percent. In 1983, 13.8 million children lived in a
poor family. Some experts believe that the government's fixed
definition of poverty understates deprivation—for example,
in congressional testimony Alice M. Rivlin picked a line at 125
percent of the official definition. One fourth of all children,
she said, live in "near-poverty households."[1] At one time,
much was made of childhood poverty in the country that de
Toqueville called child-centered. As birth rates dropped and

the women's movement gained ground, the issue came to be phrased as "the feminization of poverty."[2]

Either way, we begin with the one fifth of children who now live in single-parent families. A child born today has a fifty-fifty chance of spending a period of time with a single parent. These children and parents face a fierce array of economic handicaps. On the face of it, a single parent has only one wage to rely upon. Because single parents have, on the average, poor skills and education and because they are discriminated against, that wage is usually relatively small. Although the evidence is that they take virtually any job they can find,[3] their unemployment rate is high.

Child support helps only a little. In 1984 only about a third of single mothers received child support—an average of $2,300 a year.[4] The reasons are well understood. The income of the fathers is low, on the average. Many remarry and apply such income as they have to their new families. And courts often fail to hold fathers to stringent standards for support, either because courts are sensitive about the father's income or because they respond to the power of the contest some fathers are able to wage. Over three decades, and especially in the past four or five years, the federal government has moved with mounting force to compel the payment of support. Nevertheless, the average amount paid in 1984 was well below that in 1979, especially when adjusted for inflation. In net outcome half of the families of mothers with children are poor.[5]

Other causes for childhood poverty are low wages, underemployment and unemployment, large family size, and a problem intrinsic to the so-called family life cycle. It is a long-standing problem, identified years ago by Senator Paul Douglas, that a minimum wage earned full-time the year round is not adequate to permit a family of four to escape poverty.[6] Moreover, in relationship to family need the minimum wage has been degraded over the last two decades. At $3.35 an hour, the minimum wage just approximated the 1984 poverty level for a family of two—$6,720. Thus, it should be no surprise that, even among families in which at least one adult works regularly, those with children are more likely to be poor.[7]

A more general problem is the long-term erosion of the family wage. Until about 1960, it was thought that a man's wage or that of a single parent ought to be adequate for reasonable maintenance of a small family. Although many married women who came into the labor force in the 1960s felt that they were earning discretionary income, in succeeding years they have come to feel that they are required to work. In part, this is because the average earnings of men, which had been rising steadily, stabilized in the 1970s and then for two or three years declined. In 1981, for example, the Department of Agriculture estimated a moderate standard of living for a family of four at $25,400. At that time, the average annual industrial wage was $13,270. Two people working at the average industrial wage just managed a moderate standard of living—if neither got laid off. Thus, minimum and average wages have declined relative to family living standards, posing a new or aggravated problem for those who undertake to support dependents.

Obviously, unemployment interrupts wages entirely and is even more damaging. Only a few states adjust Unemployment Insurance to family size, as we have noted, so that benefits, which tend to be inadequate anyway, are "least adequate for household heads."[8] In general, one third of the unemployed are poor; in March 1981, when the unemployment rate was 7.3 percent, four million children lived in two-parent families in which a parent was unemployed. That family size is a factor in poverty is self-evident: three out of five poor children are in families that have three or more children.[9]

Poverty as Career
A textbook list of the qualities that cause childhood poverty provides little sense of the "career" or struggle that poverty represents. It is well understood that poverty runs a course involving simultaneous crises on two planes—family development and income development.[10] Four critical stages of this cycle are: (1) timing and circumstances of first marriage and childbearing; (2) timing and direction of occupational choice; (3) family cycle squeeze—the conflict of aspiration and need; and (4) family disorganization.

Early marriage (say, before the age of eighteen) tends to be associated with low income, poor education, early childbearing, more children, and separation and divorce. Early marriage (or living together) is not an isolated judgment; it reflects the view of two youths about their life chances. Many young people who think they can get ahead economically will trade the instant satisfaction of living together for longer-term advantage. The experience of their elders and the current economic climate affect their perception of this trade-off rather more than exhortation from afar. Early occupational choice ("hustling" included) is also counterproductive, and it tends to be forced by early marriage. Those who postpone settling into an occupation choose more knowledgeably, with better contacts and the ability to demand a higher price for their work. Personal and family income are significant because education, moving where opportunities are, and even an optimum job search all cost money.

By their middle twenties, young adults have made interlocking decisions that bind them. They have decided whether to go on in school or work, limiting what they may do later. For those who live where work is not easily found, these are the years when the decision is taken to move or to stay. Now families face the strain between income, on the one hand, and what is needed for maintenance and for realizing ambitions, on the other—the family cycle squeeze.[11] Unfortunately, income tends to develop out of phase with family need. That is, income rises over the years with job progression, seniority, and greater freedom for mothers to work, but expenses are relatively highest in the early years. To cope with this problem, people may moonlight. Alternatively, they may try to restrict their need for income—spacing children or having fewer children is an obvious strategy. Other strategies, such as borrowing money and piling up bills, have evident limitations.

At this point, some people give up such aspirations as they may have had and struggle for simple survival. Or the father (more usually than the mother) may separate from the family, possibly to try again. It is not usually quite so coldly calculated, of course. In the nature of the struggle, there has been plenty of frustration and conflict to account for separation.

The mother and children may continue to struggle, but with the cards greatly stacked against them. This has been called the stage of family disorganization. In fact, the family may seem to get itself organized for the first time in years, but it is certainly handicapped.

Thus we see the interrelationship of the choices that are made about work and family, how they flow together, and how the practical possibilities, including the money that is or may be expected to be available, influence the choices. One perceives the relevance of a concept applied to developing countries. Take-off, W. W. Rostow once wrote, awaits "the build-up of social overhead capital," together with the necessary skills and a drive for improvement.[12] Take-off for poor families requires surplus money for investment in self-improvement (social overhead capital), as well as the skill and drive more usually urged upon them.

Middle-Income Families

The same principles apply to all but upper-middle-class and wealthy families. Income starts out low for most workers and, if there are children, expenses relatively high. Child by child, the proportion of family income devoted to necessities like food and clothing rises, and family living standards decline. Something must give: expenditures on recreation and transportation and social overhead capital decline. These observations appear to hold "across all age-and-education categories,"[13] which is to say that the struggle of a broad band of young American families for decent living standards and self-improvement is being described. There has lately been alarm about the number of families dropping from middle-income to marginal status—eight million families in five years.[14] It may therefore be understood that the issue about living standards and social overhead capital for young, nonpoor families has become acute.

Programs for Families

Current income maintenance programs, even if improved or redirected, would not readily resolve this issue of income in relation to family need and social overhead capital. Among the social insurances, Survivors, Disability, and Unemployment Insurance address childhood poverty. Parental death, for which Survivors Insurance was designed, is now far out-ranked as a risk by parental separation—which Social Security does not address.[15] Moreover, all the social insurance programs relate benefit payments to prior contributions or wages. In order to protect this principle, we have noted, Social Security provides only moderate benefits for dependents and also applies a so-called family maximum—limiting the number of children for whom added benefits are paid to between 1.5 and 1.9. Most states do not provide Unemployment Insurance benefits for dependents at all. The dilemma about how to provide decently for dependents while maintaining the broad concept of wage-related benefits is, unfortunately, intrinsic to our concept of social insurance.

In addition, we have the means-tested programs—food stamps, AFDC, and a number of smaller programs. By definition, they deal only with the most deprived and at levels that are not far from pauperization, even in the best of times. They may prevent hunger but they do not provide for—indeed, the manner in which they are administered may actively interfere with—dignity and self-improvement; and means-tested programs do nothing at all for children in families with moderate incomes.

Other Western countries have social insurance and means-tested programs as we do, and they have special programs for single-parent families that very modestly supplement their income. For example, every single parent in Britain is entitled to a so-called Child Benefit Increase. More to the point, all Western industrial countries except the United States have a basic program that provides a sum of money for every child without regard to income—the family or children's allowance. These benefits represent a "significant percentage" of median wages—5 to 10 percent when there is one child and substantially more for single mothers and for families with several children.[16] Some countries provide instead or in addition an income tax credit for each child (Canada) or for a single parent (Australia).[17] The credit is payable as a tax refund to families that are not liable for taxes because of low income.

Inevitably, means-tested programs assume inverse importance in each country to the level at which children's allowances and other programs are provided. Thus, the United States spends more on such programs as AFDC and food stamps, in dollars or as a proportion of social benefits, than any other industrial country. In net outcome, in Britain and France the total income of single parents is half that of two-parent families, but in the United States the proportion is only one third. The system of children's allowances (or tax credits) and supplementary programs, taken together with other differences between countries, leave single-parent families and other families with children relatively better off in Britain and France than in the United States.[18]

There was a time when the absence of children's allowances in the United States was hard to explain;* a considerable case might still be made for such a program.[19] But time and changing social conditions probably make a refundable tax credit more desirable than children's allowances. On the one hand, very large families—the best case for children's allowances—have become less common. For example, a typical AFDC family not so long ago contained three children; it now contains two. On the other hand, aged women (and aged men as well,

---

*The major reasons that children's allowances did not spread to the United States lie in history. In Europe, they were originally an employer strategy to depress wages. Subsistence wages were adjusted to family size, thus meeting the problem of larger families without providing a general wage increase. In the end, trade unions won general wage increases anyway and the program flourished to meet other purposes; European trade unions have for years supported them vigorously. However, American trade unions opposed them at a critical time. Moreover, children's allowances were long regarded in Europe as a device for raising the birth rate. In the European experience with such efforts after 1930 it became clear that that is not how babies get made, but public perception was not much altered. When government programs were expanding in the 1960s, Americans were preoccupied with a population explosion. We were not going to enact any measure that, however incorrectly, might be thought to make such a problem worse. Finally, it has widely been supposed that children's allowances would be a Catholic measure. As the American political process goes, such a view greatly undermined chances of enactment until recently.

but women far more urgently) rival children in the desperation of their need for income supplementation. In 1980, over half of the aged women living alone had incomes defined as below or on the borderline of poverty.[20] In 1984, 2.6 million aged women had incomes below the poverty level, and almost half of aged women had incomes of less than $5,000 a year.[21] Many of these women never had their own incomes; those who did earned less than men, and those who were married outlived their husbands. Moreover, as they are older on the average than retired men, their benefits are based on lower contributions because their wages were earned in earlier years. The problem is likely to grow more rather than less serious, because more are living to advanced ages.

Finally, changing demographic patterns combine with the increasing scarcity of public funds to produce predictions, not to say evidence, of intergenerational conflict—a development not to be viewed lightly. It is attractive to meet the evident needs of the young and the old—and of middle-aged people, who are perforce linked to the needs of children and the aged—with a single public program.

To sum up, families with children have for a long time represented a large portion of the poor population—and that problem is growing. Even many middle-income families with children are experiencing difficulty. In the nature of the stages that most families traverse, the least income is available when income is most needed. For a variety of reasons connected with the economy and government policy, these pressures are particularly acute now and will be for some little while at least. Even small sums that allow for maneuverability and investment in advancement are important to young families. Yet our extensive and, despite all difficulties, fundamentally successful social insurance system has been designed with an eye to individuals. It supports disabled, retired, unemployed, widowed, and orphaned individuals, but not families. It therefore deals poorly with children as dependents and misses many children—those with single parents, for example—entirely. It is time to address a program to children and their families.

The Refundable Tax Credit

A refundable tax credit is a credit against income taxes or a cash payment to the extent that income taxes are not owed. It is usually proposed as a substitute for the personal exemption in income taxes. Personal exemptions are worth more to those who pay a higher tax rate. That is, a $1,000 exemption is worth $500 to a person who reaches a 50-percent tax rate but only $200 to one who earns less and is taxed at 20 percent. However, a $500 tax credit, or $200, or whatever is specified would be worth the same amount to every taxpayer. That would seem to be less unfair. The 1984 tax law contains an Earned Income Credit (EIC), but it is very modest, available only to those with earned income, and cuts off at $10,000 of earned income.

A Proposal. An illustration of a feasible Refundable Tax Credit (RTC) may be outlined in beguilingly few words. Legislation would eliminate the $1,000 personal tax exemption and provide instead a $400 personal tax credit. Such a credit would be reduced by 5 percent of any income in excess of an adjusted gross income (AGI) of $10,000.* (Adjusted gross income is taxable income minus a very few permissible adjustments such as moving expenses, IRAs and Keogh funds, and alimony paid.)

The existing EIC would be absorbed by this provision; that is, it would no longer exist as a separate credit. Special exemptions for age and blindness would be eliminated. Under current law, it is permissible to file one's own return and be claimed as a dependent on another return as well, if the conditions for dependency are met. Such duplicate filing would be barred. People who do not owe taxes would be entitled to refunds, as now. If the refund exceeds some stipulated figure, perhaps $1,000, it might be paid out in quarterly shares.

Implications of this particular design may be elaborated as follows. The higher one's income, the smaller the gain from such a tax credit; at some point there is a loss relative to

*The proposal is written in relation to 1984 income tax law. Except where otherwise noted, dollar levels and other estimates represent 1984 law applied to 1982 income data.

TABLE 4.1 Levels of AGI at Which the Proposed $400 Credit in Lieu of the Exemption Would Be Advantageous (under 1984 Tax Law)

Type of Family	Nonitemizer	Itemizer*
Individual, under age 65	$14,000	$14,251
Joint return, under age 65		
One earner:		
No dependents	18,800	18,838
Two dependent children	24,400	25,397
Three dependent children	26,725	27,988
Two earners (each earns 50%):		
No dependents	18,841	19,130
Two dependent children	24,864	26,041
Three dependent children	27,235	28,832
Individual, age 65 or over	14,000	14,251
Joint return, age 65 or over	18,800	15,838

*Assumes deductible expenses equal to 23 percent of gross income.
Source: Special analysis by the Office of the Secretary of the Treasury, Office of Tax Analysis, December 22, 1983.

current law. For example, an exemption of $1,000 is worth $500 per person to a family with income subject to a 50-percent tax rate. The credit proposed here would be worth $400 per person. Moreover, the credit is reduced by 5 percent of income over $10,000, so that, for example, at AGI of $14,000, the $400-per-person credit due to a filer or household would be reduced by $200 for the entire household; and the trade-off has altered. An elderly person forfeits a special exemption as well. Other variables include the level of deductions available and the family composition of the taxpayer. Taking all that into account, table 4.1 indicates the income level up to which various types of families would find the credit advantageous.

It is evident from the table that couples and families, especially those with children, would benefit from the tax credit. (Median family income in 1982 was $23,430.) The income of the aged is lower than that for younger people, but the threshold income level at which they come out ahead is also lower. Thus in 1980 the median income for aged individuals and couples, taken together, was $6,970,[22] and the threshold level from $14,000 to $18,800, depending on individual circumstance. In other words, the elderly would benefit up to relatively high incomes. Also benefiting would be those families, usually with relatively low incomes,[23] with whom the "hidden poor" aged live.* It appears that 60 percent of the people who file tax returns would find the tax credit to their advantage (see table 4.2). In addition, 5.5 million married couples and heads of households have incomes so low that they do not file returns; obviously they would find the refundable credit to their advantage.

That there are a large number of gainers and losers in the AGI class $20,000–$30,000 is an indication that in this class, under the new provisions, larger families would gain, while individuals and smaller families would lose, on the average, $319 a year. The bulk of the gain, approximately $22 billion, would go to 52 million households with incomes of less than $20,000 a year. In addition, 5.5 million households that do not currently file tax returns would be eligible for approximately $5 billion in refunds. With a few exceptions, taxpayers with AGIs exceeding $30,000 would lose by the change. Those with incomes from $30,000 to $50,000 would average losses of $720 a year, those with incomes from $50,000 to $100,000 would average losses of $1,245 a year, and so on. Tax-free investments are concentrated in these latter groups, so AGI is not nearly a complete reflection of their incomes. The net cost to the government would be a little more than $7 billion a year—$5 billion for current nonfilers of tax returns and a net cost of $2.3 billion for filers (see table 4.2). One could reduce the estimated cost to the government by netting out savings in public assistance and other means-tested programs, but I chose not to do that. These programs have been severely degraded in recent years, in entitlement and in payment levels. When savings are possible, consideration ought to be given to improving these programs.

Seven billion dollars is a lot of money, even in the 1980s.

*A term coined by Mollie Orshansky for the aged poor who are not counted as poor in the Census because the income of the household in which they live exceeds the poverty level.

TABLE 4.2 Effect of a $400-Per-Capita Refundable Credit, Together with Repealing the $1,000 Exemption, the Earned Income Credit, and the Aged and Blind Exemption, Distributed by Adjusted Income Class. Current Law Tax Return Filers Only (1984 Law, 1982 Levels of Income)

Adjusted gross income class ($1,000s)	Number of returns (1,000s)	Returns with tax reduction				Returns with tax increase				Total change in tax liability ($mil.)
		Returns		Tax reduction		Returns		Tax increase		
		Number (1,000s)	As a percent of all returns	Total amount ($mil.)	Average amount ($)	Number (1,000s)	As a percent of all returns	Total amount ($mil.)	Average amount ($)	
Less than 5	17,333	17,333	100.0%	$−7,817	$−471	0	0.0%	$0	$0	$−7,817
5–10	16,723	16,711	99.9	−6,695	−401	12	0.1	*	27	−6,695
10–15	13,836	12,197	88.2	−5,005	−410	1,586	11.5	97	61	−4,908
15–20	10,906	5,781	53.0	−2,478	−429	5,092	46.7	910	179	−1,569
20–30	16,882	4,162	24.7	−1,254	−301	12,693	75.2	4,047	319	2,792
30–50	14,288	130	0.9	−37	−286	14,113	98.8	10,200	723	10,163
50–100	3,713	2	0.1	−1	−533	3,622	97.5	4,511	1,245	4,510
100–200	641	0	0.0	0	0	599	93.5	987	1,647	987
200 and more	177	0	0.0	0	0	155	87.6	269	1,740	269
Total	94,500	56,317	59.6%	−23,288	$−414	37,873	40.1%	$21,021	$555	$−2,267

Note: Details may not add to totals due to rounding.
*Less than $500,000.
Source: Special Analysis by the Office of the Secretary of Treasury, Office of Tax Analysis, December 22, 1983.

However, a considerable argument can be made that improvement of the allowance for dependents, which this proposal addresses, is long overdue. The cost of living (and thus the cost to a family of raising a child) has far outpaced improvement in the value of the personal exemption since it was established at $600 in 1948. If the personal exemption had increased at the same rate as the cost of living it would now stand at about $2,500. If, indeed, it had increased at the same rate as the cost of living and improved wages, it would now be $5,600.[24] Thus there is a considerable case for improving the income tax treatment of dependents, one way or another.

Achievements of a Refundable Tax Credit

I sum up by reviewing what an RTC would achieve in the light of the family stresses and problems of public policy that have been outlined.

1. With respect to poverty and the chronically poor fit between the minimum wage and family need: an indication of the effect of the program on poverty among the aged and families with children may be found in estimates of its effect on the caseloads of the public assistance programs to which, perforce, they resort. In 1980, a Refundable Tax Credit as described would have provided at least equivalent income (in many cases, more income) to a quarter of the aged individuals and a third of the aged couples benefiting from Supplemental Security Income.[25] That is, they would not have had to apply for SSI. For a variety of reasons connected with program administration and the way statistics are reported, it is more difficult to estimate the effect on AFDC recipients. One may hazard the guess that 25 percent of AFDC recipients would receive at least as much from the refundable credit as from AFDC—with how much less administrative expense and hassle all around!

As for poor families that do not qualify for AFDC, a couple with one member working full time at the minimum wage has about $7,000 in earnings and, if they have two children, may receive $370 as Earned Income Credit. Instead, they would receive $1,600 from the RTC. The poverty line is just under $10,000, so the credit would bring them halfway to the poverty level. Obviously something remains to be done—by a general movement of wage levels to the point where a full-time wage supports four people at the poverty level, as in past decades; or, for any particular two-parent family, by part-time work by the second adult.

2.   With respect to the struggle of moderate- and middle-income families for social overhead capital, an indication of the effect of an RTC may be found in considering the circumstances in 1972–73 of a family of four that had an income of about $9,000 (equivalent to $20,000 ten years later).* Those were comparatively favorable years in terms of growth of GNP and unemployment rate, which is to say that families were operating in a favorable economic climate. On the average, this group of families had two children; the family head was thirty-five years old. Their liquid assets (saving and checking accounts and stocks and bonds at market value) *declined* by a little less than $80 (equivalent to $180 a decade later) per year.[26]** Thus one sees the financial pressure on such families, even at income levels approaching average.

At their income level, personal exemptions would be worth something less than $600 to each family but the RTC would be worth about $1,100. Thus, the tax credit would convert a $180 yearly loss in liquid assets into a $320 gain. This is a modest but respectable improvement in maneuverability. How much more is this so for families that, because of unemployment, lower income, or more responsibilities, experience even more so-called dissaving. Obviously, such families would show a larger gain from the Refundable Tax Credit.

3.   With respect to the social insurance dilemma about relating benefit payments simultaneously to prior contributions and to family need: the Refundable Tax Credit would act for social insurance, and indeed, more broadly, as an adjustment for family size. I have noted (chapter 3) that under current

*1972–73 is the last period for which consumer expenditure data have been published. Family income is a figure a little larger for these families than AGI.

**At the end of the year, liquid assets for these families totaled $2,227 (just over $5,000 in 1982–83 dollars).

law a one-child family receiving Survivors Insurance is greatly favored over larger families, and a third of families receiving Survivors Insurance are nevertheless poor. Apart from allowing or creating need among young families, the result is overlapping entitlement to welfare and social insurance.* Broad movement to an RTC would moderate the need created by dependents and leave Social Security and Unemployment Insurance free of the requirement to respond to these differences. Benefit payments could easily be related to prior contributions or prior work without at the same time leaving families with children in need.

4. From the perspective of each affected family over time, it may be evident that younger families with children would receive more under such a program but would, when earnings had approached a peak and children had left home, pay higher taxes than now. They would, in effect, have loaned money to themselves in a straitened period out of their own more prosperous future. And this loan to themselves—social overhead capital—would help them to make that future prosperous.

It may be obvious that a variety of alternatives are available in designing a Refundable Tax Credit. The appendix to this chapter names as possibilities retaining special exemptions along with an RTC, providing a credit at a level of $500 per person, and providing a refundable credit as an alternative to the personal exemption—at the taxpayer's choice. Data on costs and distributive effect are found in the appendix.

As with Unemployment Insurance (see chapter 3), one may ask whether the RTC is means-tested rather than mainstream. Obviously, in some broad sense the income tax tests the "means" of citizens, but it is not exceptionalistic or a means

---

*To provide an illustration with respect to the aged, Congress has been moderating benefit payments in an effort to stabilize Social Security financing. These moves have particular effect on those at the lower end of the benefit scale and will, in time, lead to more applications by Social Security beneficiaries for SSI. Because SSI brings all income up to a stipulated level, increasing numbers of retirees will find their combined benefits wholly without relation to prior contributions or wages. A Refundable Tax Credit would reduce the need for concurrent benefits and so avoid this outcome.

test in the sense used here. Whether income tax rates represent a means test depends on whether all citizens, rich and poor, are treated uniformly and whether citizens feel that the rates single out poor people. At times it has been proposed that special programs for the poor be administered as part of the income tax. For example, the Nixon administration's Family Assistance Plan was called a negative income tax. However, it incorporated a special (and especially high) tax rate for people below subsistence-level income, defined their family unit in a special way, and laid special requirements on them to demonstrate that they were at work or seeking work. Calling it a form of income tax did not make it mainstream. By contrast, the RTC creates no special tax rates or definitions—rather, it eliminates special definitions of dependency required for certain existing exemptions and special requirements for the Earned Income Credit.*[27] In the particular version offered here, it would benefit 60 percent of taxpayers. It does not meet criteria for a means-tested or exceptionalistic program.

The Political Surround

The climate that led to this particular version of an RTC was being felt in early 1984. The country was in the throes of an election campaign, but it seemed plain that, whatever the outcome, a considerable debate about tax law revision lay ahead. Projected budget deficits would force a search for savings in expenditure and, it appeared, for more revenue as well. The debate seemed likely to be influenced by extensive evidence that the Reagan years had seen a vast up-scale redistribution of income (see chapter 1) and that poverty had increased. An allied and, no doubt, more powerful influence would be alarm over and pressure from families dropping from middle- to marginal-income status.

---

*This analysis has not attempted to deal with tax administration per se, but it may be recorded that the RTC would move in a direction long urged by those who write, administer, and litigate tax law. With respect to simplification and, particularly, with respect to questions of tax equity, see references in n. 27.

It therefore seemed likely that, whatever increases might be visualized or thought necessary in portions of the tax system, care would be exercised to protect those who are least or less well to do. Special provisions favoring such people would be traded off against revenue-producing provisions. In the event, the administration's plans (at least three different versions were produced) and congressional plans as well relied heavily on increasing the value of the personal exemption to appear to benefit those with lower incomes. The administration proposed to raise the personal exemption from $1,000 (in 1986 it was to be $1,080) to $2,000.

Analysis of that proposal throws into high relief the contrast between the personal exemption and an RTC. In 1984 about one quarter of the population could be regarded as having low incomes (under $15,000); the administration's proposal would save them $2 billion. The remainder of the $40-billion revenue cost of the administration's proposal, $38 billion, would be spread among those with higher incomes—the most to those with the highest incomes. The poorest 25 percent of the population would have gotten 5 percent of the benefit of the increased personal exemption said to have been designed for them.

It may be conducive to rumination that this simple set of figures went virtually unremarked. Pro-poor congressional leaders and lobbyists supported the administration's proposal, possibly out of fear that opposition would lead to their losing even the $2 billion to be gained. They concentrated on securing relatively minor improvements, for example, in the Earned Income Credit and in the allowance for care of dependents at home. Of course, they were working in a climate in which even small gains were hard to win. Yet, the net effect of the administration's proposals would be widened inequality.

I note in passing that the $40-billion cost to the government of the Reagan administration's improved personal exemption far exceeds the $7.3-billion cost of the RTC recommended here and, indeed, approximates the cost of the "no-losers" RTC described in the appendix to this chapter.

Aid to Families with Dependent Children

/ Measures described in chapter 3 and the Refundable Tax Credit would have the effect, other things being equal, of reducing the AFDC caseload from 3.7 or 4 million to perhaps 2.5 million. Though still not inconsiderable, the remaining families would represent a more manageable administrative problem and a somewhat different population. The changes in clientele would suggest some change in AFDC policies; others need to be made anyway. However, the most important change needed is to deal constructively with the program's administrative problems. Asked what he would do about one of New York City's troubled social service programs, Mitchell I. Ginsberg, who had once directed the city's Human Resources Administration, observed, "I would add staff, supervisors, and better training. Then I would pray."[28] We begin by trying to grasp why an experienced welfare administrator would so quickly be moved to prayer.

The Administrative Problem

Virtually every literate American is aware that the AFDC program has long been regarded as "bankrupt" and chaotic. Fraud or, more generally, payment error has been only one aspect of the problem. Even when fraud does not result, procedures are confused and wasteful. Many people are denied assistance to which they are entitled, or are made to wait for assistance longer than is reasonable, or are tormented by being made to queue up, to come and go, to fetch and respond, and to struggle anxiously to understand what is going on.[29] How did we come to this?

The problem began with administering a program that has not been popular since 1940. It was contributed to by rapid expansion of responsibilities while staff grew more slowly and then, probably,[30] declined relative to caseload. From the 1950s on, caseload expanded rapidly and then exponentially for a variety of reasons: because the country was growing richer and because Congress, at the same time that it complained about rising costs, liberalized the program; because of extensive migration of blacks and other poor people from Southern states with very low AFDC standards to states where they more readily qualified for AFDC; because the financial problems precipitated by separation and divorce, which no mainstream program relieves, replaced and in time surpassed problems created by the death of a husband and father; and because the civil rights movement and the war against poverty made it possible for many people to receive assistance who would earlier improperly have been turned away.

Apart from larger caseloads, much responsibility was added deliberately and with good intentions—arrangements for recipients to receive needed social services, requirements that they be evaluated and referred for work, a system of disregarding portions of income so that recipients would feel rewarded for work, and reviews and forms that would uncover fraud. In the 1960s, applicants became more demanding, both individually and in organized pressure groups. Simultaneously, for what seemed good reason, educational requirements for the workers were reduced. At about the same time, social workers were replaced by clerical workers. The philosophy of AFDC had been that its clients were deeply troubled and needed help and guidance—that is, social work guidance. The new philosophy was that cash assistance ought to be awarded (or not) in accordance with legal qualifications; clerical employees could do that more efficiently. The serious damage in this shift lay not in the loss of professionalism or guidance but in displacing experienced workers, who were familiar with applicants, precisely when clients had become more demanding. The new income-maintenance workers were often uncertain and not infrequently frightened. The atmosphere of welfare offices shifted from friendly, paternalistic, or neutral to hostile. Staff members became reluctant to visit clients' homes, a long-standing welfare practice, and armed guards began to appear in welfare offices.

It had been the practice for workers to be assigned caseloads. That is, every recipient had a worker whose name at least she knew and by whom at least her name was known. Welfare departments now shifted to a so-called case-bank system. Recipients no longer had workers. They called the housing or employment or other specialist, or dealt with the next worker who was available. Impersonality replaced some degree of (in principle) personal attention, and responsibility in each particular case was clouded.

Caseloads continued to expand until about 1972, occasioning steady criticism of welfare departments and their staffs. In the late 1950s, Congress asked for investigations of the extent to which AFDC caused illegitimacy and juvenile delinquency. It became conventional wisdom that AFDC caused family breakup and indeed poverty. For reasons touched on above, the migration of blacks from Southern agricultural states led to an increased proportion of black families receiving AFDC nationally. Though this was never even remotely true, AFDC came to be thought of as a blacks-only program. Welfare became a major budget item at all levels of government. Health and education expenditures also increased, at times more rapidly, but welfare was labeled as the cause of fiscal problems. It was little noticed when, in about 1972, the ratio of recipients to population stabilized and then declined.

All this contributed to a drumbeat of public criticism which was a daily fact of life for those engaged in providing public assistance. Such a climate does not make for happy or dedicated work. Public dissatisfaction led to laying even more, and more detailed, requirements on welfare departments—about the pursuit of support from absent fathers, about who should be expected to seek work, about assuring that recipients had access to information about contraception. One amendment to AFDC law after another specified new ways for agencies to insure that recipients were really eligible.

All these requirements were translated first into federal and then into state rules and regulations. State public assistance manuals became so complex that hardly anyone could keep track of them. For example, a 1970 study showed that provisions especially designed to give recipients an incentive to work were not effective in part because neither staff nor recipients understood them.[31] Ultimately, staff members and even their supervisors stopped trying to keep up with regulations.[32] Applicants were even more confused by the complex requirements. In an effort to create a reasonable application process, states began developing standard application forms that ran from twelve to twenty or more pages, requiring the

submission of proofs (birth certificates, pay stubs, rent re-
ceipts, dismissal notices, doctors' statements) on every page.
An Urban Institute study showed that these appeared to require an average reading capacity at the twelfth-grade level,
but AFDC mothers had, on the average, eighth-grade reading
capacity.[33] One can visualize the impatience, on the one hand,
and anxiety and anger, on the other, that flowed between
workers and applicants.

Quite unable to comply with all that the federal government was requiring, state agencies at least implicitly came to
select the regulations with which they would comply and ignored others. For example, federal requirements to act
promptly on applications have been widely ignored and, in
one county at least, interpreted to justify *delaying* assistance.[34]
In theory, states that are interested in responsive and consistent policy should alter their practice when clients file and win
appeals. In some states, however, administrators would over-
rule administrative appeals findings. Even when states yielded
in a particular case that won administrative or judicial reversal, they frequently continued the general practice that had
been found to be improper. This policy of nonacquiescence,
extensively applied by the federal Social Security Administration, eventually required the attention of Congress and the
courts.

Federal officials can take state agencies to task. The result
is likely to be extended negotiation and occasional grudging
compliance, but federal officials themselves cannot cover all
the ground. Noting the problem, Congress prescribed fiscal
sanctions for specified violations. These generally have to do
with overpayments to ineligibles or failure to collect support
from absent fathers. The threat of financial sanction does fix
a state's attention. In itself, however, it may appear to legitimize inattention to the regulations for which sanctions are not
provided. For example, Congress has provided financial
penalties for paying those who are ineligible but not for failing to pay those who are eligible. How might Congress send a
clearer message?

Administration in welfare agencies deteriorated. A phenomenon developed that was called "churning"; that is, cases

terminated only to have people reapply within a month or two and demonstrate eligibility.[35] It is a good guess that such people have been eligible all the time and that someone—the recipient or the worker are equally possibilities—has made an error. Payment arrangements that would provide an incentive to work and other poorly understood calculations lead to payment changes that have come to seem arbitrary. Phone calls go unanswered and forms and irreplaceable documents are lost. For example, examiners in the New York Regional Office, seeking to confirm eligibility for the new ssi program in 1974, could not locate many of the records from the prior welfare program and gave up trying to do an audit.

Now public assistance staff have jobs that, in terms of meeting the need of clients or complying strictly with federal and state law, seem overwhelming. Instead, staff tend to define their work in terms of so many interviews a day, so many cases approved or closed or reviewed, eight hours worked. They also tend to play by the rules they understand for personal safety. They do not replace lost or stolen checks (suppose they turned up cashed somewhere?) or use common sense in interpreting regulations. (If the public assistance manual requires a doctor's statement of handicap, can the worker proceed just because he can see a woman has a leg missing?) As all the pressure has been against expenditure and there is little pro-client pressure, approval presents a risk and safety lies in denial. Social scientists recognize all these as intrinsic problems of bureaucratic process, but they have reached an advanced stage in welfare departments.

There is little in such performance that gives satisfaction to workers; those who seek satisfaction or the feeling of being helpful leave for other jobs. Annual turnover rates of 50 percent are not uncommon, leaving agencies with inexperienced and poorly motivated staff and extensive vacancies and obviously compounding the administrative problem. This has been the cycle of poor administration of welfare departments: public obloquy, unpopular and inadequate clients, legislative resentment, overregulation, underfinancing of staff and administration, poor worker quality and morale, and hostility and distrust between worker and client all cycle and feed one another. The problem is deep and complex and will not be rectified simply by adding staff, supervisors, and better training.

Improving Administration

An account by David Rothman[36] of the history of institutional care for sick and needy people comes to a conclusion that is applicable to public assistance. He describes how the nation has cycled back and forth between care in institutions (hospitals, asylums, workhouses) and so-called outdoor care (foster families, community support)—disappointed with each in turn and eagerly grasping at a forgotten solution that will be discarded yet again. We do not seem ever to have worked out the administrative problems in one strategy or the other in order to correct them. In the terms in which the problems of welfare administration have been cast or are likely to be cast, we cannot pit overregulation against underregulation. Both compound chaos. Nor is it a solution simply to restore the title of social worker to those who administer assistance or try to hire professional social workers for those positions (assuming that professionals would accept them). That overlooks the depth of the problem and would repeat the ping-ponging that Rothman describes.

In general, improving administration involves a steady reversal of the trend to declining administrative support—in numbers and quality of personnel and in their rewards. This would at least be made possible without additional cost by the reduction of workload implicit in policies recommended in these chapters. Improved staffing is not in itself enough, however.

Improving administration requires a sorting out of rules and regulations so that those which are important and central may be visible and enforced. With respect to the possibility of fraud, it means giving up the attempt to prevent every recipient violation, no matter how small or how large the apparatus that must be brought to bear, and moving to systems like those employed by Social Security or the Internal Revenue Service—that is, sampling techniques and exemplary punishment to discourage violation. And it means encouraging a rule of reason in administration. If the objective of law is asserted—that is, provision of benefits to those who are entitled and solely to them—workers may be permitted to use good judgment. This is not meant to suggest that AFDC should be discretionary but that, understanding whom it is meant to benefit, workers should be freed of the feeling that against all good judgment they must apply the most restrictive formal requirements. A variety of studies are available that provide detailed prescription for how to proceed correctively.[37]

It may be that all this may best be achieved by shifting the administration of AFDC from states and counties, where it now lodges, to the federal government. Among AFDC's difficulties has been a confusion between levels of government about ultimate responsibility for the way it operates. Direct federal administration would clarify that. Welfare agencies now administer a number of disparate programs, including, for example, federal food stamps. Direct federal administration would make it possible to arrive at nationally rationalized and compatible definitions of household, income, and entitlement, and so simplify administration. In substituting SSI for state-administered Old Age Assistance in 1974, a similar transfer was made comparatively smoothly. In the process, a variety of issues were dealt with that provide a precedent for an AFDC transfer. For example, a simple national level of assistance (a so-called flat grant) was provided, with states required to supplement up to previously established levels and permitted to supplement further if they wished. States currently provide a little less than half ($7.6 billion in 1985) of the total cash cost of AFDC. If administration were to be shifted, states might expect to be relieved of a large part of this cost. Cost to the federal government may constitute a substantial drawback to federalizing administration, unless it could be traded off for state assumption of other costs (education, for example) or unless there were already an overriding need to relieve state financial pressures.

As for whether entitlement should remain essentially a clerical procedure or be restored as a social work operation, in the near term the former appears to be desirable. In the first place, viewing entitlement as simple and straightforward tends to minimize even the appearance of discretion. Estab-lishing that benefits are provided in strict accordance with law has deep importance for everyone concerned—applicants, the public that needs to be brought to support these agencies, and the staff whose morale needs improvement. In the second place, change is itself difficult; one would not want to lay more change on these agencies than necessary if a turnabout is to be sought. In the longer run, it would become evident that the population receiving assistance had somewhat shifted. The mothers who have some income from work and who use the program for supplementation would tend to drop out of AFDC. It would deal more notably with mothers (and their children) and with working-age adults (and their children) who suffer from some special handicap or personal or family situation. In part, this would be a younger population and also, in part, one with a larger proportion of long-term de-pendents. It would be an even more troubled clientele than now. Once AFDC is working in an orderly fashion, it would make good sense to build a social work component into it. That need not be done by filling every line position with a social worker. Conceivably, small social work units ought to be attached to each group of income maintenance workers.

AFDC Policies

Levels of living afforded to AFDC recipients have for many years been low and have recently declined. The most that would be provided to a family of four without other income in the average state in 1983 was $368 a month—less than half of the poverty level. The real value of these payments had declined by about a third since 1970. To some extent food stamps compensated for the deficit, but the combined value of AFDC and food stamps had declined by 22 percent by 1983 and, at $536 a month in the average state, barely exceeded half the poverty level.[38]

Among the first priorities in improving AFDC would be steady movement of these levels toward the poverty line. Aid to Families with Dependent Children is the only major income maintenance program that does not automatically adjust to the cost of living, a deficiency that ought to be corrected. In estimating the cost of the Refundable Tax Credit, we declined to net out savings in public assistance, which would be in excess of $3 billion a year (state and federal savings combined). By far the largest part of this ought to go to building up payments to a level at which mothers and children might decently manage. In recent years, AFDC applicants have been required to show that the family has no more than $1,000 in assets of any sort—household furnishings, life insurance, and so forth. Entirely pauperizing families is costly to the government, let alone inhumane, as the spread of homelessness has surely shown. Liberalizing such policies would be part of a move toward more acceptable standards of assistance.

The system of disregarding a portion of income in order to provide an incentive to work has been much debated in the last decade. When the Reagan administration all but abandoned the system, it was argued that this would lead people to abandon work in order to apply for assistance. Though there may have been cases in which that happened, broadly speaking that does not appear to have been the effect of wiping out the incentive system.[39] In any case, with a substantial move to mainstream programs, relatively few women who are able to work would turn to AFDC. (Social Security, UI, and the RTC would fill the deficit between their earnings and a minimum level or AFDC level.) Thus, it would not be necessary to have a system of disregards—a good thing too, as such systems add considerable complexity. Similarly, programs that provide work as a substitute for welfare or to work off the benefit that welfare provides would seem less relevant. In any event, the combined training and unemployment benefit program outlined earlier would provide a mainstream opportunity for AFDC mothers who should or would want to move toward paid employment.

Aid to Families with Dependent Children was for many years limited to families in which a parent was absent. Largely in response to the argument that this requirement caused marital separation, Congress eventually offered states the option of extending AFDC to include two-parent families that suffer from unemployment. Only twenty-four states established such a program, and congressional requirements were so narrowly drawn that no more than a quarter million families have received such assistance in any year. An Unemployed Parent (UP) program in AFDC should not be the primary mode of relieving the distress of unemployment; that role should be carried by mainstream UI. Especially in a transitional period, however, before mainstream benefits are fully available, an effort must be made to meet the need of such families. It seems appropriate that a UP program, conceived as a backup and carefully drafted to protect families that UI and a new program for the long-term unemployed cannot protect, should be extended to all states and jurisdictions. A bill requiring all states to provide a UP program developed considerable support in Congress in 1985 and was estimated to cost only $390 million for three years.

Supplemental Security Income

Assistance to the aged (OAA), the disabled (APTD), and the blind (AB) was for many years also administered by welfare departments but escaped the build-up of public complaint that AFDC drew. To some extent these other programs reflected the same problems as AFDC—inefficient administration shared by three levels of government, extensive regulation, and variation in entitlement and payment levels. However, it was easier to sympathize with the aged or disabled client, and some of AFDC's most difficult administrative issues—whether a father who visits his wife and children is truly absent, for example—did not arise. Congress provided that, beginning in 1974, a new federal Supplemental Security Income program should replace OAA, APTD, and AB. Supplemental Security Income (SSI) has plainly demonstrated the capacity of the Social Security Administration to operate efficiently and consistently from one place to another, in the provision of cash income.[40]

We have noted that the Refundable Tax Credit would produce substantial savings in SSI—approaching half a billion dollars a year for the aged alone. Supplemental Security Income is by no means as inadequate relative to poverty as AFDC: for those who receive them all, the combination of federal SSI, Social Security, and food stamps approximates the poverty level.[41] Nevertheless, a considerable proportion of the aged—women in particular—are poor, partly because many do not and for some time many will not receive much in the way of Social Security benefits. Moreover, ssi payment levels have declined by 5 percent or so in the past decade.[42] These payment levels ought to be improved.

A number of ssi policies appear to be hangovers from Old Age Assistance and merit change. For example, the ssi ceiling on assets ($1,500 for an aged individual and $2,250 for an aged couple) ought to be liberalized and possibly eliminated entirely. The limit is intended to avoid paying ssi to rich people with extensive assets. However, assets of any consequence produce income that is in itself disqualifying for ssi, and those with substantial assets can find legal ways to manipulate them so as to become eligible if they are really determined to do so. All evidence is that the rule affects a small number of people with modest assets (worth $5,500, on the average, in 1976).[43] The government may incur as much cost in administering the rule as is realized in limiting beneficiaries. Similarly, an aged person who lives with a relative has his ssi payment reduced by one third. Apparently, Congress thought living costs are lower in such a circumstance or that the living-together arrangement represents a contribution to the aged person. Both reasons were mentioned in congressional debate, and it never became clear which was determining. In fact, it is well understood that old people who live with relatives tend to be the poorest old people; their relatives also are poor, and this is the only way they find to help. Thus, the primary effect of the one-third reduction is to reduce benefits to the very poorest aged.[44] The rule should be dropped.

The financial difficulties of aged women and of mothers with minor children are comparatively modern problems, in different ways reflecting social change and intrinsic limitations in our fundamental conception of social insurance. The problem of aged women reflects a difference between their life expectancy and that of men and a changeover from a society when women were fully expected to be dependent on men. Social Security can be and undoubtedly will be adapted to deal with this difficulty, but women who have established no work record will be living well into the next century. The problems of mothers with minor children are a consequence of family trends new to us in their magnitude. While Social Security can and should be adapted to these problems in marginal ways, it is primarily focused on individuals and considerations of equity rather than on families and adequacy. Discrimination against women in the marketplace adds to the problem of both groups, of course.

Therefore, this chapter begins with a proposal for a program that would particularly benefit such groups—the Refundable Tax Credit. Its budgetary cost to the government is reasonable, its top-down redistributive impact substantial. That is as it should be. It is a mainstream program, asking no questions and setting no conditions upon income and tax benefits that are not extensively included in ordinary tax returns. It moves with family need, providing modest increments of money when it is most required and taking it back when families generally experience less pressure. The improvements proposed in chapter 3 and the new tax credit make it possible to visualize AFDC as a substantially smaller program—at least a third smaller than it is now. (SSI, the same.) That should provide a determined administration with latitude to rescue welfare from the straits into which it has fallen. A government representing decent people cannot consign millions of citizens to be dealt with in the manner that AFDC applicants have experienced in the past two or three decades.

As mainstreaming proceeds, other means-tested programs would be improved along similar lines. For example, the question would arise (and has from time to time arisen) whether cash should be substituted for food stamps and folded into AFDC and SSI—resulting in considerable simplification all around. The arguments against doing that have been, first, that food stamps have been comparatively (although not entirely by any means) decent to apply for and use and, for people with marginal incomes, preferable to becoming involved with AFDC. Also against cashing out food stamps has been public and congressional feeling that AFDC is "bankrupt" and ridden with fraud. Improvement in the administration of AFDC might alter attitudes on both sides, but progress in this matter should probably be demonstrated before attempting to proceed with such a change. A couple of states (California is one) have experimented with cashing out food stamps. Their experience so far suggests that this would be a sound move.

It must be obvious but should perhaps be said that some of the recommendations made here represent alternatives for one another. A Refundable Tax Credit would considerably moderate the need to alter Social Security's maximum family benefit and to provide benefits for dependents in UI, and so forth. These systems are complex and dynamic. If one route to improvement is chosen, another may not be necessary.

TABLE 4.3 Levels of AGI at Which the Proposed $500 Credit in Lieu of the Exemption Would Be Advantageous (under 1984 Tax Law)

Type of Family	Nonitemizer	Itemizer*
Individual, under age 65	$15,625	$16,000
Joint return, under age 65		
One earner:		
No dependents	21,644	22,426
Two dependent children	29,962	30,862
Three dependent children	33,088	34,815
Two earners (each spouse earns 50 percent of total income):		
No dependents	22,136	22,800
Two dependent children	30,038	31,508
Three dependent children	33,720	35,419
Individual, age 65 or over:		
Without age exemption	15,625	16,000
With age exemption	16,000	16,086
Joint return, age 65 or over:		
Without age exemption	21,644	22,426
With age exemption	22,533	22,820

*Assumes deductible expenses equal to 23 percent of gross income.
Source: Special analysis by the Office of the Secretary of the Treasury, Office of Tax Analysis, December 22, 1983.

APPENDIX

Alternative Options for a Refundable Tax Credit

One might consider changing many of the design details of the proposed RTC. Special exemptions for age or blindness or the Earned Income Credit might be left intact, providing a larger gain for each respective group of people and reducing opposition to the proposed program. Of course, the cost to the government would increase. The special exemption for blindness represents a small cost, $45 million; the special exemption for age and EIC are more consequential. The former is estimated to represent a cost in 1984 of $2.5 billion in revenue forgone. (See table 4.5.) The EIC represents a cost in revenue forgone and payout in 1984 of $1.5 billion.*

One may also entertain other tax credit levels; presumably these would increase over time in any case. The consequences of a $500-per-person tax credit are indicated in tables 4.3 and 4.4. More people would gain (68 percent versus 60 percent) up to somewhat higher AGIS, and fewer would lose. The net cost to the government would be considerably higher—something over $20 billion for people now filing returns and in excess of $6 billion for current nonfilers, a total of about $27 billion.

An Elective Refundable Tax Credit

An interesting alternative would be to phase in a Refundable Tax Credit on an elective basis. Legislation would provide that individuals or families filing a tax return might elect to receive a Refundable Tax Credit of $400 per person in place of the $1,000 personal exemption available in 1984. Other provisions—a reduction of the credit by 5 percent of the excess of AGI over $10,000, elimination of special exemptions, and so forth—would then apply. Those who chose not to take the

*Executive Office of the President, Office of Management and Budget, *Budget of the U.S. Government, FY 1985, Special Analyses,* Washington, D.C., table G1. See also Department of the Treasury, Internal Revenue Service, *Statistics of Income, 1981, Individual Income Tax Returns,* Washington, D.C., tables 2.3, and 3.5.

TABLE 4.4 Effect of a $500-Per-Capita Refundable Credit, Together with Repealing the $1,000 Exemption, the Earned Income Credit and the Aged and Blind Exemption, Distributed by Adjusted Gross Income Class.[1] Current Law Tax Return Filers Only (1984 Law, 1982 Levels of Income)

| Adjusted gross income class ($1000s) | Number of returns (1,000s) | Returns with tax reduction | | | | Returns with tax increase | | | | Total change in tax liability ($mil.) |
| | | Returns | | Tax reduction | | Returns | | Tax increase | | |
		Number ($1,000s)	As a percent of all returns	Total amount ($mil.)	Average amount ($)	Number (1,000s)	As a percent of all returns	Total amount ($mil.)	Average amount ($)	
Less than 5	17,333	17,333	100.0%	$-10,137	$-585	0	0.0%	$ 0	$ 0	$-10,137
5–10	16,723	16,723	100.0	-9,654	-577	0	0.0	0	0	-9,654
10–15	13,836	13,498	97.6	-7,759	-575	337	2.4	24	73	-7,735
15–20	10,906	7,343	67.3	-4,603	-627	3,519	32.3	493	140	-4,110
20–30	16,882	8,149	48.3	-3,906	-479	8,693	51.5	2,401	276	-1,506
30–50	14,288	1,252	8.8	-379	-302	12,993	90.9	7,572	583	7,194
50–100	3,713	9	0.2	-4	-395	3,617	97.4	4,362	1,206	4,358
100–200	641	*	*	*	*	599	93.5	987	1,647	987
200 or more	177	0	0.0	0	0	155	87.6	269	1,740	269
Total	94,500	64,309	68.1%	$-36,442	$-567	29,914	31.7%	$16,109	$539	$-20,333

Note: Details may not add to totals due to rounding.

[1]The credit would phase out at a 5 percent rate for adjusted gross income in excess of $10,000.

*Less than 500 returns, .05 percent, $500,000, or $.50.

Source: Special analysis by the Office of the Secretary of Treasury, Office of Tax Analysis, December 22, 1983.

TABLE 4.5 Effect of an Optional $400-Per-Capita Refundable Tax Credit in Lieu of the $1,000 Exemption and Repealing the Earned Income Credit, Distributed by Adjusted Gross Income Class. Current Law Tax Return Filers Only (1984 Law, 1982 Levels of Income)

| Adjusted gross income class ($1000s) | Current law tax liability | | Tax liability under an optional $400-per-capita refundable credit in lieu of the taxpayer and dependent exemption, with the earned income credit repealed | | | | | |
| | | | With the exemption for the aged and blind repealed | | | With the exemption for the aged and blind allowed | | |
	Amount ($mil.)	Percentage distribution	Amount ($mil.)	Percentage distribution	Change from current law ($mil.)	Amount ($mil.)	Percentage distribution	Change from current law ($mil.)
Less than 5	$ −13	*	$−7,830	−3.5%	$−7,817	$−7,903	−3.6%	$−7,890
5–10	4,950	2.0%	−1,745	−0.8	−6,695	−2,213	−1.0	−7,163
10–15	13,129	5.4	8,195	3.7	−4,934	7,782	3.5	−5,347
15–20	17,749	7.3	15,463	7.0	−2,286	15,183	6.9	−2,566
20–30	45,402	18.6	44,581	20.1	−821	44,142	20.1	−1,260
30–50	72,645	29.8	73,036	32.9	391	72,608	33.1	−37
50–100	44,629	18.3	44,865	20.2	236	44,628	20.3	−1
100–200	22,336	9.2	22,417	10.1	81	22,336	10.2	0
200 or more	22,874	9.4	22,907	10.3	33	22,874	10.4	0
Total	$243,702	100.0%	$221,889	100.0%	$−21,812	$219,436	100.0%	$−24,265

Note: Details may not add to totals due to rounding.
*Less than .05 percent.
Source: Special analysis by the Office of the Secretary of Treasury, Office of Tax Analysis, December 22, 1983.

TABLE 4.6 Effect of an Optional $500-Per-Capita Refundable Tax Credit in Lieu of the $1,000 Exemption and Repealing the Earned Income Credit, Distributed by Adjusted Gross Income Class. Current Law Tax Return Filers Only (1984 Law, 1982 Levels of Income)

| Adjusted gross income class ($1000s) | Current law tax liability | | Tax liability under an optional $500-per-capita refundable credit in lieu of the taxpayer and dependent exemption, with the earned income credit repealed | | | | | |
| | | | With the exemption for the aged and blind repealed | | | With the exemption for the aged and blind allowed | | |
	Amount ($mil.)	Percentage distribution	Amount ($mil.)	Percentage distribution	Change from current law ($mil.)	Amount ($mil.)	Percentage distribution	Change from current law ($mil.)
Less than 5	$ −13	*	$−10,150	−4.9%	$−10,137	$−10,224	−5.0%	$−10,211
5–10	4,950	2.0%	−4,704	−2.3	−9,654	−5,172	−2.5	−10,122
10–15	13,129	5.4	5,394	2.6	−7,735	4,982	2.4	−8,147
15–20	17,749	7.3	13,260	6.4	−4,489	12,980	6.3	−4,769
20–30	45,402	18.6	41,892	20.1	−3,510	41,453	20.1	−3,949
30–50	72,645	29.8	72,693	34.9	48	72,264	35.1	−381
50–100	44,629	18.3	44,862	21.5	233	44,625	21.7	−4
100–200	22,336	9.2	22,417	10.7	81	22,336	10.8	*
200 or more	22,874	9.4	22,907	11.0	33	22,874	11.1	0
Total	$243,702	100.0%	$208,572	100.0%	$−35,129	$206,119	100.0%	$−37,582

Note: Details may not add to totals due to rounding.
*Less than .05 percent or $500,000.
Source: Special analysis by the office of the Secretary of Treasury, Office of Tax Analysis, December 22, 1983.

elective option could continue to use personal exemptions, as under 1984 law. Once the new provision had been elected by a person filing a tax return or elected on behalf of a dependent, however, that person and dependent would not again be able to claim a personal exemption. With the elective credit, no one would lose in the short run, for potential losers would simply retain the exemption. As the credit is designed to benefit people at an age and in circumstances when they really need it, over a period of time virtually everyone might be expected to participate. Eventually, with relatively little pain, the provision could be made mandatory.

Unfortunately, as table 4.5 indicates, the short-term cost to the government would be high—$24 billion for those who have been filing returns and perhaps $5 billion more for nonfilers. Table 4.6 provides comparable figures for a $500 elective refundable tax credit. As more and more people are covered by the election of a tax credit and when and if a transition is made to dropping personal exemptions entirely, costs to the government would more closely resemble those shown in tables 4.2 and 4.4.

5

Where Will Americans Live?

The nation's most severe and persistent social problems converge in a consideration of housing patterns in the United States. That urban schools so heavily serve the poor and minorities makes improving these schools extraordinarily difficult. That those who live in cities are unqualified for jobs in downtown office buildings while the work for which they are needed is miles away in the suburbs, or further, contributes to their unemployment rates. Because of the way housing is financed and housing programs are administered, segregation is a continuing pattern. It is true that there has been some movement of blacks into suburban areas, but disproportionately into houses of relatively low value and quality and not at the same rate as whites.[1] "If these trends continue," writes Robert W. Lake, "the spectre of 'two societies' . . . may simply be replicated at a new metropolitan scale."[2]

In the past three decades, we have had periods of intense attention to these social problems and of great dynamism in housing construction and distribution. Among the lessons that should have been learned is that we can solve neither these problems nor our housing problems while we concentrate disadvantaged people in urban reservations—in substandard

114

housing and shabby neighborhoods at that. Many who are expert, whether temperamentally they lean left or right or are unwaveringly upright, have grown pessimistic about improvement. Housing objectives have been mixed (concerned with the poor or middle class or with job creation), the means used complex and often wasteful, and costs high. A good deal of housing has been produced, and middle-class pressures were, at least for a time, moderated. Especially with a post-1980 view of straitened resources, there is some disposition to think that little more than triage—that is, humane rather than truly reconstructive housing policies for the poor and disadvantaged—can now be expected.[3] Unless one grasps that decently distributed decent housing is central to fair shares, to integration, and to full employment, its requirements in terms of policy may not appear to justify the effort or cost.

We begin with a review of progress to date and an attempt to define current and prospective housing problems.

The Achievement

The basic structure that would stimulate the construction of housing and direct its allocation was laid down during the depression: the Federal Housing Administration (FHA), the Farmers Home Administration, and (after World War II) the Veterans Administration—to insure mortgages for the repair, purchase, and construction of dwellings; inducements for the creation of such agencies as savings and loan associations; backup market institutions such as the Federal National Mortgage Association and the Federal Home Loan Bank Board; and tax deductions, notably for interest on home loans. A complex system of incentives and regulations tended to draw funding away from alternative investment possibilities and into housing.

In order to direct housing to the poor and disadvantaged, the government wrote priorities into some of these broad measures but tended more generally to develop targeted subsidies. Public housing was built. Direct federal subsidy for slum clearance, redevelopment, and housing rehabilitation was provided in the Housing Acts of 1937, 1949, and 1954.

Responding to rising disenchantment with these measures, by the 1960s the federal government moved to offering tax advantages to private developers of low-income housing and supplementation of the rents that the poor could pay. When President Nixon launched his "new federalism," a number of these subsidies were combined in Community Development Block Grants (CDBGs), providing local governments with a large measure of discretion in their use. In the last few years, the old subsidy programs have virtually disappeared. In their place are CDBGs and experimentation with housing allowances—direct payments to or on behalf of families that cannot afford standard housing.

Housing production climbed by fits and starts—with what the President's Commission on Housing ponderously called "the extreme cyclicality of housing construction."[4] For example, shifts of resources occasioned by our involvement in Vietnam caused a substantial contraction of housing construction, but the programs embodied in the Housing Act of 1968—following on the civil disorders of that period and concurrent with the sweeping recommendations of the Douglas and Kaiser commissions[5]—produced a two-thirds increase in the number of new housing units per year between 1970 and 1973. In the long run, total housing units started built up from around three hundred thousand a year in the early 1940s to over two million a year in the early 1970s.

Effects on family living have been impressive. In 1960, one household in eight lacked complete plumbing facilities; by 1980 that proportion was down to one in forty. In 1950, the average household had 1.5 rooms per person; it now has 2 rooms per person,[6] and the rooms are larger. The number of newly established households is a function of birth rates and marriage and divorce, to be sure, but also of housing availability. Half of the twenty million new housing units added in the decade of the 1970s represents a devolution of larger into smaller family units—old people living separately, young people the same, and so forth.[7] The proportion of families that own their homes—less than half before World War II and about three out of five in 1960—crept up to two thirds. In one way or another, all these figures reflect improvement in average housing quality and opportunities for families to live in the manner they wish.

The Problems

Four types of housing problems are identified: residential segregation, inadequate housing of poor people, the steady climb of housing costs, and an approaching crisis in overall supply.

Segregation

Residential separation by social and economic differences did not appear in the United States until the late nineteenth century.[8] All but a few people walked to work; therefore "most areas of the new big city were a jumble of occupations, classes, shops, homes, immigrants, and native Americans."[9] The development of alternative modes of transportation made it possible for those with more income to live further from work, particularly as new homes tended to be built on outlying, open land. Older housing available for reuse filtered down to those who were poorer and tended to be in the city center. Effect became cause: the population of a neighborhood came to determine the value of the housing, prompting or reinforcing the inclination of the advantaged to resist incursions into their domain. With time and advancement, immigrants and others who had been relatively poor tended to disperse; the influence of national background on where people lived declined. It was not so with color, however, which continued to dictate or confine choices about location.

By their very power and productiveness, the post-depression instruments of housing policy contributed to racial separation. Because tenant farming was declining and for other related reasons, three million blacks left the South between 1940 and 1960. In that very period, large-scale suburbanization, facilitated by FHA, VA, and the rest, was under way. Whites moved up and out, and blacks moved in. It is not more secret than other government secrets that government housing agencies, taking a "conservative" view of housing values and of their social responsibility, actively discouraged racial mixing in residential development.[10] Private lending institutions, more influential than the government in this area, played the same game.

When, finally, first President Kennedy (1962) and then Congress directed the government to avoid discrimination (1964) and to act affirmatively to achieve fair housing (1968), exclusionary practices were defended in depth: their personal biases aside, homeowners were convinced that desegregation would cost them money. Metropolitan areas were politically segmented, with independent municipalities controlling planning and zoning within their boundaries. Banks and builders were not inclined to take unnecessary risks with their investments. George Romney, President Nixon's Secretary of Housing and Urban Development, received his education in this matter when he accepted the congressional mandate and undertook a vigorous Open Communities program. It stirred up such a political storm, producing so much contrary pressure on him from the White House, that he backed down step by step. Eventually he asked bitterly, "What the hell is the Administration policy?"[11]

The direct subsidy programs, addressed to low-income families and therefore disproportionately to blacks and other minorities, were shaped by the same dynamics and reinforced them. When middle-class neighborhoods resisted public housing development, planning authorities turned to center-city locations. Large center-city tracts had, in any case, been taken over for urban renewal; it rapidly became clear that prospects for private or mixed development were not bright. Thus, locating public housing in heavily minority areas not only raised less opposition; the government owned the property, was uncertain what to do with it, and found locating public housing there less costly than buying suburban sites. Developers using government subsidies tended to locate housing in low-income areas for similar reasons. Banks redlined center-city neighborhoods, denying private funds for home purchase or improvement.[12] Meanwhile, the old cities in particular were experiencing economic decline. Low-income population and declining industry spelled a heavier cost for social services and a low tax base simultaneously.[13] Why would anyone who had a choice live with declining schools, poor sanitation, and inadequate police protection? Answering to a perception of other advantages, obviously some middle-income families located in the center city and some neighborhoods gentrified, but overall a process had developed that meant a heavy concentration of those who had no choice—that is, the poor and minorities.

In 1970 the federal government undertook an extensive experiment with housing allowances, intended to direct subsidies to low-income families and to replace subsidies that had moved through banks and developers. The new program was justified in part as a measure that would facilitate dispersion or desegregation: beneficiary families would be in a position to pay for standard housing wherever they could find it. In the event, researchers concluded "that the experiments negligibly affected racial and economic integration."[14] Independent experiments in providing subsistence income to needy families came to a similar conclusion: beneficiary families tended to disperse residentially but without effect on segregation.[15] Even with modestly adequate income, the dynamics that had been set in motion, not to mention discrimination, steered families to segregated living. As some of the housing of low-income people deteriorated beyond livability or was replaced by public buildings or office buildings, families doubled up or pressed into nearby suburbs. The move to the suburbs, viewed purely statistically, contributed to a spurious appearance of desegregation. Reports of the 1980 Census may be read to indicate increased segregation since 1970.[16] One study, limited to cities with one hundred thousand or more blacks in 1980, arrived at an index figure for segregation of 81—compared with 87 in 1970.[17] Thus, one may also judge that there was a slight decline—during a decade, however, that followed vigorous open housing legislation and saw a striking increase of 27 percent in the total number of occupied units. Analysts have lately developed a vocabulary to describe the effects of the ongoing process—"the separated society," "the duplex society," "two societies," "the two-cities phenomenon."[18]

Low-Income Families

Superficially considered, reviews of housing subsidies for the poor and figures about overall housing achievement may leave a misleading impression of the net effect on poor families. In earlier years, congressional liberals tended to collect in the legislative committees of both Houses and were responsible for the programs enacted. On the other hand, conservatives tended to collect in the appropriations committees, and so actual appropriations were far less than the authorizations that were won.[19] In any event, annual budget authority for housing assistance dropped from $27 billion in 1980 to under $10 billion in 1983[20] and was slated for further cuts in 1985.

Then, resistance by entrepreneurs and government agencies at various levels have impeded the development of the low-income housing that was actually funded. For example, in 1949 Congress established a six-year goal of constructing 810,000 units of public housing; by 1955, only 212,000 had been started. Construction from the Depression to date provides the nation with a stock of subsidized housing of almost five million units. But so-called very low income families, defined in housing legislation as having less than half of the median family income, numbered twenty-one million in 1979. In sum, it was estimated in 1980 that federal housing subsidy programs served 15 percent of all the households in need of assistance.[21]

Not commonly viewed as a housing program (but over the years, probably contributing more than any other to poor people's housing) is public assistance. During the 1970s, formal levels of welfare support declined by about a third in real money. Because other changes took place simultaneously (new rules about how to calculate the income of recipients, for example)[22] the decline in average payment level was substantially steeper than one third. In the first years of President Reagan's administration, existing levels of welfare funding and of the programs more narrowly viewed as housing programs were even further reduced.[23] Thus, those with little income were not even in the same competitive position with respect to private housing as they had been. (Subsidies authorized in earlier years continued to provide a small build-up of housing in the early 1980s, but the pipeline is expected to go dry by 1990.)

If poor people's subsidy programs and their income are less than they may appear to be and declining, the hope for improvement must lie with what George Sternlieb has described as flooding the housing market—a phenomenon that he believes occurred in the 1970s. He puts the argument as follows: "The basic way we house poor people and moderate-income people in the United States is precisely the same way we provide them with automobiles, and that is by a filtering-down process which has been enormously successful. Using any criteria that we can count, whether it is plumbing or persons per room, or what-have-you, we have had . . . an enormous increase in the quality of housing for just about all Americans."[24] Such an argument brushes aside the 3.5 million units of subsidized housing that were produced between the Douglas and Kaiser Commission reports and 1981. One may wonder where we would be without them. Also, it overlooks the question whether low-income people are sharing equally or more nearly equally in general improvement in standards—a question with which, in the view taken here, one must be concerned. The filter-down strategy—a strategy as old as the struggle for decent housing for poor people—directs attention precisely away from the issue of fair shares. "You can see that poor families now have more space," it says. "Never mind how much more space everyone else has." And so forth.

In any event, this argument also overlooks the most practical considerations. First, filtration requires that the real estate market operate in a situation of stable demand and continuing supply. However, poor people in general—not just welfare recipients—have less money than they had. Between 1978 and 1983, their average disposable income dropped by 9.4 percent.[25] At the same time, they face more rather than less competition for decent housing. For example, a study of the nation's principal cities reports that the second reason (after declining construction) for declining availability of low-income housing is "increased demand from higher-income renters"—not filter-down, but filter-up![26] And we have noted that the production of housing is volatile. That is, it is governed by issues of grand economic policy, such as war and government deficits, that are extraneous to consumer need for housing and so does not answer to need or demand, as classical economics would have it. *answers to profit which may be different*

Second, filtration requires that the housing market operate without substantial impediment. Segregation is the notorious barrier to free movement of property, but there are other barriers as well. Location is one constraint: a surplus of housing in one city with high unemployment will not induce filtration in another city with a housing shortage. Other barriers have to do with the availability of housing to large families, to families with children, to single-parent families, and to welfare recipients. Such groups make up large proportions of the poor population; studies over many years have shown that they are widely excluded and pay more for the poorer housing they find.[27] Third and last, housing that is sold, converted, and put to uses for which it was not initially designed exacts a price from the families who live in it. Houses and apartments that have been divided up usually wind up poorly designed. The neighborhoods populated by trickle-down "are characterized by overcrowding, poorly maintained buildings, high crime rates and inadequate public services."[28]

It is no surprise, then, that very low-income families are still in trouble. Of twenty-one million very low-income families in 1979, almost four million were living in physically inadequate housing, and another eight hundred thousand were crowded.[29] That is, almost one quarter suffered from the types of deficiency that many people think no longer exist. An unpublished study by the Department of Housing and Urban Development indicates that conditions have deteriorated since 1979.[30] Worst off of all low-income families are the elderly, those under thirty years old, families headed by women, and blacks and Hispanics.[31] The average waiting period for public housing is eighteen months, and for a so-called Section 8 certificate—authorizing a supplemental payment for rent—over two years. The certificates, in any case, are widely unusable because recipients cannot find housing that is acceptable to the program in quality and price.[32]

In recent years, doubling up of families has been increasing again. The number of families living with others as "subfamilies" rose by 100 percent between 1978 and 1983, and the number of unrelated individuals living with others increased by 20 percent,[33] developments that must so far have been concentrated among the poor. Despite the fact that it is illegal and risky, doubling up is occurring extensively in public housing.[34] Doubling up, particularly when the landlord discovers and reacts to it, is said to be a major factor precipitating homelessness in the United States.[35] Homelessness is of course the primordial housing deficiency. Estimates of the number of homeless people in the United States have ranged all the way from 250,000 or 350,000 to 2 or 3 million. Whatever the number, no one doubts that the problem has increased dramatically in recent years. First among the causes of the problem, identified in a study of ten large cities, was "lack of housing affordable by low-income people."[36]

In short, while physical deficiency of housing is less widespread among the poor than it was ten or twenty years ago, it is still common. Crowding too is a problem—no doubt more serious now than the 1980 Census counted. Stark homelessness has seized the imagination or conscience of the nation in a manner not known since *The Grapes of Wrath* appeared. Moreover, there is a new problem, at least new in its depth for poor people and in its spread to those with middle incomes; that is, the steadily rising portion of income that housing consumes. I turn now to that question.

Affordability

Almost two thirds of American families own their homes; in general, owners have higher incomes than renters. From the end of World War II through 1972, median family income in the United States kept pace with the steady rise in the price of new homes. That is, year by year the median price of a new home remained at little more than twice median family income. Translated into monthly payments on a mortgage, this meant that the average family could expect to pay out about a quarter of its income. In 1973, prices of new homes took a sharp upturn relative to average income; by 1985, the median price of a new home was approaching three times median family income. Moreover, mortgage interest rates displayed a dismaying tendency to rise despite a declining and then more nearly stable cost-of-living index, adding to the burden of higher prices for dwellings. A sixfold rise in fuel costs in the 1970s also added to the burden. By 1984, the average proportion of family income required to purchase a new home had reached 35 to 40 percent.[37] For the first time in decades, the proportion of families owning their homes registered a decline (to 64 percent in 1985); and the rate of foreclosure on home mortgages promised to exceed the record set in the recession of 1973.

What was responsible for this substantial shift? Government policies aimed at restraining inflation had driven interest rates up (including interest on construction loans). In 1984 and 1985 they declined, but not nearly to earlier levels. A rich array of tax incentives for non-housing investment and deregulation of savings and loan associations diminished the advantage that housing had enjoyed. That, too, increased interest rates for home mortgages. Baby-boom children were coming to adulthood and creating buyer pressure that bid up prices. As potential buyers with moderate incomes felt the effects of the affordability gap, builders concentrated on more expensive homes. Despite occasional campaigns to increase the efficiency of the home-building industry, for various reasons there was little success, and general inflation was reflected in the cost of homes.

Moderate- and low-income families are, naturally, more likely to be found in rental housing. The expenditure of all renters of housing has been rising. "Between 1950 and 1976, the proportion of renters spending 25 percent or more of their income on rent rose from 31 to 47 percent" and to 53 percent in 1985.[38] Four out of ten rental households have "very low income"; the large majority of them were paying over half their income for shelter.[39] Between 1973 and 1983 median costs for all families that were renting dwellings increased from 22 to 29 percent of family income.[40] The rental market reflects some of the same forces as the construction of owned housing, and others besides, that is, special incentives for conversion to ownership and severe limitations on the profit that can be made.[41] For example, as the population of rented housing became relatively poorer, raising rents and collecting them became more difficult. The pressure on renters' incomes and on the supply of rental housing can be summed up in a single pair of figures: If the nine million families with incomes of less than $7,000 a year who were in rental housing in 1980 were constrained to find rental housing at 25 percent of their income or less, they would have found themselves competing for five million units.[42]

A famous housing study during the Depression in Stockton-on-Tees, England, compared the death rates of families who had moved to modern dwellings and of families who had remained behind in slums. The death rate for those who moved increased substantially over the rate of those who remained behind; it may be imagined that the difference caused some stir. In the end, it was established that families in new housing were paying twice as much rent just when they lost work. Because their income was marginal, higher rent led to poor nutrition—thus, better housing to a higher death rate.[43] The study illustrates the fact that, contrary to a ranking of priorities that one may arrive at a priori, poor people pay what they must for housing first, and then pay for food and clothing with what remains. Upon reflection, it may readily be understood why this is so.[44]

Recent experiments with a government housing allowance point to the same phenomenon. Eligibility for an allowance required a family to spend 25 percent of its income and to improve its dwelling or move to a dwelling that would meet minimum standards. Much to the surprise of almost everyone involved, fewer than half of those who might be eligible even applied, and those in the worst housing were least likely to apply. More likely to apply were people who, upon making a relatively simple repair, could receive an allowance that replaced part of what they were already paying out. Researchers concluded that 3 to 8 percent of the allowances was converted into improved housing and the remaining 92 to 97 percent was used for general income maintenance—that is, to free money for other purposes. Queried about what all this meant, nonparticipating families said they liked their neighborhoods or didn't feel like moving. Obviously the budgetary issue far outweighed the issue of housing standards.

Perhaps one may recast this material along with earlier material in this fashion. By fits and starts, housing standards

have been raised considerably since World War II; adequate
housing has replaced much that was inadequate. That has
been achieved at costs reflected in higher prices relative to
income—that is, costs rising faster than the general standard
of living. Middle-income families are feeling that pressure.
This will doubtless be reflected in a turning to rental, to doubling up, to withdrawal from social overhead capital (see
chapter 4), and so forth. Some low-income people have had
substandard housing replaced by standard housing at higher
cost; even those still in substandard housing must therefore
pay more. Compounded by the fact that their real income was
simultaneously declining, they have been placed under budgetary pressure from which they escape in any of the ways
indicated. Those who do not escape these pressures, presumably, in greater or lesser degree pay the penalty exacted in
Stockton-on-Tees half a century ago.

Once Again, an Approaching Crisis

Much of what has been outlined spells an oncoming crisis
in the provision of housing. Investment in housing construction and purchase is no longer stimulated by incentives and
regulation, as formerly. Morton J. Schussheim assesses the
prospect as follows:

> The financial world has changed . . . and the terms at which
> funds can be borrowed for housing will not be as favorable. . . . As
> mortgage pools and secondary market facilities take on a larger
> share of mortgage financing, home borrowers will have to com-
> pete head-to-head in the capital markets with muscular bor-
> rowers—business corporations and the Federal government itself.
> Monetary and fiscal policies that generate expectations of a resur-
> gence of inflation and high interest rates would be particularly
> adverse to the housing sector.[45]

In mid-1984 the interest rate once again reached almost 15
percent and then declined somewhat; anxiety persisted that
with a large government deficit, it would rise again. In general, it is calculated that every 1-percent rise in interest rates
adds $2,000 to the annual income needed to buy a house. Put
differently, every 1-percent rise means 100,000 to 150,000
fewer housing starts a year.[46] Housing starts, which had

showed substantial recovery from under 1 million in 1982, struggled fitfully to 1.8 million in April 1985, a far cry from the 2.6-million-a-year goal established by Congress in 1968 or even the more modest 2.2 million that experts say are required to replace abandoned housing and meet the needs of new families.[47]

One would think that the generous production of the 1970s created some reserve housing, but only for the relatively affluent. Unfortunately, rising financial constraints affect especially the young families who, as we have noted, tend at best to spend a little more than they earn. As for rental units, there is no reserve at all; there is rather a serious shortage already. At the end of 1979, almost half of the vacant units had no bedroom or one bedroom, and 43 percent were more than forty years old.[48] Yet, in the 1980s some ten million more people than in the 1970s will reach the age of thirty—an age group that forms families and makes independent housing arrangements.[49] The Joint Center for Urban Studies estimated that 1985 to 1990 will see an average increase of 1.3 million households a year.[50] Meanwhile some housing will disappear and other housing will fail to connect with demand because of neighborhood, region, or other reasons. By doing a calculation with such figures as these, one concludes that we need to attain housing production of 2.2 million units a year. Nor does that address the problem of twenty-one million very low income families, most of them currently in trouble about housing.

Adjustments will be made. In an effort to produce buyable or rentable housing, the standards in space and facilities that have become customary will be cut back. Just as more families were formed than was expected a decade earlier, in the 1980s fewer than are expected will be formed. Families are already doubling up;[51] one may expect the development of a literature on "how to live with your in-laws" and "living with your children can be constructive." It is arguable to what extent this will be acceptable. "The new problem," writes George Sternlieb, "will be to cushion the shock of reduced housing quality in the middle class. The long line of housing improvement . . . has aborted."[52] Facing this set of issues, or, more exactly, declining to face it, the President's Commission on Housing expressed confidence that, unassisted, "the private housing market adjusts to provide homes in changing numbers, size, and tenure as the needs of households both grow and change."[53] Decent people will wish to do better than that.

The remainder of this chapter deals with the choices that will have to be made—in stability and scale of effort, in providing the investment in housing that will be necessary, and in strategy—to produce explicit objectives such as integration and a better share of housing of good quality for poorer families.

Stability and Scale

The "extreme cyclicality" of housing production creates a set of problems all its own. It builds a skilled work force that is from time to time abruptly dumped into extended unemployment. It discourages investment in expensive equipment, though that might lead to more efficiency in building. As builders are caught in a downturn or glimpse an upturn, some go in for "creative" financing. States and localities counter by developing costly requirements for issuing building permits. In short, "a more stable housing cycle would lower housing prices."[54] Moreover, volatile production creates chaos in the distribution of housing. The cycles respond to land values, inflation or deflation, interest rates, and a variety of other qualities only distantly if at all related to demographic trends and housing need. The President's Commission on Housing observed that "there has always been debate about whether a social product as important as housing should serve as a balance wheel for the economy."[55] Setting aside the question whether housing has successfully served such a function (the President's Commission thought not— lately, at any rate), stable housing production is itself a desirable goal. In addition to efficiency and the advantages for construction workers and builders, it would facilitate a more orderly flow of housing to deal with unmet and emerging needs of families. The key to nonsubsidized private production, writes Henry B. Schechter, is "to provide a less volatile, more adequate supply of mortgage funds that leave housing affordable."[56]

It is a curious coincidence that, across the world, an objective of eight to ten new housing units annually per thousand population appears to meet the needs of the underhoused, new families, and families moving up or down or changing location or housing style. In underdeveloped countries, the ratio reflects primitive need, in wealthier countries mobility and rising standards. The United Nations has estimated that countries in Asia, Africa, and Latin America need to produce housing at this rate—though few have brought that off. Obviously situated very differently, industrial countries also balance pressure for housing against other domestic needs. As it turns out, Western industrial countries have all produced housing at a rate that ranges from five, six, or seven units per thousand (Italy, the United Kingdom) to ten and even twelve units per thousand (Federal Republic of Germany, Sweden, the Netherlands).[57] In its best years, 1972, 1973, 1977, and 1978, housing production in the United States approximated the higher rates. In recent years of worldwide economic difficulty, these rates have widely declined.

It has been argued that in the United States the boom production years drew too much from the nation's economy for housing and are therefore responsible for the affordability gap, if not for undermining the growth rate of the economy generally.[58] This displays a somewhat parochial view of the significance of housing; the economy's difficulties were deeper and more far-ranging than housing alone might account for. As for the affordability gap, it is a function not only of rising prices for dwellings but of family income that declined in real terms for two or three years and in relative terms for several years more, all for reasons remote from housing production. In fact, over the years most Western industrial countries have invested more in residential housing than the United States, either as public expenditures on housing as a percentage of the total public budget, or as total investment in residential housing as a percentage of gross domestic product.[59] It seems reasonable in terms of our own past capacity to perform and of the investment of other, somewhat similar countries that the United States aim at a steady-state investment of 5 to 6 percent of GNP. That is to say that a new welfare state would have not only a housing objective—perhaps eight to ten newly constructed and rehabilitated units annually per thousand population—but an investment standard to make this practical.

Investment in Housing

If such an objective and standard are to be realized, continuing flows of investment in housing will have to be encouraged. In addition to the disappearance by the 1980s of the sheltered position of shelter, in terms of direct subsidy, Reagan administration policy cut back the government's investment in credit for housing. For example, administration proposals for fiscal 1984 included a $10 billion cut in housing credit insured or advanced by the Farmers Home Administration, the Federal Housing Administration, and the Government National Mortgage Association.[60] We begin with a government subsidy of housing that has not been cut back and has, indeed, been expanding rapidly.

The income tax deduction for mortgage interest and property taxes represents a large cost to government—about $40 billion in 1983. That single-year cost was more than "the total of all the assisted housing payments ever made under all HUD assisted housing programs." In 1979, almost 60 percent of the value of the deduction went to taxpayers in the top 10 percent of the income distribution.[61] In 1981, households with income over $50,000 received an average of $3,200 in such subsidies, while households with incomes under $10,000 received subsidies averaging $1,353.[62] Obviously, the income tax deduction measurably contributes to inequality. Moreover, analyzed from the same perspective as experimental housing allowances—that is, the extent to which the government subsidy achieves housing objectives—it would undoubtedly turn out that the mortgage interest and property tax deductions are a highly inefficient means of producing the upgraded housing and that, as with the allowances, 92 or 97 percent of the cost serves an income maintenance purpose (for the rich, to be sure), freeing money for other purposes.

In the past few years, several people have proposed substituting a tax credit for the deduction. Properly designed, such a credit would work out to the benefit of eight or nine out of ten taxpayers and could yield a substantial net gain to the government as well.[63] The saving, Anthony Downs calculates, could be enough to pay for a nationwide housing allowance entitlement program,[64] a proposal not favored here, but nevertheless an indication of the magnitude of funds available. Moreover, analysis of economic effects suggests that such a tax credit would "provide a boost to the construction industry, and improve the quality of housing for lower-to-middle-income households."[65] Without moving to a tax credit, even so modest a change as a $5,000-a-year maximum on the mortgage interest deduction—that is, limiting the deduction to mortgage interest payments of a little more than $400 a month—would have saved the government $6.5 billion in 1984 and affected fewer than 5 percent of taxpayers.[66]

Somewhat related are proposals to limit the use of Individual Retirement Accounts as an escape from taxation. In the sense that it discourages savings that might be used to buy a house, the IRA is "anti-housing."[67] We should provide instead for housing-related IRAs (presumably renamed)—that is, for the accumulation of savings free of taxation, provided that they are to be used for family housing. In order to avoid exploitation of housing-related IRAs by the relatively well-to-do, they would be limited to homes of modest cost or, possibly, to first homes. The United States is one of the few major countries without such a provision. I noted in chapter 3 that $35 billion was transferred to IRAs in 1983 and the same amount in 1984, and that it is in any case undesirable to subsidize their rapid growth for retirement purposes.

Apart from direct government subsidy, a number of strategies concerned with interest rates are available. Some economists tend to favor wiping out the preferential treatment of housing as an investment, partly because they enjoy the capacity of money when unconstrained, unlike the democratic inclination of water, to seek its highest level. In any event, economists are much at odds about how interest rates in general can be brought down and what the fallout of various strategies will be. Without entering this general argument, a number of strategies particular to housing are available.

In the late 1970s, states and local governments began selling tax-exempt revenue bonds that were, in turn, used to provide low-interest mortgages to home buyers. These are beneficial as investments mainly to those with good incomes, and so the practice is justifiable only if the homes that are financed go to lower- or moderate-income people. That was the original goal, and Congress's intention when it passed a law regulating the bonds. In practice, unfortunately, most loans were made to middle- and upper-income households. "For the most part, these home-buyers' incomes and the prices of homes they purchased were similar to those of buyers under the Federal Housing Administration's subsidized mortgage insurance program."[68] In extending such legislation, therefore, Congress would need to specify an upper limit on the prices of homes for which such mortgages could be available. As rental housing is of most concern to low-income families, revenue bonds should continue to be available to state agencies to stimulate construction of low- and moderate-rent dwellings. Fees and other costs associated with these bonds have been unconscionably high—as much as half the proceeds[69]—and would require regulation.

Another possibility follows the model of the Brooke-Cranston Emergency Home Assistance Act, offering government subsidy for below-market interest-rate financing for moderate-income housing. Once again, it would be important to establish maximum sales prices and mortgage amounts for such a program and to make it available as well for moderate-income rental housing. As construction costs are also a problem in producing rental housing, it would be useful to provide a construction loan program at an interest rate representing the cost of funds to the government. Such loans would be fully repaid at the completion of construction.[70]

The income tax proposals in chapter 4, substituting tax credits for tax deductions and offering tax relief largely to the less affluent and to younger rather than middle-aged families, would tend to provide revenue that might be used to rent or buy housing for those with poor to middle incomes. It is the way funds would be spent that would be critical in moving us toward a fairer distribution of decent housing. The interest-rate programs defined above are examples, and other examples will be offered. However, the housing objective and investment standard that have been specified are not meant to be limited solely to those with moderate incomes. Unless interest rates come down a good deal, as many hope but few expect, the credit capacity of government agencies like the Farmers Home Administration will need to be built up again substantially and used as a moderating influence on interest rates for home construction and rehabilitation. Another method of increasing the credit available for housing includes requirements for all thrift institutions or pension funds to include a specific proportion of home mortgages in their holdings.

Strategic Choices in Investment

By choice or by default, the nation settles a variety of issues of strategy in housing policy—subsidy of builders and rehabilitators versus subsidies that help to pay the cost to the consumer, stimulation of new housing versus rehabilitation, and a preference for owned or rented housing.

With respect to the choice between builders and consumers, government policy was for many years a straddle. Public assistance was provided for the poor; for others the price of housing was moderated by such devices as mortgage insurance. At the same time, though not in the same magnitude, public housing was built and other kinds of subsidy provided that produced housing for the disadvantaged. After World War II public housing got a bad name and, later, other subsidy programs were widely abused. For example, "there have been many instances where purchasers of rehabilitated housing under the Section 235 program have been exploited by real estate operators."[71] Abuse apart, analysts concluded that subsidy to the builder was very expensive per unit. By the 1970s the government was turning from direct subsidy to a search for methods of helping to meet the rent or mortgage payments of needy families. Experimental Housing Allowances represented a major move in this direction. Possibly the move also represented accumulated weariness—the wish to lay out a sum of money, whether large or small, and be discharged of responsibility for what ensued.

However, experience with the experimental allowances was discouraging. In the first place, although they are a good deal cheaper per tenant than construction subsidies, they do not necessarily accomplish the same objectives. For example, they do not appear to increase the supply of housing, nor do they provide housing in specific regions of great need or for specific target populations like the aged or the disabled.[72] That is, allowances may be cheaper in general but are not a cheaper way to achieve specified housing objectives. A more balanced, broad appraisal is that direct subsidy is efficient in periods of low building activity and is relatively expensive when construction is robust.[73] Second, as noted, the benefit of the allowance is felt almost exclusively in terms of affordability; its contribution to raising housing standards is minimal. Third, in the words of the borough president of Manhattan, in tight rental markets the effect of allowances would be that "the rent levels of existing worn out housing will go up."[74]

Finally, in terms of the objectives offered in chapter 2, the major new "housing allowance entitlement program," of which proponents write[75] would be the wrong way to go. Income ought to be provided, when it needs to be provided, in mainstream and not in income-tested programs—that is, in expansion and correction of the general income-maintenance programs—social insurance and the tax system in particular. Henry Aaron, expressing some sympathy for this point of view and facing the issue squarely, comes down in favor of a housing allowance program because of congressional preference for "earmarked income-tested benefits" and because "subsidizing commodities permits political alliances to develop between advocates of assistance to the poor and producers of the commodities."[76] As a Briton might observe, "this is too clever by half." Political judgments such as these, when sound, are sound from month to month and perhaps even from year to year. They are notoriously undependable over the long run; witness the fate of income-tested programs after 1981. They have played their role in producing some of our now deeply rooted, malfunctioning, and even mischievous public policies.

In short, a new welfare state would return to straddling the issue of subsidy versus mechanisms that substitute for income. The latter would be fostered in the manner outlined in chapters 3 and 4, but there is no objection to continuing a modest program of housing allowances. This is especially suitable during a transition period while the gap between the cost of housing and the income of poorer people is being reduced. At the same time, construction subsidies are desirable to stimulate construction and rehabilitation during periods of low housing activity, to provide housing for poor and moderate-income families when there is significant need and it appears not to be attractive to private entrepreneurs, and to provide housing in specific regions, for special populations, or for special purposes such as voluntary racial integration.

On the issue of new construction versus rehabilitation, there has come to be general agreement that maintenance and rehabilitation of the existing housing stock require priority. For some, this represents pessimism about the capacity of our society to invest substantially in construction or doubt that interest rates will come down—but there are other reasons as well. Other things being equal, rehabilitation is cheaper, by about $7,000 per unit in a recent study.[77] Certainly proper maintenance is cheaper. Indeed, subsidy programs that spurred building but not rehabilitation or maintenance have contributed to the abandonment of sound structures.[78] On the whole, for reasons that may be obvious, homes owned by their occupants have suffered little compared with rented dwellings. Many sound rental units have been lost when a tipping point was reached (in terms of tax depreciation, collectable rents, and maintenance costs) at which it is profitable, in the cool term used by analysts, for owners to disinvest.

Rehabilitation cannot meet all needs, of course. For example, almost half the housing inventory of the Northeast and North Central regions of the country is forty-five years old or more. Only 20 percent of the inventory in the South and West is as old. Thus, rehabilitation cannot deal with need in all regions. Furthermore, units available for reuse tend to be concentrated in the inner city. If housing programs are to lend themselves to racial integration, units will need to be provided in suburban and exurban areas as well. There are also issues such as life style, family size, and special need to be taken into account.

Finally, it should not be supposed that priority for construction or rehabilitation is exercised solely by allocation of federal subsidies or preferences. Writing of rental housing, Anthony Downs lists these additional ways of encouraging more intensive use of existing housing: local government tax abatement for a period; change in zoning laws and housing codes to encourage the division of large, older single-family homes into multiple dwellings; local government tax credits, rebates, and other incentives; and selective enforcement of housing codes to allow for different levels of quality in differing neighborhoods.[79]

With respect to ownership versus rental, the long-term increase in home ownership in the United States expressed deeply rooted personal preference and has advantages from a public point of view. In particular, owners are more likely to maintain and improve their properties. However, it will take some years to overcome the difficulties in supply of purchasable housing that have come upon us, and rental housing is even more acutely in short supply. Existing rental units are more subject to deterioration and loss, for reasons that have been touched upon, and they are subject to conversion to owned dwellings as well. In addition, rental housing is more important to the poor—though it is also important to middle-income families who rent while they accumulate funds for purchase, or for other reasons having to do with preference or family circumstance. All this is to say that we must focus on maintaining and upgrading the supply of rental housing and cannot assume that improvement in the supply of owned housing will meet all needs.

A variety of strategies that would help have been noted, including those proposed by Anthony Downs (above), making certain that federal and state below-market rate loans are open to use for rental housing, and reducing the incentive that federal tax deductions create for ownership as opposed to rental. Apart from these, it has been proposed that rent control (a phenomenon occurring mainly in New York, New Jersey, and some West Coast cities) be abandoned, in order to allow rents to rise to a level that would encourage the maintenance and construction of rental housing.[80] That rent controls contribute to the loss of rental housing may be readily understood. On the other hand, it is difficult to encourage this course while so many families cannot afford the rental housing they are occupying or seeking. In fact, cities have learned that, without controls, investment in rehabilitating low-income housing may lead to rent increases that force the poor tenants out.[81] An appropriate strategy might rather be to seek in other ways to increase the supply so that rent controls may in time be dropped without severe, widespread consequences. It is not to be doubted that, in a free market society such as ours, controls compound the problems of supply.

Other important, though special, strategies are available. For example, many aged people now live in homes that are too large for them and too expensive to maintain, in communities zoned to prevent multifamily living. It would serve these old people well if they were permitted to divide their homes into two or three units, in one of which the old person or couple would presumably continue to live. Zoning change is required, much of it in suburban communities that never conceived of this issue. As some of the aged have few assets except the equity in their homes, low-interest loans or devices for turning some of their equity into liens collectable at death may be required to pay for modest conversion costs. Housing supply would expand, additional income would be provided for the aged person, and the mixture of older and younger families could have practical advantages for both. Moreover, the development of senior housing complexes and the expansion and coordination of existing housing for the elderly and nursing home programs would free units that are now too expensive or too large for their elderly occupants for other age groups facing a tight market.[82]

Urban Areas and Low-Income Housing

Housing deterioration and shortage are extensively characteristic of older cities; moreover, in the major metropolitan
areas, problems of housing are interwoven with other tena-
cious social problems. Taking into account demographic
trends, economic prospects, and the manner in which the several problems of declining cities and regions reinforce one
another, further losses of housing stock may be unavoidable;
even Southern and Western cities will probably slow their
rates of growth. A long roster of initiatives has been traversed
in attempting to correct these problems. The following lessons
may be said to have been learned from the series of policy
failures.

1. "One of the continuing social functions of large
cities—helping society cope with and upgrade its poorer
citizens—will require sustained infusions of outside resources, especially from the federal government." It is the
nature of the problem that the cities do not have sufficient
resources of their own. A corollary lesson reinforcing the
main point is that "certain policies cannot be effective unless
they are carried out on a significant quantitative scale." For
example, a thousand new housing units properly planned
may change or stabilize the character of a neighborhood,
while a hundred units would be overwhelmed by the forces
leading to deterioration.[83]

2. Because problems vary from city to city, general measures turn out to be poorly designed to achieve a particular
city's objectives. Also, the willingness and capacity of powerful
local forces to distort the impact of programs intended for the
disadvantaged should not be underestimated. Therefore, "in
order to improve any particular condition such as unemployment or housing, it is much more effective to aim policies
directly at the condition than to attack decline in general and
hope the effects will 'spill over' or 'trickle down.' This is especially true of fiscal distress, which is only slightly relieved
by . . . nonfiscal measures."[84]

3. If the inner city is the focus, peripheral vision must
nevertheless attend to the metropolitan area. One reason that

inner cities decline is, after all, that their decline serves powerful metropolitan interests. Policies designed to restore inner
cities have to take metropolitan impact into account and have
to engage relevant suburban interests. This is particularly the
case with respect to any hope of moving toward integrated
residential development. A corollary here is that segregation
has become the hinge on which urban revival turns. As long
as housing values and neighborhood desirability are influenced by color and, conversely, as long as specified neighborhoods or entire cities must bear the concentrated burden of
dependent and pauperized populations, improvement in
housing—not to mention public services, school systems, and
employment opportunities—will be very nearly impossible.
The past thirty years have taught that lesson, if no other.

Policies that are attentive to these lessons tend to fall into
three overlapping categories: (1) policies and practices that
permit and, more than that, offer incentives for residential
dispersion; (2) the provision of resources and incentives for
the maintenance, rehabilitation, and construction of housing
of appropriate standard and price; and (3) so-called empow-
erment mechanisms.

Residential Dispersion

The converse of the earlier observation that residential
separation is defended in depth is that a policy of dispersion
cannot be pursued successfully with a single strategy or by the
use of powerful, distant authority alone. One key to strategy is
an *inclusionary* policy—defined as including "the development
of low- and moderate-income housing among many and often
conflicting values to be served by local government."[85] Part of
the pressure toward such a policy should emerge from the
federal government, in firm and continuous enforcement of
anti-discrimination statutes. National administrations have
executed a steady retreat from such enforcement[86] since Secretary Romney suffered his humiliation, but in a new welfare
state the position of the national government would not be in
doubt.

At the same time, it would be important to engage state
and local interests in seeking the kinds of changes that are

desirable—planful provision for multifamily development, zoning that encourages inexpensive development, and so forth. Federal benefits for low-income development may be allocated in part to suburban areas that would use them; grant-in-aid funds for housing, economic development, and public services may be made contingent on planning for low-income development.[87] Financial incentives for construction and rehabilitation that are developed with priority for dispersed housing can prove attractive to real estate interests. Many such ideas have been developed and described with care.[88] Suburban areas are facing unplanned and uncontrollable development and fiscal difficulties that were once confined to center cities. They may now have a different incentive for participating in such programs.

At the same time, "political considerations . . . dictate that suburbs be offered some protection against concentrations of subsidized housing, apartments, and mobile homes."[89] This is partly a matter of accepting, not to say encouraging, comparatively small and scattered development. Integration will, in any case, not be served by recreating ghettos in the suburbs. It is also partly a matter of scale, for the pressure of minority and low-income populations on small numbers of dwellings may be virtually irresistible. Housing that is made more widely available frees particular communities of the sense that they are being singled out and will be taken over. With developments of relatively large scale, the issue of "benign quotas" is likely to arise— that is, whether it is acceptable to limit the proportion of minority, welfare-dependent, or single-parent families in order to preserve integration and economic viability. This is a sophisticated and, for some, exquisitely difficult civil rights issue. Yet it is difficult to see how, in a transition period at any rate, integration may be achieved without resort to such devices.[90]

Downtown, inside the cities, comparable measures are required. Such practices as "block-busting" by real-estate interests and redlining (that is, defining areas of the city as high-risk in terms of mortgages) by thrift institutions have to be confronted. Answering to political pressures as well as to apparent convenience and economy, local housing authorities have tended to reinforce segregation in their placement of new housing. This is contrary to law and would need to be discouraged and, if necessary, penalized. City subsidies and other preferences have to be used in a more businesslike fashion to achieve municipal objectives. Norman Krumholz puts the matter as follows: "Cities must learn to be less profligate in giving away the local tax base through tax abatements and exemptions designed to attract businesses. There is no evidence that the $1 billion given away annually by states and cities to lure businesses has any real effect."[91] Krumholz recommends hard bargaining in exchange for such subsidies: employment of low-income workers (with performance guarantees), investment in low-income housing, and so forth. Integration in inner cities will not be achieved by adding only low-income housing, of course. A portion of the preferences or incentives that are made available for middle-income housing (tax preferences for housing rehabilitation, for example) should be available only if used in center-city locations.

Listing such mechanisms may be wearying to a reader; humanity suggests a small digression. In a public meeting not long after the Supreme Court's decision on school desegregation in 1954, Margaret Mead considered whether the change would be too abrupt for the American people. It was an argument widely heard at the time that public education was necessary first—Americans were not ready. "Nonsense," she said; "in our attitudes we are the most volatile people in the world. Yesterday we were practically at war with the Soviets; later we were bosom friends; now we are on the road back to enmity. Yesterday the roles of mothers and fathers were sharply defined; today *Life Magazine* carries a cover photo of Elizabeth Taylor, Eddie Fisher, and their new baby, in which it is hard to tell from their expressions which is mother and which father."[92] The ensuing years have provided other examples of overnight shifts in attitude. Many who have reviewed the civil rights record since 1954, in housing particularly, have concluded that segregation is deep-seated in the American ethos and not likely to be changed. It is well to remember that residential segregation was itself a radical change. We are changeable; change is our way of life. In any event, the alternative to seeking such change systematically is to embrace an impossibility—social progress in the face of continuing segregation.

Means and Ways

A number of the proposals that have been made here would operate to enlarge the housing supply inside the cities and for low-income families elsewhere. The fundamental need is to improve their relative income; we have dealt with this in other chapters. In the section on investment, changes in the income tax deduction for mortgage interest and real estate taxes and in provisions governing IRAs were discussed. These would chiefly affect the capacity of moderate- and middle-income people to purchase housing and might redirect some to rental housing. More careful use of tax-exempt revenue bonds for housing and below-market interest rate financing would have more consequence for low-income families. Federal, state, and local subsidies for rehabilitation and construction would be effective, provided that they are carefully designed and are allocated to neighborhoods and populations that require preference. (For example, one effect of replacing categorical subsidy programs with Community Development Block Grants was "to shift spending priorities out of low-income census tracts and into middle- and upper-income census tracts.")[93] It is the assumption here that the revisions in income tax deductions suggested earlier would (modestly estimated) recapture $15 billion in revenue annually and would pay for expanded subsidies.

A wide variety of methods that have not been mentioned are also available. The experience of past subsidy programs (nos. 221–d–3 and 236, for example) has not wholly been disheartening;[94] a scrupulous reading of experience will show how they might be revised and used to good advantage. Also promising would be an adaptation to housing of the so-called Urban Development Action Grants, that is, substantial one-time grants for low-income housing paid out at the initiation of a project and awarded competitively. Anthony Downs has proposed the development of a roster of high-deterioration zones of cities; all business deductions for rental housing in such zones would be disallowed unless accompanied by local certificates of code compliance.[95] The National Commission on Neighborhoods devoted eight pages simply to listing recommendations that would facilitate reinvestment in urban neighborhoods by banks and private businesses.[96] A recent book discusses the hundreds of thousands of homes and apartments that are owned and controlled by the federal Department of Housing and Urban Development and how they might be managed more productively. Many of them are underused, and not a few are vacant and deteriorating.[97] These experiences and proposals are not endorsed here in detail nor, indeed, necessarily put forward by their authors for blanket endorsement. They are a repertoire through which an administration should sift to develop a vigorous program.

Two sets of ideas require the most urgent consideration. One concerns public housing, the other housing decline and abandonment.

Public housing. Well over three million people live in 1.2 million public housing units, almost a third in large cities and the remainder in smaller cities and towns. Public housing is not a single program, historically; it is a single vessel into which diverse wines have been poured. In the 1930s, public housing was intended for families who voluntarily sought to improve their housing but could not afford private rentals. They were not regarded as dependent. In the 1940s, the program was redirected to provide housing for war workers. Following the Housing Act of 1949, it was oriented to those having the most urgent housing need, many of whom turned out to be depressed, untutored, and dependent. From the 1960s on, little public housing was constructed, and that devoted mostly to the least offensive among the poor—old people. Existing public housing grew older, requiring more extensive maintenance, but federal subsidies for the now unpopular program did not keep pace. Part of the funds needed was provided by raising the rent requirement in 1984 from 25 to 30 percent of the tenant's income.

Not all policy change was at the direction of Congress. To the extent that public housing found its sites chiefly in land cleared for urban renewal, large areas were devoted exclusively to public housing. The growing suburbs successfully confined public housing to the city core. After 1954, segregation became a more open insult. The steady passage of years produced a greater proportion of Americans who had never experienced poverty or were trying to put it out of mind. They contributed to a more critical, if not pious, view of public housing. Those who were inside suffered daily evidence of failure in the conditions and people that surrounded them and, in some places, turned on one another.[98]

In the course of these developments, public housing has extensively been mystified—stereotyped, made into a legend, and freighted with homilies (about the perversity of the poor or the inevitable failure of public policy, as one prefers). Pruitt-Igoe in St. Louis, the prize-winning high-rise project that turned out so badly that the government leveled it, imprinted an indelible image of squalor and failure on the public mind. Yet only 10 percent of all units are in large, high-rise projects. Extensive waiting lists testify that poor people regard public housing as superior to anything otherwise available to them. The variety of social and economic conditions to be found in public housing was described by the President's Commission on Housing as follows: "The social and physical problems among public housing projects vary considerably. Some projects are in good condition with few or no significant problems; others must be considered troubled because of their general condition and/or management problems. . . . A 1979 HUD study found that 67 percent of all public housing projects were untroubled, with another 26 percent relatively untroubled."[99] The average cost of the projects, the Commission observed, "is not out of line with private rental housing. Some projects provide housing for low-income tenants at less cost than private market housing and represent efficient use of federal resources." Other projects have much higher federal costs.[100]

There is no reason to permit these 1.2 million units to decline into dilapidation and unusability. Maintaining them and restoring those that require restoration lie well within the capacity of the federal government and the housing authorities that are responsible. The per-unit, per-year subsidy on projects for which capital financing bonds (of forty years) have been paid off is the lowest possible housing subsidy for comparable housing that is available in any manner. Essentials of restoration have been laid out in the findings of an Urban Institute study. They include an improved administrative system, incorporating incentives for good management and, where feasible, encouraging tenant participation in management; replacing the current system of maintenance subsidy with a simplified system based on the number and type of tenants and the local cost of providing services; diversification of tenant populations, accompanied by more thorough screening of tenants and firmer enforcement of occupancy standards; and providing funding for a comprehensive improvement and modernization program.[101] This last would cost about $1.5 billion.[102]

Such a program would do little to dilute the ghettoization of existing public housing. Some part of construction and rehabilitation subsidies should be allocated to expanding the supply of public housing, in particular where new policies make it feasible to disperse these units. One promising source for expansion lies in the development of a program to prevent housing deterioration and abandonment and to make constructive use of units otherwise likely to suffer such a fate.

Decline and abandonment. Housing that has been withdrawn from use and is returned to supply constitutes a large proportion of newly available housing. When new housing completed was at a high level in 1974, 1978, and 1979, returns to supply were almost a quarter of new construction; when, in the intervening years, new housing completed dropped off, returns climbed to 39 percent of new construction.[103] Returned housing includes substandard housing that has been improved, large units converted into smaller ones, and dwellings converted from nonresidential use. The proportions—23 percent or 39 percent of new construction—dramatize the importance of focusing on dwellings that are on their way out of the housing market.

In all, we lose perhaps 240,000 inner-city low-income units each year.[104] Much of this loss is avoidable. In large measure, it represents tax advantages to the landlord for a finite period, with this incentive reinforced by increasingly impoverished tenants and the rent they pay. At some point it is profitable to disinvest and, ultimately, to abandon a no longer salvageable structure. In some measure also, housing loss represents a thinning out of center-city population, so that a higher income market does not claim these units. Why is it profitable to lose one's investment while money is being put into building elsewhere? Because much has already been earned and, presumably, because different entrepreneurs are losing and gaining. Concurrently, neighborhood forces assert themselves. A neglected or abandoned house leads to other abandonments, not to say to arson and vandalism.

It is not necessary to lose all these dwellings, but timing is crucial. It is important to begin reclaiming a building before neglect has proceeded very far; it is vital to address the neighborhood as well when decline is just becoming evident.[105] Desperately pressed by problems of neglect and abandonment, in 1978 New York City took the problem on seriously with a series of measures. Code enforcement was strengthened and procedures for seizing tax-delinquent buildings simplified. A variety of approaches to taking ownership and restoring buildings was developed, including encouragement of tenant ownership and involvement of nonprofit organizations in management.[106] Organizations such as Neighborhood Housing Services and National Neighbors have spread a network around the country of teams of people who have demonstrated facility in bringing together the various elements—government, banking, real estate interests, local organizations—that make such development feasible. Many of the localities mix private funding with CBDG funds or appropriations under new Dodd-Schumer legislation to support such development. Funds now available will need to be enhanced. Devices such as linking business deductions for real estate to code compliance should help.

On the whole, cities have been reluctant to consider property acquired in this way as public housing. They have sought rather to auction it off to private interests, in some cases virtually giving it away, or to turn it over to low-income management. That may be a sound course at times. At other times, depending on the terms of the transfers, such a course can

easily lead to further exploitation, mismanagement, and abandonment. If we are to make progress with this problem, the
bargaining position of the municipality or local housing authority will be strengthened by a willingness to own and manage such properties, when that appears to be sounder business. That may be particularly true of New York City, which,
large though it is, has had a superior record of managing
public housing. At the very least, such a course will provide a
yardstick against which to measure the efficiency of the free
market.

Decentralization and Empowerment

Decisions with regard to housing and neighborhood should,
as much as or more than any other, be sensitive to local decision-making and citizen views. Especially when their interests
are at stake, joining and organizing come readily to middle-
class groups. Not readily nurtured among alienated, poor
people, citizen participation was nevertheless spreading by the
middle-1960s. In large part, this flowed from requirements
written into early legislation for urban renewal, the war against
poverty, and "model cities." Unfortunately, citizen participation was tied programmatically to a direct federal relationship
to cities. For philosophical reasons and because cities tended
more than states to be under Democratic administration, the
Nixon government turned back to conventional federal-state
relationships. For more direct program reasons as well, federal
interests shifted from these programs, and citizen participation
by federal requirement dissipated.

However, more truly spontaneous grassroots organizations
appeared to take its place. Some were carried over from the
civil rights movement; others were stimulated or supported
by private foundations and church groups such as the Campaign for Human Development; many sprang up in response to perceived local threats to the neighborhood. In
their nature, many of these groups are transitory; others
appear to have taken root. There is extensive activity across
the country, though it is difficult to enumerate precisely;
much of it is concerned with neighborhood preservation and
housing restoration.

Neighborhood and broader citizen organizations may or may not have formal (that is, government-recognized or government-accorded) status. They may or may not manage housing, though large-scale housing programs seem to operate on a citywide or metropolitan-wide basis, perhaps for reasons of efficiency. Three levels of activity may be distinguished. First, citizen organizations may function to identify local needs (traffic signals, improved trash collection) and to press for their satisfaction. They may organize block watches, weatherization and paint-up programs, and so forth. Second, citizen organizations may be identified by local authorities and asked for advice with respect to decisions that impinge on the neighborhood or, in a nonurban area, town or county. That is a desirable approach but, absent a requirement by a funding source, not widely practiced. Officials understand that, once solicited, advice may not lightly be disregarded. Moreover, officials unfamiliar with local organizations and their dynamics readily fall into traps—presenting an issue poorly and reaping the consequences, or finding that a citizen group feeds back little but the viewpoint of an articulate individual or small group of people. Perhaps the soundest approach to encouraging citizen exchanges with officials about local needs and priorities is to proliferate the type of self-organized group described above. As they make representations to relevant officials, the officials perforce gain experience in such exchange. The financial costs of stimulating such groups are modest.

A third level of activity takes place with groups formally constituted to deal with planning issues that affect them. The range of their authority varies from an obligatory period for providing advice to the exercise of a veto on certain kinds of decisions—amendments to zoning status, placement of special facilities in their area, and so forth. After all, participation is best exercised when accompanied by power or, conversely, difficult to sustain when frequently if not always frustrated. Yet it is not self-evident that local organization decisions should always govern. For example, such groups have widely opposed the placement in their neighborhoods of facilities for the handicapped and of public housing. Thus, it seems reasonable to limit the power delegated to such organizations by providing that it will not prevail if it is incompatible with law or with overriding municipal, state, or federal objectives. Such a proviso can, of course, be used to nullify the authority delegated; much rests on according basic respect to the purposes of a delegation of authority and not abusing the privilege to override.

The best hope for these organizations lies in their own vigor and determination and in providing such support as is needed from nongovernmental sources. Housing legislation should nevertheless specify circumstances under which advice or approval must be sought from relevant citizen groups.

We have come a long way with respect to housing in the United States, but poor people have at times gained and at times lost ground, especially if one thinks in terms of shares. A net assessment would depend entirely on the points in time selected for comparison. The distributive issue becomes particularly painful for us now because disadvantage is spreading to families once viewed as middle class and because the homes of young people do not match the expectations they have learned from their parents. We face four problems in particular: continuing segregation, substandard and crowded housing among low-income families, a growing problem of affordability, and a severe and increasing shortage of available housing. Yet we have demonstrated a capacity to achieve the goals set forth here: substantial rehabilitation and new construction (with progressively high standards of quality) at the rate of eight to ten dwellings per thousand population annually, and stable investment in residential dwellings of 5 to 6 percent of GNP.

Though it is an important element of the national enterprise, housing is in general produced by small entrepreneurs and purchased or rented by smaller ones—that is, by families and individuals. Planning is complex for another reason too—because grasping the effect of policies on fair shares requires tracing advantage from investment through to the outcome for beneficiary families. For example, carefully designed tax-exempt revenue bonds for housing, while they should increase housing availability for low- and moderate-income families, would provide tax-free income to relatively well-to-do investors, thus tending to skew the income distribution toward the top. Policies that benefit the relatively rich may be socially worthwhile or not depending on whether they produce standard housing for five years or twenty, and depending on who lives in it.

I have tried to be sensitive to such considerations. In addition, recommendations here move toward racial and economic integration (real movement will take some time, to be sure), and choices have been made for mainstream as opposed to income-tested policies. To the extent possible, means-testing has been avoided in recommendations for the provision of basic income. With respect to seeing that a fair share of housing, especially subsidized housing, goes to those with low or moderate incomes, targeting is to be sought by size, price, and location of the dwelling rather than by tests of family income. Still, some programs—public housing, for example—will incorporate income tests. Until considerable progress has been made toward full employment and mainstream income maintenance, more income-tested housing will be necessary than is really desirable. Full employment and selective decentralization of decision-making would also be facilitated by the recommendations offered here.

Notwithstanding the emphasis in these pages on meeting the needs of low-income people, the policies recommended will tend to provide better, more affordable housing for all but the rich. The rich may find, as they sometimes do on visits to Western European countries, that lower levels of social tension benefit them too.

6

The Public's Health

The situation of health policy in the United States is not unlike that of housing policy. A great deal of energy and money has been invested, producing a sometime sense of substantial accomplishment but also a sense of frustration and impotence. We careen from one objective to another, failing with or indeed undermining last year's objective while we struggle with this year's. Neoconservative and radical analyses of health policy converge in the view that only incremental changes are possible, and even these are severely constrained by the interest groups involved—providers, consumers, agencies of government, insurers, and so forth.[1]

Many analysts and advocates now concentrate on desirable technical or incremental improvements in policy, and a small band argues that only with a turning away from capitalism will real improvement be possible.[2] Some put forward incremental proposals while simultaneously expressing deep skepticism that this is the way to go.[3] That the technology of medical care has greatly improved and that Medicare and Medicaid have eased problems of access for poorer people tend to support the position of health policy pragmatists and optimists. However, these gains were made in a period when the nation literally poured money into health service delivery. As funds are limited and even reduced, the gains are perceptibly being lost and meanwhile new problems are created.[4]

In order to peer into the future, it is peculiarly important in this field to have a sense of how much deeper the problem goes than cost and how we got here. I therefore begin with a rapid outline of the development of health service delivery policy (much of this review based on Paul Starr's recent book)[5] and a review of a variety of efforts to move toward the nation's fundamental if fluctuating objectives of quality, reasonable cost, access, and equity. Quality and reasonable cost are more or less self-defining. Access refers to the capacity of people to seek and use services; the stark existence of services at geographic or bureaucratic distance does not satisfy this objective. Equity is related to access. It means that, assuming the supply of medical personnel and hospital beds is always limited, they are used by people of all classes and types (urban, rural, rich, poor, young, old) roughly in accordance with their number and medical need. Obviously, access and equity are a refinement of the objective of fair shares.

Descent (or Ascent) of Health Service Delivery Policy

Between 1920 and 1950, the struggle over a system of health services was waged between two groups. On the one side were reformers interested in the poor, organized labor, and rural populists whose cooperative movement pioneered prepaid comprehensive health care. On the other side were employers, the insurance industry, and organized medicine. The first group sought a national system of health insurance. The latter, respectively, regarded the payments that would have to be made for such a system as in effect wage increases, or they wished the business for themselves, or they feared infringement on the patient's freedom of choice and the physician's professional autonomy. Pressure for some sort of breakthrough was steadily building because of "rising costs of hospital care and the new salience of such costs for middle class families."[6] The issue might have been joined in Franklin D. Roosevelt's administration but, evidently fearing that it would bring down his Social Security program, Roosevelt postponed a confrontation. It appears that he meant eventually to press for health insurance, but he never did, for reasons that included World War II.

Meanwhile, hospitals had encouraged and indeed financed the development of Blue Cross and Blue Shield. Commercial insurance companies, edgy about insuring for health care, took heart from the successes of the Blues. Thus took shape a development that was to satisfy organized medicine, the insurance industry, employers, and those with middle incomes. As Starr puts it, "[i]t was not exactly an open and fair contest; the dominant institutional, professional, and class interests biased the outcome in their own favor."[7] Harry S. Truman proved to be an enthusiastic advocate of national health insurance, but by that time middle-class pressure was somewhat diluted,* and the country had entered a vividly anti-communist period not hospitable to "socialized" medicine.[9] The failure of health insurance in Truman's administration, writes Starr, meant that the medical profession won the argument and "health insurance in America would be predominantly private, but it left open what form a private system would take."[10]

By the early 1950s, the dominance of hospitals and their allied Blues began to be qualified. Unions bargained aggressively for improved health plans. In turn, this led to higher costs that unions had difficulty restraining, and it provided some of the impetus for the subsequent spread of prepaid group practice. The Blues had been paying providers, but commercial insurance companies were willing to pay the patient. The Blues had used a single premium scale for all groups. Commercial insurers offered variable rates adjusted to the risk that particular groups presented, thus picking off the low-risk, low-cost groups. Forced to compete, the Blues "became increasingly incapable of providing protection to high-risk groups like the aged."[11] Because the institutions

*For example, arguing that income tax deductions can serve public purposes, Senator Daniel Patrick Moynihan observed that the exclusion of employer-paid health insurance premiums from taxable income "probably forestalled national health insurance."[8]

that dominated these developments had no special reason for restraint, costs started to move upward; at the same time, major population groups were failing to benefit equitably from the improved capacities of health service providers. The early political and economic successes of organized medicine and its allies were setting the stage for a major intrusion by government into what they regarded as their preserve.

In the wake of World War II, with government revenues readily available and a general determination to deliver on the promise of a better world, the nation embarked on four major health care developments: hospital construction, costing $13 billion in fifteen years; medical research, particularly within teaching hospitals—a preoccupation of medical schools since the Flexner Report of 1910; and expansion of Veterans' Administration and of mental health programs.

Reflection on these developments, taken together, may suggest at least two conclusions. First, largely they served and in any event did not threaten established health service delivery interests. Second, while these developments met readily apparent needs such as hospital obsolescence, shortage of beds, and the care of large numbers of newly returned veterans, taken together their effect on health service delivery as a system was not considered and was mainly accidental. For example, the Hill-Burton Construction Act tended to correct the inequitable distribution of hospitals among states but favored middle-income communities within states. In time, it contributed to the excess of hospital beds within large cities, which in turn contributed to uncontrolled health care costs. And teaching hospitals' devotion to medical research tended to produce a withdrawal from primary community care,[12] an effect not sharply evident until medical schools were subjected to the financial pressures of the 1980s.

Because dominant interests were served and broader national objectives were not considered or, at any rate, not brought into play, by the 1960s there emerged three distinct sectors of medicine: the physician faculty members of prestigious hospitals and schools; the physicians who moved to or opened their practices in suburban areas and did well, generally, but were dependent on their patients; and a relatively small number of the least prestigious practicing in urban ghettos and rural areas. The implications for patient care must be obvious: location and income determined access to and quality of medical care, and the cost of care was most influenced by the sector of medicine that was least interested in controlling it. There was also an implication for the national system or absence of system. Western European countries and Canada, at different points in time and with differing ideological objectives, had used extensive investment in health care to restructure and integrate their systems.[13] In the postwar period, the United States had once again forgone the opportunity to do this. On the contrary, it expanded and strengthened elements of the existing system that would presumably oppose restructuring.

The stage was set for the demands of the 1960s for health care reform and the accommodationist strategy reform would pursue. On the one hand, medical enterprises had been greatly expanded and "demanded to be fed."[14] On the other hand, reform in terms of access and equity—that is, from the point of view of the disadvantaged—had long been delayed, and the Kennedy-Johnson climate was hospitable to reformers. A variety of new initiatives were introduced, ranging from the attempt to renew and encourage family practice as a specialty to the multibillion-dollar Medicare and Medicaid programs. Proof in such matters is always arguable, but there is little doubt that the aged in particular and the poor in general made gains relative to other population groups in the use of medical care. In the same period, indicators for these groups, the infant mortality rate, for example, showed improvement. The major initiatives were developed in a fashion that would accommodate established medical interests.[15]

Medicare appeared to have been won over the strongest opposition of organized medicine, but not without paying a price to that opposition. In the end, "the administration of Medicare was lodged in the private insurance system originally established to suit provider interests. And the federal government surrendered direct control of the program and its costs."[16] As a result, in time cost of care would come to be defined as the overriding health policy issue, many of the access and equity initiatives would be abandoned, and Medicare and Medicaid would be curtailed.

By the mid-1970s private insurance companies, facing employer and consumer pressure, found themselves joining with government to promote increasing regulation by health planning agencies, professional review of medical practices, and so forth. The Nixon administration adopted and promoted a once-liberal idea, Health Maintenance Organizations (HMOs), an attempt to demonstrate a competitive model that would provide superior health care and yet be more efficient. However, regulation and HMOs proved to be dismissable by what had become commanding health industry interests. Moreover, although unremarked for a time, the decade saw the growth of a new "medical-industrial complex": a "network of corporations engaged in the business of supplying health care services to patients for profit—services heretofore provided by nonprofit institutions and general practitioners."[17] In dollar volume these were supplying about a quarter of all personal health care services, and growing rapidly.[18] By 1985, they owned nearly 10 percent of the nation's hospital beds.[19]

Corporate, for-profit medicine was a new wild card in health care[20] but, appearance apart, not entirely new. Notwithstanding all the hotly debated proposals to introduce competition into health care, it should have been plain that competition required no assistance. In effect, the government's policy had always been to allow market forces to shape health care delivery. That the physicians and hospitals had been called independent professionals and nonprofit organizations tended to mask their pursuit of self-defined aims using strategies shaped by purchasers—patients, private insurance payments, and for some time now government payments. Charity patients were accepted as long as their costs could be shifted to the others, and for many years they were.

Still, the spread of corporate medicine led to anxiety about the capacity of employed medical practitioners to distinguish between an institution's and a patient's objectives. Moreover, for-profit institutions would presumably now openly decline to accept patients who could not pay the full cost of care,[21] placing nonprofit and public institutions at a competitive disadvantage. That is, the latter, already in financial difficulty, would be flooded with charity patients. Between 1979 and 1982, 170 public hospitals closed their doors,[22] and in the teaching hospitals that had provided a very large proportion of charity care and were now financially stressed, such care began to be rationed.[23]

It is worth embarking on a new paragraph to observe that professional autonomy, the redoubt from which organized medicine had fought its battles, has been extensively compromised. The justification for professional autonomy offered by Talcott Parsons, long influential among theoreticians, was that the physician is privy to special knowledge about the patient and therefore cannot be expected to brook interference.[24] As Pamela Doty observes, "[h]owever, this view has increasingly been challenged both in theory . . . and practice."[25] The physician may know more about how to treat a particular patient (although even that argument has been undermined by consumer education and peer review), but he or she stands on no special eminence with respect to health policy—whether $2 billion a year should be spent on kidney dialysis and transplants, for example, or on prenatal care for poor women. As for practice, physicians and hospitals have come to be extensively constrained by government regulation and the impact of competitive forces. The medical profession is well prepared by tradition to resist government regulation, for all the good that has done, but is ideologically ill prepared to resist corporate pressures. Patients' freedom of choice, too, faces erosion as a result of the pressures that have developed. Never quite assured under Medicaid as a practical matter, freedom of choice was abandoned in principle in 1981 federal budget legislation.[26]

All these developments are merely early signs of the sea that is running. It is not to be supposed that physicians will totally lose control over their practices; nonprofit and corporate hospitals cannot operate without their good will and cooperation. "Nonetheless, compared with individual practice, corporate work will necessarily entail a profound loss of autonomy."[27] The principle of professional autonomy owes much to a folk image of the country doctor, and probably he was not to survive in any case. What must be deeply grasped, however, is that no one—not organized medicine, not providers, not the government, and not consumer groups— sought the system of health care that at any recent stage we have had. It is tempting for Americans to believe that we can fix things with some new incentive or more powerful regulation. If one thinks about the long development of health services, however, it is impossible to avoid the conclusion that the central error was absence of a vision of the whole system and determination to arrive at it. There were slogans, to be sure— competition, access, mainstream, right to health care—but beneath that level of generality no agreed-upon view of what the system ought to look like.

Advances and Increments

Having engaged in a broad historical review, it is useful to consider more particular program tactics that have been applied and their effects. I begin with a few words about the four objectives of a health care system: quality, access, equity, and reasonable cost.

It is conventional wisdom and possibly a fact as well that at its best American medicine is the best in the world. Over the years, a large majority of the population has expressed the view that our system of medical care required "basic" or "fundamental" change. Yet simultaneously a large majority expresses confidence in their personal physicians and medical arrangements.[28] This level of approval is testimony to the quality of medical training, the status and skill of practitioners, a constantly advancing medical pharmacopoeia and technology, and the resources invested in all of these. No part of this encomium goes unqualified. Some schools are better than others. Many physicians lag behind their professional literature and advancing knowledge; not a few suffer addiction and other pathologies without being constrained from practicing.[29] Also, there is evidence that surgery and other specialist services are needlessly performed.[30] These are problems that might be expected to arise; they qualify but do not essentially alter the overall assessment.

A more deep-seated qualification deals with the organization of medical practice. Although overall there is no shortage of physicians, it is increasingly hard to come by "the primary-care practitioners able and willing to care for the broad and ordinary problems of illness in the population, which constitute the major part of the illness burden."[31] This is partly because of a long-term shift of physicians from general to specialty practice, so that there are too many surgeons, for example, though too few family doctors. It is also partly because "health care has been tilting towards hospital-centered management,"[32] which shifts care away from general practitioners and, as already noted, away from the community. Thus, Americans express high levels of confidence in receiving care for acute illness but not for routine needs or chronic illness. In general, patients are treated ad hoc for discrete illness, without adequate management over the course of months or years. In particular, "preventive services are highly fragmented and inadequate."[33] The emphasis of American medicine on cure rather than prevention is a long-standing, deep-seated problem.

Access to medical care is limited by two kinds of factors, financial limitations of the patient and organizational limitations of the system. The number of people financially unable to secure care declined for a number of years, especially after the enactment of Medicare and Medicaid. By 1983, however, the number of people without insurance coverage of any sort had climbed to 35 million—mostly the unemployed but also the self-employed and workers in small, low-wage firms.[34] The increase was partly produced by unemployment (with accompanying loss of coverage) and partly by mounting employer resistance to providing health insurance coverage.[35] One in ten American families spent more than 10 percent of its income on health care. "More than 3 million families, or 7.6 million people, had truly catastrophic out-of-pocket expenses exceeding 20 percent of family income."[36] Obviously, the uninsured and those who spent too much are not the only ones who are deterred from seeking medical care. On their margins are the inadequately insured and those who cannot spare or who feel they cannot spare the 10 or 20 percent.

Moreover, as insurance programs protect themselves by requiring patients to share costs in one way or another, some insured people seek care less often and some not at all[37]—this is the very purpose of cost-sharing.

Organizational limitations have to do with geography and the kind of system in which people seek care. Overall figures on physician oversupply mask their scarcity in rural areas and urban ghettos. For example, the ratio of physicians to population in Manhattan is quite good, 1:164, but in Harlem it is 1:4,500.[38] Those people who seek care in stressed systems such as public clinics and emergency rooms wait longer for an appointment, wait longer in the office when they arrive for an appointment, and are less likely to receive continuous care.[39] In 1982, 10 percent of the population could not name a usual source of health care, and a larger number—twenty-eight million people—had trouble getting health care. In 1983, one out of seven American families believed that they needed care but did not or could not obtain it.[40]

The reasons for lack of access—financial incapacity, lack of insurance coverage, rural or urban ghetto location, and reliance on stressed portions of the delivery system—more or less determine on whom inequity falls hardest. They are "the poor, the aged, the disabled, and racial minorities; their numbers are increasing and their need for health services is high relative to the needs of other populations."[41] Because of the way insurance and government coverage tend to be written, hospital care is more likely to be used equitably by disadvantaged groups; dental care is relatively least used.[42] The disadvantage of low-income and minority children with respect to health services begins before birth and is reflected in health indicators: "The gap between black and white infant mortality rates not only continues but is increasing." "In the past decade the black/white ratio for low birth weight (directly linked to inadequate health care for the mother) has increased from 2.03 to 2.19."[43] In short, classically disadvantaged groups—the poor, the minorities, the uneducated, children, and those who live in areas with poor medical facilities and personnel—do not have equal access to the fine medical care that is available in the United States. In the end, there is striking disparity in their use of care, especially in relation to their demonstrably larger need. "My own view," wrote Victor R. Fuchs, "is that we must quickly come to grips with the tremendous inequality in our nation."[44] That was in 1974.

The final national objective with respect to health care is reasonable cost, and costs have been rising by almost any criterion. Hospital costs went up almost fivefold between 1970 and 1983.[45] The percentage of GNP spent on health care has doubled in the past twenty-five years and gives promise of doubling again by 1990.[46] Without producing higher marks on indicators of overall health, expenditures in the United States now exceed those in countries whose health care systems Americans have tended to deprecate. In 1984, about $1,500 per person was spent for health care in the United States whereas the comparable figure in Japan was $500, in Great Britain $400, in France $800, and in West Germany $900.[47] Cost is a serious problem—in its effect on willingness to deal with other health objectives, if not in itself. However, it will not be ameliorated by going on here with the statistical evidence.

The Last Surge of Reforms

The reformist period of the 1960s was, in the field of health care at any rate, characterized by accommodationist, incrementalist strategies. Those who wished to restructure the system had struggled fruitlessly for thirty years or more. Though some health care radicals continued to press their arguments, particularly around the struggle that ended with enacting Medicare, and although radical arguments could be and sometimes were made for particular strategies, the day and the decade went to the pragmatists. Sufficient time has passed for scholars to attempt judgment on that strategy in relation to the four objectives of health policy. It is instructive to consider their conclusions.

A careful and systematic piece of work by Charles E. Lewis assesses eleven reform efforts initiated during the 1960s.[48] These were efforts to improve primary health care, by increasing the number of providers and altering their geographic distribution and by relieving the financial burden on patients. Some were older efforts that had faded from attention and were renewed in the 1960s. I comment on these briefly, taking advantage as well of other published evaluations.

First in the Lewis listing is loans for medical-school tuition that would be forgiven if, upon graduation, the new doctor established practice in an area of physician shortage. The author sums up his conclusion about impact as follows: "Marginal: Most effective in reinforcing motivations of those with prior decisions to locate in these areas."[49] Factors undermining the program's effectiveness were the option of paying back the subsidy in lieu of meeting the commitment, the government's failure to enforce the commitment provision, and its inability to keep physicians down on the farm after they had seen Paree (medical school). Among other things, Paree represents better learning opportunities and higher salaries—presenting a medical-care work-force problem observable across the world.[50]

Second in Lewis's list is rural preceptorships, exposing students to general medical practice in rural areas. Evaluation of this reform resembles that for loan forgiveness. "Preceptorships, as presently constituted . . . deserve to be available for students with appropriate interests. They should not be expected to alter the effects of a system of education-socialization that emphasized institution-based specialized practice." The impact in this program, too, is assessed as marginal.[51]

A third intervention, family practice, was an attempt to deal with the loop-back relationship of medical education and medical practice. The disappearance of general practitioners having been identified as a problem, earlier efforts to interest medical students in general practice had been undermined by its declining status, the disappearance of role models in medical school, and, inevitably, specialist opposition. Now family practice was to be promoted as itself a specialty, and financial incentives offered to create residencies and special departments in hospitals and medical schools. Fortuitously, just as this intervention was launched, the new Medicare program created a large demand for primary care and so contributed to the possibility of the strategy's success. So, too, did the concurrent inflow of women into medical schools, abetted if not produced by affirmative action programs. Women, proportionately more than men, opted for family practice.

Lewis was hopeful about this effort but thought it too early to make a judgment.[52] In fact, by 1984 family medicine established itself with about 10 percent of all residencies, yielding first and second place only to internal medicine and surgery.[53] Whether, in the face of professional hostilities and other institutional interests, family practitioners were widely practicing the family-oriented, continuous, comprehensive care that was intended has not yet been carefully studied.[54] There is evidence that their practice is more versatile and painstaking than that of older general practitioners who had not had family-practice residencies.[55] In any event, if family practice has carved out a niche for itself, it has not much affected other practitioners or institutions.

Fourth was a series of efforts to increase the number of physicians. Turning from its postwar emphasis (hospital construction, research, and so forth) to problems of medical personnel, the government provided a series of grants that would expand facilities for medical education and subsidize the tuition of medical students. The hope was that increasing the supply of physicians would direct proportionately more into primary care and general practice, into the geographic areas of most severe medical need, and would alter curricula in ways that would orient students to important issues such as preventive and community medicine, geriatrics, and occupational health. More physicians were certainly produced, but none of the other consequences seems to have followed.[56] "There is a little evidence," writes Charles Lewis, "that merely increasing the output of physicians by medical schools, that is, altering the supply, will have the desired effects of redistributing physicians among specialties or geographic areas, or both. The principles of the free-enterprise market do not apply to the working of health services." Effects of the programs were "minimal, if any."[57]

Three other interventions were an attempt to develop new health practitioners, the development of a National Health Services Corps (NHSC), and investment in Children and Youth

(C&Y) projects. In some ways, these are quite different strategies. The first was, or was soon conceived to be, a sophisticated attempt to move medicine in the direction of more holistic practice. Practitioners would be trained and legitimized to undertake activities that do not interest physicians or for which physicians do not have time—for example, health education and counseling. The NHSC and C&Y projects were more straightforward attempts to direct health services, volunteer in one case and paid in the other, to areas with special need. All three interventions suffered similar fates. Generally, they were underfunded—eventually, if not from the beginning. They were undermined by interorganizational opposition and struggles, especially when public interest cooled. As a consequence, they had difficulty in recruiting and retaining the best medical personnel. Fitzhugh Mullan, an advocate for the National Health Service Corps, wrote bluntly that such programs "are ultimately fingers in the dike. The predominant mode of health service delivery in this country remains private practice."[58] To the extent that they were funded and otherwise able, the three interventions served the people they were meant to serve, but it cannot be said that they substantially affected access or equity of health service delivery.[59]

In the minds of the framers of the poverty program's Neighborhood Health Centers, this intervention directly addressed the inadequacies of existing health care and might, by example, reform it.[60] The centers were to be neighborhood-oriented, comprehensive, and would include prevention. Community involvement was to be encouraged. In the outcome, there was great variability in achievement from one center to another; for example, rural centers tended to suffer from isolation from other medical facilities. Lewis sums up: "They achieved considerable impact on access to care for the limited populations they served by dealing with all barriers simultaneously. They also have had an impact on 'The System' that they confronted, and these effects (consumer participation, use of community outreach workers, etc.) are still being felt."[61] That the centers served "limited populations" is a cryptic statement of a large truth: plans had called for one thousand centers serving 25 million people by 1973; instead, forty centers were serving 720,000 people. Paul Starr explains that policy makers chose to push Medicaid over Neighborhood Health Centers. "Medicaid simply had the advantage of institutional compatibility. It covered what would otherwise have been bad debts for hospitals and raised no challenge to private interests in the health sector. Although Neighborhood Health Centers managed to survive (and even grow in the late seventies), they never became more than a marginal alternative."[62] We note in passing that studies appeared to show that the neglected Neighborhood Health Centers were more cost effective than Medicaid.[63]

In contrast with the Neighborhood Health Centers, Medicare was framed as a financing mechanism alone. In final legislative bargaining, indeed, language was included that said that "nothing in this title shall be construed to authorize any federal official or employee to exercise any supervision or control over the practice of medicine" in any way.[64] I have noted that administration was placed in the hands of "fiscal intermediaries," who turned out to represent established provider interests. With Medicare's introduction, however, costs of care rose sharply over prior years and then continued to rise much faster than the Consumer Price Index. By 1970, the "nothing shall be construed" clause notwithstanding, the government began a series of attempts to limit use of the program and its costs—including definition of reasonable charges, performance guidelines, and peer review of medical practice. None of these appeared to have much effect.

The public's attitude was becoming generally anti-regulatory; nevertheless, in 1984 the government turned to a set of regulations that hospitals found radical and upsetting—so-called prospective reimbursement, or DRGs (Diagnostic Related Groups). Patients were to be grouped by diagnosis and hospitals paid a flat amount based on the diagnosis. Presumably, the implicit incentive would be to treat patients as efficiently as possible in order to make a profit or, at any rate, not lose money. Experts promptly predicted that other effects would be to shift hospital costs from Medicare to private insurance, to admit patients who would once have been treated on an outpatient basis, and to find ways not to admit at all patients who appeared to be money-losers.[65] "The net result," writes Mark C. Hornbrook, "is a two-class system of health care in which lower income groups receive less care and have less control."[66] Karen Davis has continued to observe that "one serious mistake of both Medicare and Medicaid was the decision not to initiate reforms of the health care system, to control costs and promote efficiency. Instead, these public programs joined private health insurance in contributing to the spiraling costs of health care."[67]

Cost aside, Medicare chalked up impressive achievements. The percentage of the aged who saw a physician at least once a year climbed from the pre-Medicare rate of 68 percent to 83 percent in 1984. All but 7 percent of the aged claimed a regular source of medical care. The aged were "successfully integrated into mainstream American health care."[68] To be sure, the program benefited the nonpoor aged more than the poor, and program cuts made in the 1980s were clearly going to sharpen the disparity.[69] From its beginnings, Medicare altered medical priorities in other ways that had barely, if at all, been foreseen. It was obvious that the aged would use a larger share of health care. It was not foreseen, however, that 9 percent of Medicare's beneficiaries would account for 70 percent of its services, or that almost a third of its annual expenditures would go for terminal care.[70] This surge of payments into the last months of life accounts in part for recent medical-ethical-legal debates about who controls decisions about heroic measures that prolong life.

One must say in sum that Medicare has achieved impressive results in expanding health care for the aged in general, though in the long run probably not as much for equity among the aged as might have been hoped from such large expenditures. On the other hand, it has been a major factor in increasing the cost of health care. Apart from the problem that this intrinsically represents, it appears to have driven other national objectives in health care out of mind. As always, eventually we shall be forced to consider those objectives again, when they may have become even more difficult to achieve. Meanwhile, Medicare has moved the health care system around in ways not considered at all. For example, the

public has reacted uneasily to arguments that thoughtful decisions must be made about how to ration health care.[71] Yet
Medicare was itself a powerful rationing decision—amplifying
the claim of one group instead of directly restraining the
claims of others—and no one has been uncomfortable on that
particular score. Finally, the autonomy of organized medicine
has been much interfered with, even for practitioners who are
truly resistant to administrative pressures and financial incentives. The dynamics at play in a free enterprise health care
market were far more powerful than promises of free choice
and professional autonomy. Many people received care; that
was good—but the system wound up in a state of crisis.

A companion measure to Medicare, Medicaid was a "legislative sleeper,"[72] adopted by Congress with little debate or
grasp of what it would mean. Administered by states in compliance with federal guidelines, Medicaid was intended to provide comprehensive care for some of the poor and nearly
poor under the age of sixty-five—the so-called medically
needy. Until about 1975, states seemed to be moving toward
this objective, extending coverage further into the medically
needy population and expanding the list of medical services
that would be provided. This trend was reversed in ensuing
years, and by the 1980s states were cutting back severely.[73]
From the time of its adoption, the cost of the program moved
steeply upward—partly of course because Medicaid played its
part in lifting costs generally; partly because Congress (apparently unaware of the consequences) was liberalizing AFDC and
SSI, automatically according Medicaid coverage to new client
groups; and partly because states and providers saw in Medicaid a way to pay for nursing homes for the aged. In 1980,
well over a quarter of program expenditures went for nursing
home care for the aged.[74]

Effects on access and equity bore some resemblance to
those for Medicare. By 1976, poor children averaged 65 percent more physician visits than in 1964, a much faster improvement than for other children.[75] The aged apart, by 1980
Medicaid was paying for most of the health care provided to
nine million poor children, four million of their parents, and
five million disabled people.[76] Nevertheless, 60 percent of the

poor were not reached by Medicaid. Of greatest concern were the uncovered "6 million children and almost one million pregnant women with family incomes below the poverty level."[77] Effects of the program in terms of equity were odd. Because federal law required that welfare recipients be covered, it was the nonwelfare medically needy who failed to get medical care; worse than simply not being helped, they too faced increased costs. Because federal financing was available only if matched by state funds (and despite a preferential matching arrangement for poorer states) there "was a redistribution of medical-assistance income from lower to higher per capita states."[78] Analysts who live with such figures will already have inferred that, as it turned out, whites benefited more than nonwhites.[79]

At the heart of its design, Medicaid was different from Medicare in that it was means-tested. Its consequent vulnerability was signaled by an administration statement as early as 1969 "that the slogan, 'Let's get everybody into the mainstream' should never have been used in connection with Medicaid."[80] In fact, increased costs built up resistance to Medicaid so that, by 1984, twenty-five states were requiring recipients to pay a portion of the cost of eyeglasses, pharmaceuticals, dental care, and so forth. States moved to limit eligibility in a variety of other ways, received federal permission to specify where recipients should go for care, and then cut back on services that would be provided.[81] Restriction of eligibility for AFDC had itself reduced Medicaid enrollment by over a million.[82] Even prior to all this, Charles Lewis wrote in summary: "Although Medicaid provided a somewhat broader medical-assistance program, in terms of coverage and benefits, it has not resulted in a uniform program nor, apparently, in a significant decrease in financial barriers to access to primary care for low income persons."[83]

One unanticipated effect of Medicaid was to divert low-income patients from the private offices of physicians to emergency rooms and public clinics, where cost of care is much higher. Thus, researchers were startled to learn that reducing Medicaid fee scales led to higher costs: disaffected physicians refused Medicaid patients, who sought care in emergency rooms.[84] The uncovered poor perforce turned to hospital-based facilities.[85] The implications of all this for comprehensive care or continuity of care must be obvious, and fragmentation of care was reinforced by restrictions on allowable service. Meanwhile, Medicaid had developed into an indispensable financial support for teaching hospitals, those specializing in children's services in particular, and for nursing homes.[86] Once more, an eminently practical and practically unconsidered increment had created a dynamic that would call for its own reform and simultaneously created a dependence that would impede reform.

Finally (the last strategy in this review), the HMO is characterized by Doty as a "fundamental-rational" strategy—that is, a strategy seeking radical change and based upon relevant knowledge rather than power or consensus.[87] When the Nixon administration decided to promote HMOs as a centerpiece of health policy, it defined them as "organized *systems* of health care, providing comprehensive services for enrolled members, for a fixed prepaid annual fee."[88] Financial incentives in such a system would be to provide preventive, office-based care—representing improvements in access and quality for the patient and less cost overall. As HMOs would spread, many of the health system's failings—fragmentation, overspecialization, excessive reliance on hospitals—would tend to be corrected. Yet HMOs could be promoted under the banner of free enterprise, "creating viable, self-sufficient businesses."[89]

Analysts appear to agree that the very advantages of the strategy—that it would rely on reason rather than political power and that it would displace established interests—contributed to its undoing; moreover, the sponsors were naive about organizational and political power.[90] What some called the "anti-HMO act" that emerged in 1973 incorporated conflicting pressures. For example, HMOs were required to offer a single "community rate" for high- and low-risk people. Yet it was expected that HMOs would compete in premium rates with relatively unconstrained insurance companies. It was not the first example of radical or perfectionist ideas of technicians being adopted and then transformed and domesticated by the political process. A similar theme may be traced in the history of Medicaid.[91] Health Maintenance Organizations languished. Efforts to provide a workable law in succeeding years provided further evidence that the social goals of HMOs were incompatible with their free enterprise framework. In the ten years ending with 1981, enrolled membership had grown from 3.5 to 10.5 million,[92] not impressive in light of the effort and government money that had been invested.

The basic concept of the HMO worked—or could work. A ten-year study by the Rand Corporation showed that health costs for HMO members were 25 percent lower than for others with fee-for-service arrangements, mainly because HMO members used hospitals less.[93] Evaluation seemed to show that HMO enrollees were at least as satisfied and received at least as good care.[94] However, HMOs also faced professional hostilities and were opposing a deep-lying shift to hospital-based medical care. The HMOs that succeeded, Kaiser-Permanente in particular, were organized in a particular way (relying solely on full-time medical staff, for example) and staffed by people with a strong ideological commitment. There was no assurance that others, organized differently and for other motives, could achieve the same results.[95] Indeed, it had been pointed out that the very incentives that should promote preventive, office-based care might in profit-motivated HMOs promote poor care. "From a bookkeeping point of view," said Harry Schwartz, "an HMO has an equally strong interest in having its seriously ill patients die quickly and inexpensively."[96]

With the Reagan administration renewal of a drive for competition in the provision of medical care—now in the context of strong restraints on fee-for-service programs—HMOs experienced a surge of growth. Between 1981 and 1984, almost five million members were added, and it seemed likely that three million more would be added in 1985.[97] In this period, large organizations, profit and not-for-profit, began to dominate the field. States were encouraged to use Medicare and Medicaid funds offered in competitive bidding to private contractors. It was as if nothing was learned, even in the short run. In the early 1970s, for example, the state of California had contracted with fifty-four prepaid health plans for service to about three hundred thousand Medicaid enrollees. Within a couple of years, a committee of the California State Assembly concluded that only a handful of plans "were providing a quality of care commensurate with the tax dollars they were receiving."[98] One bears in mind that such arrangements effectively trap the patient in the HMO.[99] A considerable scandal blew up, involving fiscal irregularities and improper links of nonprofit and profit organizations, leading first to massive attempts at regulation and then to abandonment of the program. Nevertheless, Arizona went the same route, from competitive contracting for group prepayment in 1981 to scandal in 1984.[100] Ohio appeared to be going the same course just one year later.[101]

California turned to a somewhat different system of competitive bidding and limiting patients to so-called preferred provider organizations. Critics observed that "a two-tier level of health care is evolving in California in which the poor get a lower standard of care than the affluent."[102] In Cleveland, nonprofit hospitals, concerned that the spread of HMOs would exacerbate their problem of empty beds, began to consider establishing their own HMO. Paul Starr pointed out that such a development promised to undermine the most economical aspect of successful HMOs, that is, scrupulous restraint about the use of hospitalization.[103]

What seems plain about post-1980 developments is that the HMO, a sound concept on its own terms, was being swept up in heated competition for outpatients and inpatients that would alter its premises and outcomes, though as this is written no one can know how. All the presumed advantages of HMOs were at risk, and they were not changing the overall delivery system but were certainly subject to being changed by it.

Laissez Faire and Overregulation: The American Way?

This decade of incremental strategies in health policy, coolly considered, may be regarded as a set of the most expensive demonstration programs ever conducted in domestic social policy. What might be learned? Charles Lewis wrote that "most of the programs focused on one barrier [to access] have either failed to demonstrate the desired impact or else have created secondary, almost intolerable side effects. The multibarrier approaches have demonstrated impact but have proved politically and economically unfeasible."[104] This is because we have long had a market economy in medical care, in which lately the government has been a powerful player—but only one player. Practitioners, hospitals, insurance companies, the pharmaceutical industry, and corporate medicine (the newest entrant) are other players. The incremental improvements that are launched may be sidelined and allowed to wither away (as the National Health Service Corps and Neighborhood Health Centers are being allowed to do); or they may be allowed to grow slowly but without affecting health service delivery (family medicine, for example); or, especially if really substantial, improvements may be transformed and caught up in market processes (the medical personnel programs, Medicaid, HMOs). The increments that the market uses may become essential to it, so that withdrawing or altering them when their problems are perceived presents political problems equivalent to wiping out sectors of the defense industry.

Those who formulated these incremental reforms were not necessarily oblivious to the risks. Some believed that they could out-think the market—but inevitably they failed. Some argued for carefully formulated, incremental steps that build up to fundamental change. In their view, the failures of the 1960s were failures of poorly conceived incrementalism.[105] Still, it is hard to imagine a time when more creative energy, more resources, and more public good will would go into the creation and support of an incremental strategy; the hope that it can be designed much better may be a special case of expecting to out-think the market. Finally, perhaps it has seemed that incrementalism and pragmatism were the only game in town—and so health planners played it. Lester Thurow summed up the basic problem as follows (possibly sounding harsher in quotation than in context): "In the process of doing what they do, markets . . . create and alter values. In an environment dominated by the market, doctors and hospitals would become income maximizers—nothing more and nothing less."[106]

A second lesson is that the inevitable response of the public and government to failed expectations, particularly if these fail in a manner that is genuinely scandalous, is tougher regulation. That has been the experience with HMOs and Medicaid. But regulation, although it is costly and may interfere with prompt and appropriate health care, also tends to be caught up in market forces—it is allowed to languish (as peer review of hospital practices did) or turned to the advantage of one competitive player or another (as many predicted would be the fate of DRGs). The underlying trend over the past decades to steadily increasing regulation, incorporating financial penalties, seems clear.[107] In the manner of psychiatrists practicing "paradoxical therapy," dissatisfaction with regulation produces a prescription for more regulation, which in turn produces revulsion and a swing to laissez faire; and we embark on a new phase of an old cycle. Surely it should give us pause that, in the words of David Mechanic, "we have developed more regulation and cumbersome bureaucratic procedures than would be necessary for a completely nationalized system. The amount of regulation in comparison with the English National Health Service is staggering, and the typical private doctor in the United States feels the heavy hand of bureaucracy far more than his British counterpart."[108]

A third lesson is that when attention shifts from equity or quality to cost or waste, another virtually automatic reaction (particularly at this distance from the 1930s—see chapter 2) is to move toward or strengthen means-testing. Means-testing in Neighborhood Health Centers was carefully specified in the original legislation; in Medicaid in the early 1980s it was made more rigorous. It was proposed that even Medicare should be means-tested. Although such proposals usually rest on arguments of efficiency and equity,[109] the underlying issue is rationing.

In terms of overall policy, five methods of rationing are available: (1) controlling overall supply by budget allocation combined with planning controls—as in controlling the number of physicians or hospital beds or the availability of special equipment; (2) pricing—allowing services to be bought by those who, in effect, can win a bidding contest; (3) cost-sharing, really a special form of pricing; (4) an assortment of administrative devices that reduce utilization, for example, waiting lists for elective surgery; and (5) means-testing—separate programs or budget allocations for welfare recipients or those regarded as medically needy, while the supply to others is determined by pricing or, at any rate, separately. One may observe that the first method, controlling overall supply, appears to provoke the least sense of injustice and resentment. "As long as the 'rationing' is implicit, it is tolerable."[110] Another way of putting this is that decisions are more easily accepted that appear to be made impersonally, for example, because costly equipment is not available.[111] It is easier for the physician, too, if society rations through policy rather than expecting each doctor to weigh cost-control in the calculus of what treatment to recommend.[112]

Directing ourselves to the initiatives reviewed above, we may observe that gains were made in access and equity because of the very magnitude of the sums that were invested, but in the 1980s even these gains were broadly at risk. Because programs had set out to deal with issues of access and equity incrementally, without focusing on the whole system, costs were distorted. One reaction was to cut back most sharply on programs already means-tested while simultaneously expanding the use of means-testing as a rationing device. That is, more people were asked to qualify in terms of financial need for programs that simultaneously were being reduced. As an incidental but consequential result, some of the institutions that had been built up to serve them closed or passed into management with other objectives.[113] Such moves elicited a broad spectrum of support. For example, in 1982 a distinguished group of private-sector representatives suggested that "Medicaid and Medicare should be reassessed. As a check on demand, consumers should pay more for services, and the United States should explicitly address the prospect of creating a multi-tiered health-care-delivery system that would distinguish between patients who could pay and those who were dependent on public support."[114] This is a chilling statement; perhaps hypocrisy would have been better.

Lesson four is that incremental strategies tend to aim at one or two of the four objectives of national health policy, but the market is most interested in growth and profit (or at least no loss). Thus access, equity, quality, and reasonable cost are lodged in legislative preambles, but in real life the struggle for resources overwhelms them all. That much has been said above. One reason this happens is failure to elevate the technical and organizational views of experts (which often serve at least to initiate proposals) to the level of public discussion, where naturally they would suffer the risk of political repudiation. On the other hand, with political debate conducted in terms of slogans (broadened access, government interference) and institutional interests (the threat to private hospitals, free competition), the public never becomes educated about underlying issues or able to cohere around deep or broad reform. One painstaking analysis of four major health policy initiatives concludes that they have gone aground on either a failure of knowledge or a failure of political power—that is, each of the initiatives studied failed to wed knowledge and power. Moreover, the development of public consensus is itself a determinant of the success of an initiative; that is, consensus helps to disarm subversion.[115] With the calm and felicity of an author putting the last words to a 500-page volume (about HMOs), Lawrence Brown expanded the point thus: "Making policy is inescapably and properly a political project, one undertaken in the unsettling foreknowledge that although there are endless social transitions to be mediated, there are no right answers to discover or learn."[116]

Finally, I note a few of the unintended and largely unforeseen consequences of the objective-by-objective and sector-by-sector policies of the 1960s. There has been a considerable shift of resources and services not only to the aged (which was or should have been foreseen) but into terminal care. Considerable reinforcement was provided for an already evident shift from office-based to more expensive hospital-based care. The cost of all medical care shot up so much more rapidly than the cost of living as to crowd all other considerations from the minds of experts and the public. Public hospitals, teaching hospitals, and Neighborhood

Health Centers became inordinately dependent on Medicaid in particular, a source of support that, in the inevitable reaction, would be cut back severely. The funding mechanisms that had been set in place provided a considerable boost to the expansion of corporate medical care. Last, the professional autonomy of physicians and the patients' freedom of choice suffered substantial erosion.

Is Deep Reform Possible?

I have traversed two lines of thought, one historical and long-range and the other based on the outcomes of the particular health program initiatives of the 1960s. One must conclude that incrementalism and pragmatism (but what is a pragmatism that inevitably fails?) produce a medical care system that is like an idiot savant—brilliant in limited ways (in technology, in the skill of its best practitioners) but unable to control its own direction or to be a responsible servant of general public interest. Unexpected lurches of this system quite often defeat acknowledged objectives of health policy and overall objectives as well, including fair shares, mainstreaming, decentralization, and integration. As to the last two, localities and citizens can hardly feel that they control health care if physicians, health institutions, and legislators themselves feel not in control. And it is well understood that a two-tier or multi-tier system of health care will scatter across the land waiting rooms in which the patients are virtually all black, or all white, or all Hispanic.

At each stage, moreover, resistance to systematic change gets dug in deeper. This is no longer merely because portions of the system become dependent on existing arrangements; whole communities and regions become dependent. Economically depressed Camden, New Jersey, built a hospital primarily, it appeared, for the employment it would provide. A proprietary hospital in Cleveland, the Cleveland Clinic, is the largest private employer in that depressed region. Threats to such hospitals draw resistance from labor, management, and civic officials. Thus, the analogy to the defense industry is by no means overdrawn.

The point about reinforcing impediments to structural re-organization is peculiarly important. In some ways, it should be acknowledged, Europe rates higher marks than the United States in indicators of health or effective health care systems. Yet there is not a "simple correspondence between capitalism and medical care, at least not in organizational and financial structure."[117] That is, the differences between capitalism and socialism do not alone account for variations in health and health care systems. We delude ourselves if we root the nation in an ineffective system, thinking that that is an affirmation of capitalism or free enterprise. Part of the variation has to do with life-style and environment, to be sure.[118] But a significant part of the difference flows from the extent to which each country, using the lever of substantial new investment, early or late, succeeded in reorganizing its institutional structure for health care delivery.

It is the nature of social and policy sciences, dismal sciences all, to suppose that established trends or recognized states of equilibrium may be projected indefinitely into the future. They are decades behind the natural sciences in accepting and undertaking to study uncertainty and random events. Possibly for that reason, gross unlikelihood of deep reform is conventional wisdom.[119] Then why would one think there is a reasonable chance for change? To begin with, because there is a widely shared sense of crisis about health care. For example, Arizona's Director of Health Services staked his hope for an improved system on "the integrity of physicians, as well as fear of malpractice suits" (an interesting coupling), while simultaneously Dr. Clyde W. Kurtz, onetime president of the Arizona Medical Association, observed that "self-policing isn't working."[120] An economist concludes that professional "norms have to be expanded to include cost control. . . . If the medical profession fails to do this, sooner or later the United States will move to a system of third-party controls. Something will have to be done."[121] All those quoted deal with ethics as if they should or could command the heterogenous free market, much as other analysts return again and again to better-designed financial incentives, and still others to demonstrating the merits of prepaid group practice or comprehensive neighborhood delivery. But all have a sense that "something will have to be done."

In all this, the public is hardly monolithic; rather, it is "schizophrenic." While the American public is generally satisfied with its *personal* health care arrangements, almost one quarter say that "our health care system has so much wrong with it today that 'we need to completely rebuild it.' " Three quarters subscribe to an evidently more moderate statement—that the health care system "requires fundamental change."[122] The views of practicing physicians are very influential, perhaps more than the views of any other leadership group—yet they are less and less influential year by year. Two thirds of the public say "they are beginning to lose faith in doctors."[123] That is both an indicator of the sense of crisis and a suggestion that organized medicine's influence on policy development may be declining.

These are attitudes; what are material changes? As patients find that they must change personal arrangements for medical care anyway—because of preferred provider and sole source plans and so forth—satisfaction with personal arrangements will become a less important counterweight to general dissatisfaction with the health care system. The interests of physicians are changing as well. It should not be supposed that physicians are inherently opposed to restructuring. For example, early in the century the American Medical Association and State Medical Societies favored proposals for national health insurance. It was only in time that they were persuaded that such plans were against their interests. In Great Britain, "the strongest advocates of change [that led to the National Health Service] were the voluntary hospitals and the British Medical Association."[124] British medicine was hoping that a reorganized system would provide the resources and opportunity to take advantage of medical frontiers that were, at the close of World War II, just being opened up.

As for contemporary American medicine, it finds increasingly compromised the very principles that it thought existing arrangements would assure—professional autonomy and free client choice. "Ties between doctors and patients are so much weaker" than they were, partly because specialization interrupts continuous relationships and partly because medical corporations and the insurance industry have joined the government in imposing controls.[125] Moreover, the independent, solo practitioner who once characterized American medicine is of declining significance.[126] There were 88,000 physicians in group practice in 1980, but 140,000 only four years later.[127] Of all physicians, 86 percent were in private practice in 1931, 68 percent in 1959, and only 58 percent in 1980.[128] Physicians are increasingly becoming members of bureaucracies anyway, and the reasons that they so long opposed structural reorganization no longer apply, certainly not with the same force.

Further, I have noted that in 1983 one in seven American families said they needed care but could not get it, and a presumably overlapping 10 percent spent more than they could afford for health care. These are in general the poorest Americans, and the poor do not make health policy; yet those who fail to get the care they need now make up, say, 20 percent of the population. Perhaps more important to this argument, circumstances are changing for middle-income Americans, who, we recall, fueled early drives for fundamental reorganization until they found their interests met in other ways. Of the twenty-nine million Americans under sixty-five years of age in 1979 who lacked private health insurance, three fourths were not poor. The next four years added six million people to the pre-retirement, uncovered group, partly because employers had started to restrict health coverage.[129] Medicare and private insurance plans have also undertaken to control costs through cost-sharing, restricting benefits, and other methods of discouraging utilization. All this is to say that the system is unwittingly alienating a significant part of the alliance that has so far prevented institutional restructuring—the alliance that the system once unwittingly put together.

These incremental changes come together now by the kind of chance our accommodationist pattern promotes. Powerful opposition notwithstanding, this coming together may produce an opportunity for deep and constructive change that requires to be nourished. If this is to happen, however, voices must be heard more and more clearly than they so far have been, and alternatives need to be outlined. In the next section, I name two.

Reform How?

If deep or institutional reform shortly becomes feasible, in form it ought to escape the most serious errors of past years. In particular, reform cannot be sought incrementally. The overriding lesson of the review in this chapter is that increments are assimilated or subverted by an overwhelmingly powerful health industry market.

National Health Insurance

Structural reform may be more or less far-reaching; the major alternatives are well understood. At the least, the term implies national insurance—a financing mechanism that covers virtually everyone in the country. It makes feasible a national budget for health care, allocated in the ways that appear important: by region, by type of institution, by specialty or general practice. Planning would be made feasible—it would, indeed, be unavoidable. Public ownership of facilities is not implied in this alternative, nor would physicians in independent practice be required to alter that arrangement.

All primary and specialist care and hospitalization for all residents or citizens would be reimbursed in accordance with established scales, which may, of course, be renegotiated from time to time. Such a system precludes payments supplemented by individuals; in that case, universal payment would become merely the base from which individual fees depart. It does not preclude a certain amount of "opting out," that is, patients who forgo government payment and have their own arrangements with physicians and hospitals. If opting out were to take on large proportions, however, many of the best-known or most skillful practitioners and well-to-do patients would tend to opt out, leaving the impression if not the fact that the universal system is second class.

One set of prescriptions for a program of national health insurance, in this case based on an evaluation of a program of preventive care for poor children, is as follows: (1) Eligibility must be universal—that is, not means-tested or confined to contributors. (2) It must provide comprehensive services, including a range of health-related support services. (3) It must make "maximum use of providers of comprehensive care" and provide incentives for the development of such programs where they do not exist. (4) It should emphasize preventive programs and provide outreach and transportation for health care where those are needed. (5) It must assure quality of care. And (6) it must provide strong federal leadership and authority to build an optimum health care system.[130]

Canada embarked on a national insurance system in the early 1970s, and, despite occasional difficulty, it appears to have achieved widespread acceptance. For one thing, the proportion of GNP Canada was spending on health care (roughly the same 7-plus percent as the United States at that time) virtually stabilized under the plan. Over the same decade in the United States, in contrast, proportionate expenditures on health care continued steadily upward. Paralleling a trend in the United States, in 1984 Canada converted federal financing into block grants to the provinces but nevertheless maintained universal, comprehensive coverage. In the United States, sustained efforts have been made to arrive at a similar system, notably the 1970 Health Security Plan of Senator Edward Kennedy and representative Martha W. Griffiths. The years that followed produced successive compromise proposals that would have undermined universality, accepted substantial cost-sharing, and once again placed fiscal management in the hands of insurance companies. These were offered in order to get a bill enacted, obviously, but would possibly have been fatal to cost control and a firm grip on national planning.

In any event, the opportunities of 1970 have not necessarily survived into the 1980s, and it is important to assess the workability under current conditions of a plan based solely on the financing mechanism. The prospects for planning and equity of a single national financing mechanism for health care seem untarnished—if anything, more lustrous—as we painfully learn the lessons of addressing the failures of the health care system. However, the health industry (despite cutbacks) has now become adjusted to very high costs; and a substantial segment of the public has developed very high expectations and is accustomed to making considerable personal expenditures for medical care. Such people might opt out of a national plan in large numbers, even at high cost. In the train of such a development would come two-tier care, with penurious financing of the lower tier and a variety of other damaging consequences. Moreover, the blossoming of for-profit medicine raises the spectre of a new version of a two-tier system. The for-profit tier would limit itself to a relatively low-risk, low-cost population; the other would struggle, as now, to provide more difficult and more expensive care (and possibly to teach medicine at the same time), but with no greater resources. Yet, national health insurance offers the possibility of an effectively planned system with minimal ideological strain for Americans. It may be that the difficulties can be worked out.

United States National Health Service

More far-reaching would be a United States National Health Service, for which physicians and other health personnel would work and which would assume ownership of health facilities. Obviously, a USNHS means a national budget for health care, systematic allocation, and planning. In Great Britain, which has operated such a system since World War II, the hand of government is not very heavily felt. Patients select a local physician for primary care; they change from one to another if they like. The physician receives an annual payment from the government for each patient, regardless of how much or little care is used (but payments are higher for the aged, for example). The physician recommends specialist attention or hospitalization as indicated; in this too patients are not involved in paying for care. British investment in facilities has been much less than in the United States and so equipment and facilities are less modern. (Cost of care is much lower as a result.) Also, patients may wait weeks or months for elective surgery; this is an indirect rationing mechanism, of course, and a product of planning choices about investment. Nevertheless, the British are widely satisfied with their National Health Service. At the end of 1980, the major private insurance schemes in Britain enrolled about 6 percent of the population,[131] indicating impatience with the NHS among those who could afford impatience, but this hardly constitutes a major threat to the system. Despite severe budget problems, Britain's conservative Thatcher government left the structure and functioning of the Health Service virtually untouched.

A bill to establish a United States National Health Service was introduced years ago by Representative Ron Dellums. It has had respectable (the American Public Health Association, the Gray Panthers) but not widespread support. A Health Service in the United States would operate quite differently from Britain's: it is a different time now in a thousand ways; we are a larger, more diverse country; it would be established for our contemporary reasons, not for theirs in the 1940s. For example, the Dellums bill is heavily oriented to local control, a choice in keeping with our general movement toward decentralization. We would probably develop such a plan with state or even local control, and possibly with quasi-governmental (for example, public authority) ownership and management. Still, state variations in the capacity to set standards and the national trauma about health costs, not to mention other controversies, might lead us to strong federal regulation. "Health care," Jack Meyer observes, "makes price regulators out of everybody, liberals and conservatives alike."[132] "Paradoxically," writes Rosemary Stevens, "we may yet see a health service in this country which is subject to a greater degree of national control than in Britain."[133] In short, a U.S. National Health Service might wind up at once both more local and more federal than Britain's.

Why would people be less likely to opt out of a Health Service than out of a national insurance scheme? A Health Service could so dominate health care—for example, assuming a degree of supervision of urban, teaching hospitals—that it would seem inconvenient and counterproductive to opt for private care, though of course some might do it. A Health Service would have other recourse open to it, such as expecting medical students who had been extensively subsidized to spend some period of time as Health Service staff. Inclination to opt out of a USNHS and out of national insurance as well could also be discouraged by eliminating income-tax deductions for health care for patients and employers.

A program that sounds broadly like a cross between national health insurance and a United States National Health Service has been proposed by the National Association for Public Health Policy.

> The federal financing program should cover the entire population; provide all needed services, including dental, mental, and long-term care; emphasize prevention, home care, and rehabilitation; and fund all services without deductibles. . . .
>
> The program should be financed by progressive taxes [and] payments to practitioners should be made only through community health centers, group practice prepayment plans, and individual practice association plans.

The association further stipulates that prevention is important and planning should be organized on a regional basis. "The medical care program should be democratically administered by federal, state, and local health departments."[134]

It may be obvious that, apart from trying to merge the two sets of ideas, extensive variation of either basic type of national plan is possible. In the end, selection of a basic plan does not by any means settle issues of quality, access, equity, or reasonable cost. Questions of access and equity are still being fought out in the British plan.[135] Whether hospitals would become more community-centered again, whether care would tend to move out of hospitals and back into offices, whether more resources would be provided in urban ghettos and rural areas would be determined by planning decisions year after year. One deep reform or the other simply provides planning control so that all issues can be settled within a single framework, but that capacity to settle them in a single framework is everything. So, at least, the record seems to indicate. Moreover, either system would provide a capacity to ration care by the system's structure and the way it would operate, that is, implicitly—evidently the method that tends least to make people feel that they are deliberately being denied the very stuff of life.

As Lawrence Brown observed, settling on a plan is inescapably and properly a political project. A decent citizenry will address it politically—with the best technical advice, to be sure. Health care has long been highly political, of course, but what has not been political—what has possibly tended to be disguised—is the intention to secure deep change and the reasons for this intention. Thought and study are required to place such plans before the public with sufficient care so they may be understood. How to move with respect to deep reform will not be settled in a year or two. If a current national administration is cool to such ideas and would not undertake such work, it is difficult to imagine a more perfect project for foundations or other voluntary institutions. It will, of course, take an informed public, undoubtedly with a sympathetic administration, to enact such a plan; in the end, only an informed public will sustain reform.

Incremental improvements are not offered here. In the short term, particular ones may be very desirable; in the long term, taken together, they will not deliver on promises that may be made for them and will compound our problem. When we move into deep reform, we shall then have to take pains that its internal design give shape to the several objectives of a new welfare state—fair shares, mainstreaming, and the rest.

7

Education for Community

James P. Comer

The essence of a democratic social system is individual freedom. But individual freedom without concern for the rights and needs of others is antithetical to the maintenance of a democratic society. A deep sense of fellow feeling, common purpose, and mutuality—a sense of community—must be promoted by institutions and their leaders at several levels. The same is true for the individual's acquisition of the capacity and discipline to act according to a sense of community. The family and its social network—parents, religious and social leaders—may be powerful sources of community from birth to maturity.[1] The leaders of the larger society, through their behavior and the policies they establish, help or hinder the efforts of families and these social networks to promote community.[2]

In a literate society based on science and technology, the role of formal education in providing individuals with attitudes, capacity, and discipline for thinking and acting out of a sense of community is second only to that of the family. An educational system, appropriately focused and managed, can counter forces that work against a sense of community in the family and in the larger society.[3] It was this function that

Thomas Jefferson, the most influential advocate of popular (public) education in America, had in mind. Indeed, its capacity to promote community allowed public education to be rationalized under the general welfare clause of the United States Constitution.[4] Jefferson wrote,

> If a nation expects to be ignorant and free, in a state of civilization, it expects what never was and never will be. . . . I look to the diffusion of light and education as the resource most to be relied on for ameliorating the degraded condition, promoting the virtue, and advancing the happiness of man [people]. . . . When I contemplate the immense advances in science and discoveries in the arts which have been made within the period of my life, I look forward with confidence to equal advances by the present generation, and have no doubt they will consequently be as much wiser than we have been, as we than our fathers were, and they than the burners of witches.[5]

Jefferson's interest in education for the enrichment of all and for the promotion of community and the general welfare of the society was never fully accepted by some Americans. To this day an elitist perspective remains strong.[6] In addition, the support of science, technology, and commerce remains the only legitimate goal of education for many. The arts have not been fully appreciated as a form of academic learning and a vehicle for the betterment of humankind.[7] Indeed, many people, including many educators, feel that the improvement of humankind is not a responsibility of public education; this function, they believe, must be carried out in the family and its social networks.[8] Such a perspective ignores the constitutional rationalization for public education. In this scientific and technological age one cannot, without adequate personal development, obtain the level of education necessary to participate in the commerce of the society. Implicit in Jefferson's reasoning is the notion that public education is the instrument of government that helps create and maintain democracy and community.

Much of what is called educational reform today abandons the intent of the early advocates of popular education. It is a violation of the constitutional rationalization for public education; it will not adequately serve the interest of commerce;

and it will not promote a greater sense of community and democracy. I include proposals and policies with the greatest currency such as the exclusive emphasis on academic subject matter or "back to basics," merit pay for teachers, and tuition tax credits or voucher payments for students and their families.[9]

In this discussion I will review some of the major forces working for and against community in American society. I will explore the way these forces have helped create both significant problems and major successes in American education. I will then consider why current proposals and responses in public education fail to address the constitutional mandate for the creation of a national sense of community. Finally, I will outline the basic principles and mechanisms necessary to achieve a national sense of community and to facilitate the principles of American democracy.

Community and Anti-Community Forces

Several anti-community and community forces are cited elsewhere in this book and are central to its thesis. A wide gap in a person's position relative to others and high expectations in the face of limited opportunity work against community, as do private and governmental activities which lead to a sense of chaos. On the other hand, full employment, selective decentralization, and racial integration will help to reestablish community. A review of the interaction of these factors over time will be helpful in considering the way inadequate education maintains anti-community forces.

Employment and income sufficient to provide for basic family needs, and the psychosocial well-being that comes from being able to do so, increases the probability that children will be raised to acquire the attitudes, capacity, and discipline necessary to create a sense of community in their lives.[10] Self-production of essential goods and services or a system of income transfer that does not significantly reduce one's dignity is necessary to achieve the same outcome when work is not possible.

Prior to 1900, employment or self-production of life's essentials—food, clothing, and shelter—was possible for most people without elaborate government or private planning and program development. The latter gradually became necessary between 1900 and 1945, and the need grew rapidly after 1945. Before the twentieth century, the level of scientific and technological development limited communication and travel. Americans lived in small towns and rural areas; even large cities were more like collections of small towns. Work and play were usually local and often based in family or social networks. Leaders or authority figures—parents, employers, ministers and rabbis, teachers—were likely to know each other personally; they more often trusted and respected each other as a result.

These conditions made it possible for these authority figures to establish and maintain local attitudes, values and customs. Rarely were sources of "truth" to be found beyond a local community. Major policy decisions—work, play, the quality and quantity of education and other services—were made locally. These conditions permitted bias and abuse, but they also provided a sense of place, predictable sanctions, clear expectations, and a sense of community—even if one's status and condition in that community were not the most desirable. Under these circumstances the school was a natural part of a community. The hierarchical organization and authoritarian style of leaders in the larger social system, neighborhood, and families also existed in schools.

Throughout the twentieth century, but particularly after World War II, technological and scientific changes began to liberate the individual from local sanctions and controls. Radio and television, greatly increased information sources and their penetration; automobiles, improved roads, and air travel made it possible for people to work and play long distances from home. Locally owned stores and services were gradually replaced by impersonal chains; relatives and friends who had worked in stores for a lifetime were replaced by teenagers working for minimum wage who moved on as soon as they could.

Sources of information literally came from around the world and often competed with local attitudes, values and customs. Decisions and policies affecting local life were more often made by strangers whom one could not trust and respect like local people. As a result of these changed conditions, authority figures, both local and national, lost influence. What was right and wrong, good and bad for the individual, community, and society was more often challenged. Several generations of people who were better educated, in large part because of the public education system, were less accepting of the status quo.

Bias and abuse of particular groups and individuals became less tolerable and more easily exposed and censored under the changed conditions, but expectations became less clear and a sense of place less palpable. National policies and practices in housing, health care, education, and other essential services were not established to promote a deep sense of fellow feeling and common purpose—even though such national standards are more necessary now than in the prewar period when conditions allowed a sense of community to emerge and prevail naturally.[11]

These changes were largely determined by the country's movement from an agricultural society to an industrial, and finally a post-industrial, one. This movement decreased the number of low-education and low-skill jobs that nevertheless paid a living wage.[12] Simultaneously, an international labor pool developed. The increased competition for jobs made education a ticket of living-wage employment even when it was not necessary to do a particular job. These circumstances threatened the well-being of individual and family and worked against a deep sense of fellow feeling and concern about others. These same forces have created significant problems in American education.

Education Problems

Much has been said about "the crisis in education" in America. But the American system of popular or public education has been remarkably successful. Especially before World War II it served science and the arts well and, along with affluence based on industry, it helped to create an intelligent electorate.[13] But when transportation and communication advances after the war reduced the sense of local and national community and the power of authority figures, public schools did not make the necessary adjustment. There were changes in training and certification standards, teaching methods and content. But the school organization remained hierarchical and its management style remained authoritarian. Inadequate attention has been given to relationships and interactions of people in schools. Thus, there was no response to the most significant change in American life—the decreased power of authority figures to influence or control student, staff, and parent behavior.

People born after the war are exposed to more information than their prewar counterparts. They see many different models for behavior. They are more often mobile, moving beyond the scope of influence of parents and emotionally important others. But they are no more mature than young people of the past. Thus, they are in greater need of help and support in managing their emotions and in analyzing, integrating, and acting on the information and stimulation around them. But the changed nature of modern living has reduced the contact between mature and emotionally important adults and young people.

Physical distance and distrust between staff and parents, among staff, and between staff and students is a big part of the problem. The necessity for each group to fight for rights and opportunities they are due by virtue of their citizenship has intensified the problems in the relationships. Wherever there are racial, religious, income, and style differences between the school staff and the community it serves, the potential for conflict is high. This problem has been complicated by the fact that many young people who prior to 1940 would have dropped out of school and taken jobs now stay in school because such jobs are less often available.[14] Style and performance expectations more often differ between such youngsters and school staff.

Schools of education generally do not select teachers for their ability to inspire or motivate students. They do not counsel students to drop out when it is obvious that their ability to relate to others is not adequate. They generally do not teach staff and administrators even elementary child development and psychological concepts and skills, let alone help them learn to apply them in the classroom and school. They generally do not help teachers learn how to work with each other, support staff, and parents. They do not help them learn to create a learning climate or ethos in their buildings.

Most school systems—when not influenced by political, religious, racial, sex, and other such considerations—select teachers on the basis of their academic achievement and their personality. The personality criterion of greatest significance is whether the interviewers find the applicant "likable." The consequence of the education and selection process is that many teachers and schools are not prepared to address the learning needs of the space-age child, family, and community, particularly when the family is under stress of one kind or another and is less able to provide children with school readiness skills.

Learning requires modeling and imitation and is facilitated by positive identification with the teacher.[15] These interactions in place, the teacher is able to promote development along the critical pathways necessary for school success—social, psychological, moral, speech and language, and cognitive-thinking-academic, or school learning. A negative interaction between teacher or school and child often leads to the student's rejection of the academic program of the school. It reinforces undesirable behavior and promotes acting out. Such youngsters, in an effort to meet their own psychosocial needs, seek adequacy in areas other than academic learning.

Teachers and administrators, unprepared except through intuitive understanding and responses, generally respond in culturally sanctioned ways, through punishment, criticism and low expectation. The ensuing struggle further limits the possibility of positive imitation and identification and often leads to a downhill academic and social performance course for the student. It also leads to professional disappointment, disillusionment, burn-out, and lower performance on the part of the staff.

Vandalism, drug abuse, cheating, and many other habits which do not contribute to the betterment of humankind exist in schools—both public and private—serving some of our most affluent and highest-achieving students.[16] But many such youngsters receive a level of intellectual and social skill development at home which allows them to perform well academically in spite of other problems. And most are exposed to a level of opportunity and privilege which, they eventually come to realize, can best be maintained through a reasonably high level of academic performance. This also limits the misbehavior of these young people, both in and out of school. And, obviously, many young people from every socioeconomic level function well.

Children from families in economic distress are often well cared for physically, but their parents may not be able to give them the kind of preschool development that will lead to academic success, even when they aspire to potentially available opportunities. Some such young people are prepared to achieve in school but attend schools in which the staff, other students, or both, make high-level academic learning difficult. Children from the most stressed and troubled families often enter school greatly underdeveloped along the pathways most necessary for academic success.[17]

A disproportionate number of students from the most stressed families are from minority groups which have experienced the greatest amount of cultural trauma—disruption of family and social network organization and exclusion from the policy-making institutions of the larger society. For example, blacks denied political and economic power experienced severe educational deprivation during the period of greatest social and economic mobility in America, up to the 1940s. As late as the 1930s, four to eight times as much money was spent per capita on the education of white children as on the education of blacks. Similar extreme disparities existed in higher education.[18] Thus, in the 1940s when a high level of education and skill was needed to compete successfully in the job market, undereducated blacks were forced to the bottom of the occupational ladder. This, coupled with the aftereffects of slavery, abuse, and racism, made it difficult for many black families to provide their children with the preschool experiences necessary for academic success.

These historical and behavioral problems constitute a much greater crisis in education than sagging SAT scores, lowered standards, the IQ scores of teachers, and other questionable concerns. Who knows what the ideal IQ score of teachers should be once it is above the threshold necessary to master advanced learning? Much more is involved in career and life success than SAT scores, IQ level, and school grades. To over-emphasize and promote such concerns, probably of limited relevance, is misleading, harmful, and unfair. Most important, continued attention to the academic aspect of education alone will not enable us to recreate the sense of community that existed in the past. "Back-to-basics" education will not promote the general welfare and facilitate our democratic social system as public education was intended to do.

Current Reforms

Current advocates of educational reform, seizing the moment of national concern and confusion, are alarmed about the wrong failures. For example, the generally useful but unbalanced report of the National Commission on Excellence in Education argues that academic achievement by American students is putting us at a competitive disadvantage economically.[19] But a well-researched report by the Educational Visions Team of the New World Foundation shows that there is no crisis in academic achievement among American students relative to their counterparts in Japan and Western Europe.[20] The top 9 percent of American students who typically hold high-skill professional, technical, and managerial positions achieved as well as the foreign students. The report also found that "there are no critical skill shortages looming in the professions which will dislocate economic development."[21] Ironically, the only profession in which a shortage is looming is in teaching.[22] And this, in significant part, is due to the inaccurate findings about and unjust attacks on the profession.

The New World Foundation report states, "the crisis is in our failure to provide even minimum levels of quality to the school population which is working class and poor."[23] It reports 50–80 percent dropout rates in the inner city, and one million teenagers who can't read above the third grade level. It finds that 13 percent of all seventeen-year-olds and one third of all adults are functionally illiterate, that 28 percent of all students do not get their high school diplomas, and that 50 percent of all college entrants drop out in their first year. A disproportionate number of these underachieving young people come from working-class, poor, and minority families.

The continued underachievement of schools serving low-income and minority youngsters reinforces the sense of an irreducible gap in socioeconomic position and further limits the opportunity to develop a truly integrated society. Attention to the achievement of low-income and minority students has been marginal. Indeed, both groups have been largely ignored or written off. Almost none of the "reforms" being proposed and implemented will address the needs of low-income and minority students.

Abandonment of these students will destroy efforts to establish a national sense of community and democracy for all. It would be a costly step backwards. The only way a democracy can be maintained is to promote, sustain, and preserve hope and opportunity for all. The growing crime, violence, dependency, alienation, and anger in our society have resulted from permitting hope to die in too many.

A major shortcoming in the thinking of conservative educators and advocates of reform is the tendency to ignore the critical relationship between the social climate and the ethos of a community and its schools and the preparation and readiness of children to learn.[24] Learning is thought of as a mechanical process that can be turned on and off by the student at will, as if he or she were a computer. This leads to inattention to the context of education—interactions among the people in a school building—and excessive attention to the content of education. Thus current proposals for reform related almost exclusively to curriculum, content and achievement standards, teaching methods and credentials, and the like.[25] The conservative approach to socially based problems is to isolate and punish the "bad eggs" and, as it relates to teachers, provide financial rewards to the "good eggs."[26]

Let us examine the major proposals more closely, beginning

with the back-to-basics movement. Even during the height of social change in the 1960s and 1970s, almost no school stopped teaching basic academic skills. Schools changed the curriculum, attempted to involve young people in decision-making, experimented with new classroom designs, and made a number of other changes in an effort to motivate students who were not greatly involved in the academic program of the school, to the point of not attending and dropping out when possible. Mistakes were made, but it would be a bigger mistake to toss the baby out with the bath water.

One charge of conservative reformists is that too many nonacademic subjects have been introduced into school programs, the arts and athletics being their favorite targets. But rarely do the arts and athletics—frills in the minds of some educators—detract from the educational mission. When properly integrated and carried out, they are intrinsically educational. They motivate young people for academic learning and can help create a sense of community.[27] Moreover, there is growing evidence that overemphasis on basic skills does not promote the kind of higher-order thinking needed by effective professional, technical, managerial, and even general workers.[28] Indeed, if education does not provide high-level thinking skills—how to observe, analyze, and evaluate—the public will not be able to select candidates, programs, and policies to promote community and democracy. Too many people identify with and support powerful authority figures in a manner appropriate only for young children because they do not have higher-order thinking skills. Such people are easily manipulated.

A second currently popular reform is to increase the time per day and per year that children must attend school. In the name of raising standards, children are also often required to take more academic subjects. These changes could be worthwhile, but often they are not, because the underlying problem is not being addressed. Many students are not enthusiastic about academic learning. Requiring them to take more academic courses or to spend more time in school will not make them more enthusiastic about learning. In many situations, there is inadequate time for academic tasks, not because these subjects are not taught, but often because of behavioral and motivational problems. Most often, inadequate management has failed to allow the staff to tailor the academic program to the needs of the students. Research on effective teaching suggests that such tailoring increases student interest, improves learning, and decreases behavior problems.[29]

A third reform gaining currency is merit pay for teachers.[30] It is argued that merit pay will motivate teachers and improve accountability. This is an attractive free market concept but has limited effectiveness even in the marketplace. In schools and other public service institutions it can be directly anti-community in effect and may do little or nothing to improve teaching and learning. While all teachers want and deserve a living wage, most are not motivated primarily by money or they would have chosen another profession. Most are motivated by the opportunity to use their skills effectively, to aid the academic and social development of young people, and to make a constructive contribution to society and be appreciated for it. Teachers' performance declines when these ends are frustrated.[31]

Merit pay, then, does not address the underlying problem and, indeed, may contribute to it. Cooperative staff planning, mutual respect among staff members, and fair play in all aspects of school life are needed to promote effectiveness. A teacher who is excellent one year, because of personal or family problems or other reasons, may not be so the next. He or she may need the support of colleagues to perform adequately during stressful times. But jealousy, animosity, disagreement with the merit pay selection criteria and process, charges of bias, favoritism, and the like can poison the relations among staff, decrease staff satisfaction, or preclude any opportunity to establish a sense of collegiality in a school building. More effective ways of promoting accountability will be discussed below.

The voucher system—a tax-supported payment for attendance at a private school—is another free market approach. This would legitimize and fully institutionalize an already existing two-tier public school system—good public and private schools for the affluent, second-rate ones for the poor—separate and unequal, but this time by class rather than race. Because tuition would not be fully covered and private schools not readily available, or comfortable and cooperative, there would only be a token inclusion of the poor and minorities. Thus the vast majority of capable minority students would be trapped in second-tier schools.

Such an approach would remove the incentive and responsibility to understand and address the growth and development needs of students and, in turn, improve second-tier schools. Indeed, a frequent student management mechanism in some private and church schools in localities under social or environmental stress is to threaten to send a youngster back to a troubled public school rather than to respond appropriately to his or her needs. There is no pressure for a voucher system outside large, heavily minority population centers. Parents in such centers who pay taxes for public education and also tuition at private schools, and politicians who are more responsive to this constituency than to the poor, are the major proponents of this approach.

That there is a crisis in education must be nevertheless acknowledged. A number of innovations developed over the past twenty-five years—mental health concepts and support staff, integration, open classrooms, compensatory education, such nontraditional programs as sex education and drug abuse prevention, school breakfast and lunch, various management programs—have been less effective than predicted. Despite these developments, educational problems persist and grow. Thus, it is understandable that some believe a return to the narrow function of the prewar school—academic teaching—will restore order and excellence in education. But the needs that promoted these programs in the first place have not gone away. Let's look more closely at the progressive approaches.

Mental health personnel—social workers, psychologists, counselors, and so on—were introduced to schools largely in response to the kind of problems postwar social change produced. Reflecting their disciplines, they focused on students *after* they performed in an undesirable fashion. Inadequate attention was given to the social system—program organization, management, and personnel—as a cause of performance and behavior problems. For these reasons, and also because their training did not prepare them to apply mental health concepts to the social system, mental health personnel were never fully integrated into most school systems. Recent research suggests that treating schools as social systems and applying mental health concepts to improve the climate and ethos is a more efficient and effective way to prevent performance and behavior problems than working with students after such problems are manifest.[32]

School integration was a necessary and major educational change. Segregated schools symbolized separate purpose, suggested inferior worth and ability of blacks, promoted anti-community attitudes and practices, and engendered intergroup conflict. Once local control of attitudes, values, and customs was lessened by scientific and technological changes and black discontent could not be contained, school segregation had to be eliminated or we would have experienced severe societal conflict.

On the other hand, school integration will not be successful without significant political and economic integration, which is necessary to allow black families to create an atmosphere of motivation and skill acquisition conducive to academic success for their children. Political and economic integration is needed to overcome resistance and racism in personnel, parents, and students. Without it, school integration often leads to separate and unequal educational experiences within physically integrated schools. It may precipitate antagonistic racial interactions and promote white flight or sustained and serious conflict.[33]

In the meantime, research shows that school programs can be developed which greatly improve the performance of low-income students.[34] I am not suggesting that school integration is an error. But education which provides the appropriate level of academic skills and prepares students for community and democracy—coupled with political and economic integration efforts—will facilitate future racial integration much more than elaborate efforts to put minority and white children in separate and unequal education programs in the same building.

Open classrooms, time-block scheduling, team teaching and a number of other organizational and teaching changes are being used in an effort to make education less bureaucratic and more responsive to the needs of individual students. They are intended to stimulate more diagnostic and creative teaching, to make students more responsible for their own learning, and to promote more higher-order thinking. These approaches work, but they are difficult to maintain in stressful environments. They are often not well integrated into a comprehensive plan and thus do not produce the "bang for the buck" they are capable of. They wax and wane in effectiveness with the enthusiasm of the teachers involved.

Compensatory education programs—Head Start, Follow Through, Upward Bound, and others—were developed in the 1960s in response to the black community's push for civil rights and equal opportunity. In the late 1970s such programs came under attack when some research suggested that they were not useful.[35] But now there is clear evidence that they can work.[36] The real problem is that less than 25 percent of eligible students participated.[37]

Even in these programs the emphasis on academic skills is usually not matched by an appropriate emphasis on social skills and personality development, particularly after the preschool years. Yet attention to these areas is often necessary to allow low-income students to achieve academically. Efforts to link middle- and high-school students with the larger social system—an important motivation technique for low-income students—are often not a part of such programs.

A number of programs addressing needs of students at all socioeconomic levels—drug abuse prevention, sex and family life education, school breakfast—have been introduced. But these too often are not carefully integrated into existing school operations and are seen as "add-ons" by an already burdened staff. Understandably many educators feel that they are being asked to do too much. In an effort to control these mushrooming responsibilities, elaborated management programs have been introduced. But because most staff are not prepared to participate in management activities, they often get caught up in paper-and-pencil assessment and the management approach itself is seen as a time-consuming add-on with little benefit. Management programs are also being used to force a kind of accountability and level of skill development which cannot be forced. They must be nurtured and developed in other ways.

While the innovations of the 1960s and '70s have not fully met the needs of modern education, they were more realistic responses to changed societal conditions than current proposals to narrow the educational focus. It is suspicious that such proposals are being pushed at a time when well-documented research shows that education of the poor and minorities can be greatly improved; yet there is almost no discussion of their needs. Furthermore, current proposals do not address the issue of education for community and democracy. Academic excellence without an emphasis on promoting a sense of community at every level of our society will not facilitate American democracy and will not carry out the mission of American education.

I now turn to the kind of education that can help us achieve this mission.

Education for Community and Democracy

To meet our constitutional mandate, education must provide students from every socioeconomic level with the experience and skills necessary to perform well at work and play, as family members and heads of households, and as citizens. Adequate performance in these areas is necessary to maintain a climate of community, to promote the general welfare, and to develop our democratic society. School-based education must reinforce and build on child development begun at home. It must compensate for underdevelopment and provide an alternative to students who have had experiences and hold skills different from those required for academic and life success. In order to do so, the school must provide models for relationships and behavior required for individual achievement and a sense of community and democracy.

A positive climate of interaction among parents, staff, and students permits students to imitate and identify with the adults in the social system and facilitates greater acceptance of its established attitudes, values, and customs, including those surrounding academic learning. More mature staff may serve as models, guides, and moderators. The mature and caring adult-student relationship helps make learning worthwhile even when it is not intrinsically exciting. Parental approval and support of school activities reinforces staff efforts. Concern for the rights and needs of others, or a sense of fellow feeling, common cause, and mutuality can take place. In such a climate or ethos students can grow and develop along the critical pathways necessary for life success.

A staff that understands child development and how to organize and manage their building as a social system is best able to create a climate that facilitates learning among the greatest number of students. Unfortunately, it is precisely in these critical areas—child development and school management—that the instruction of teachers and administrators is most deficient. Thus, many teachers—no matter how intelligent and initially committed—are not prepared to help create the educational context necessary to allow the students to make the most of the academic content.

When bankers lose money, they make an adjustment. When products are defective, manufacturing firms examine both the material and the process. When a patient remains ill or dies the physician or the medical profession searches for new cures. But when students underachieve and act out in response to their frustration—particularly if the student has been designated as less capable or desirable by the society—school staffs often assume that the problem lies in the student or his or her family, income, race, or religion, not in the process of education in the building. Not surprisingly, this is rarely the assumption in public or private schools serving children from middle- and upper-income families. Indeed, the best private schools are organized and managed much like modern businesses, analytical and participatory.

The difference in attitude and approach to different groups is directly related to our cultural commitment to independence, often distorted and carried to extremes and expressed as individualism without common cause and fellow feeling. The abuse of this important and useful American value has led to countless rationalizations for privilege and denial, reflected in commonplace notions like "anybody who works hard enough can make it," "the cream always rises to the top," and so on. In schools the argument often heard is, "anybody who doesn't learn at a high level or behave in an acceptable fashion is either not able or simply not trying— and therefore deserves what he or she gets" . . . or doesn't get. Independence and hard work are important in all social systems. But cooperation and support of child development to the point where independence and hard work is internalized as a value is equally important.

The Yale Child Study Center School Development Team worked with the staff and parents of two elementary schools in New Haven, Connecticut, using the positive approach, attitudes, and beliefs described above. The schools served neighborhoods that were 99 percent black and largely low income. Student achievement moved from the lowest in the city in 1969 to the third and fourth highest level in 1984 without significant change in the neighborhood conditions.[38] The students in the two schools are now twelve and nine months above grade level on standardized achievement tests. Attendance and behavior also dramatically improved. The process is now being used in other New Haven schools and elsewhere in the country. Other innovative programs with both low-income minority and middle-income predominantly white schools have shown that academic achievement and social behavior in public schools can be greatly improved.

The key element of the program is a school-based management team sensitive to child development and relationship issues. Such a team, rather than a singular principal attempting to manage the environment of the school, represents an adjustment to changed societal conditions. It moves the primary responsibility for leadership from the central office throughout the building, involving all mature participants in decision-making, more necessary in our modern complex society which accepts authoritarian direction less than in the past. This permits the traditional management functions—

identification of problems and opportunities, strategic planning and program implementation, evaluation and change—
to take place without disrupting the unique autonomy of the
classroom teacher.

When teachers and parents on the school-based management team are truly representative of their groups, this mechanism recreates the kind of interaction, trust, mutual respect,
and common cause that once existed among authority figures
in and around schools. It permits all involved a sense of
ownership with its accompanying commitment and responsibility for the outcome of school activities. The work of this
team generates and sustains the climate of cooperation, common cause, fair play, and community needed to optimize the
performance of all involved.

This social context promotes accountability in a more palat-
able way than the authoritarian iron hand that is resisted by
many better-educated Americans. The approach has little of
the risk of merit pay. In fact, cooperative goals and program
implementation promote a higher level of performance by all
staff. In my experience this approach has the effect of improving the performance of both the lowest-level achievers
and the higher but still underachieving students. Thus, each
student achieves success at the level at which he or she is
capable.

A school-based management team is in a position to tailor
its program in response to the special needs of its students. In
our New Haven work, during what would have been elective
or free time, we developed a Social Skills Curriculum for Inner City Children in which we integrated the teaching of social skills, arts, and academics into life activity units—politics
and government, business and economics, health and nutrition, spiritual and leisure time. This gave vitality, meaning,
and immediacy to the teaching of traditional academic skills.

The program permitted the staff to assist students directly
in their social, psychological, verbal, cognitive-academic, and
moral development. It provided numerous opportunities to
promote high-level thinking to prepare the students to live in
a democratic community. The same can and should be done
to aid middle- and upper-income students, who are better

prepared for academic challenge but often not able to cope with the social challenges of their complex society.

School-based management also addresses a serious limitation to the utilization of research findings in education. Much that we know about parents, school staffs, and students, teaching and learning, never gets utilized because there is no mechanism for adequate integration of this knowledge into the school program. The same problem exists for support services, both professional (social work, psychology, special education) and operational (aides, custodians, parents). Because of the lack of responsive management, these resources are underutilized and support staff and teachers often feel unwanted, undervalued, and undersupported.

The professional support staff are experts on child development and relationship skills. When they cannot share their knowledge with their teacher colleagues, most of them focus only on students. This is wasteful. Many teachers are not helped to respond to students and parents more effectively. As a result, they are unable to serve as role models and guides for students; some even generate student behavior problems. When this is the case, there can never be enough support staff. It is more productive and less expensive to make provisions for the support staff to help teachers respond effectively and to help them develop a social system sensitive to child development and relationship issues which prevents behavior problems. There would then be fewer students with serious behavior problems, more manageable for the support staff. Teachers could also enjoy greater professional satisfaction.

The school-based management team is not a fad, an all-too-common response to education problems. It is a different way of working, more comprehensive but not unlike the widely hailed "quality circles" and other innovations often used in manufacturing in Japan. The best-managed American businesses have also moved in this direction over the last fifteen years, and many schools have instituted practices borrowed from professional management. But most school staffs are not prepared for involvement in participatory management. This leads to rigid adherence to management rules and techniques and inadequate attention to the unique needs of each child.

A well-functioning school-based management team focuses on child development and learning, utilizing management, child development concepts, and support staff to make this focus possible. The staff can then respond to problems and opportunities on an ongoing basis like the staff of a well-run bank or manufacturing firm. As they develop a climate, academic program, and staff tailored to the needs of the students, the school program gradually improves. It is then possible to take advantage of new findings, to plan ahead, and to be more creative.

Educational Establishment

School staffs must be selected and trained appropriately in order to respond effectively to the needs of their students. Schools of education must provide future teachers with the experiences and skills which will enable them to help students grow along the developmental pathways necessary for them to achieve life success. But not everybody can be a teacher or school administrator. Again, child development theory and research tells us that a large component of learning takes place through imitation and identification with the teacher—particularly in the critical early years, but later on as well. For this reason, some of the brightest and the best, defined by elitist educators and advocates as those with high IQs and grade point averages, should not be teachers or administrators. People who do not like children or who cannot be fair and supportive to students from different backgrounds and with different ability levels should not be in schools. Teachers should be selected for their attitudes and behavior as well as their intelligence and academic achievement.

All would-be teachers should be exposed to a teaching environment early in their educations. Many students of education discover too late that they are not comfortable with children or schools. Their effort to survive as teachers under these circumstances is a source of difficulty for their colleagues, parents, and students. There is a vast difference between the theory of teaching and child development and its application in the classroom. This is one reason why so many young teachers feel that their training did not prepare them to teach. Early exposure to a school environment or at least simulated experiences, could enable the future teacher to learn to apply theory to real-life situations.

Would-be teachers should be encouraged to enter other careers when there is evidence that they are not suited—intellectually or temperamentally—to be a teacher. The intellectual and academic criteria are obvious, the temperamental and attitudinal ones less so. They should be based on the mission and method of the school. All teachers should be able to relate to children and adults involved in their education and to promote a school environment of community and democracy. School boards and responsible management should select and extend tenure on the basis of the above criteria. School administrators should be selected whose performance reflects the best of these criteria—not because they are males, politically well connected, or because they hold a degree in administration.

If teachers, administrators, social workers, psychologists, parents, and other support staff are to work together in management and academic and social planning of schools, their training should either simulate these conditions or provide real opportunities to experience them. Professional support staff should learn how to prevent as well as treat students' behavior problems. The lack of such early training makes it difficult for teachers to utilize existing services fully and for support staff to contribute positively to the social climate of a school.

Society, Local and National

We cannot expect to have a good educational system without adequate financial and social rewards for school people. In a mobile society, it it not rational to allow financial support for education to rest on the resources of local communities alone. Americans educated in the poverty-stricken rural school systems of yesterday now compete for jobs that require high levels of academic and social development. It will take more than money to create a desirable educational system, but a national system of support of education is required to insure the level of quality necessary for social stability now and in the future. Unequal levels of financial support for education across the country are unfair and immoral.

On the other hand, *social* rewards for school staff are probably most effective when they come from the local community rather than the national. In my experience, teachers appear to be most satisfied when the parents of the children they teach— and the students themselves—are appreciative of their efforts. Genuine interest in education on the part of school board members and school managers—more than nuts and bolts administration—is also very important. Recent efforts to make public school education an interest and focus of local business and government is a step in the right direction. But such a relationship must include more than the donation of hardware and other miscellaneous financial support. Responsible local leaders must join educators in thinking through and supporting the academic and social mission of the school.

Extremes of support across the country are also a function of de facto segregation. Integration is required because it fosters community, because students learn from life more than they do from the classroom, and because divisions of power, class, and color interact. In large degree, integration in schools is a function of residential integration (see chapter 5), but there are steps that a decent people can take while that necessary process proceeds. Among them are strict enforcement of federal and state anti-discrimination laws, the use of magnet schools as an incentive to (not as a substitute for) integration, and voluntary assignment of students into and out of the core city.

Popular or public education was created to improve the human condition and/or general welfare and to extend and maintain democracy. To do so, public schools needed a dual but mutually reinforcing focus on the academic development of students and on their general development as human beings.

The nature of neighborhoods during the agricultural and

early and middle industrial periods made this dual focus natural for many schools. Fellow feeling or community could exist even when there was unfairness and abuse of various groups. This permitted an almost exclusive focus on academic development. When neighborhoods changed because of technological advances in transportation, communication, and other areas, schools failed to adjust and, as a result, failed to meet the needs of many students, particularly low-income and minority students.

Innovative school programs—particularly those allowing flexible responses at the school building level—across the country show that it is possible to provide adequate education for students from all socioeconomic levels. But to establish improved schools, changes in organization and management at the local level and improved preparation of staff is necessary. A systematic effort to make schools an important part of the interest and effort of local community leaders is also required, as is adequate and equitable financial support.

8

Policies for
Decent People

The United States is not alone in joining people with diverse national, religious, and ethnic backgrounds and providing them with an overriding sense of nationhood. Even relatively small countries like Switzerland, Great Britain, and Belgium have faced the problems of diversity with more and less success. As in every country, the problem in the United States has special qualities. One is the history of slavery and Civil War that adds passion and complexity to our race relations. Another is the ambiguity of class advantage and disadvantage that plagues some and motivates others even as we deny that we are a class society. Facing such problems, the issue is how to allow all or most citizens to feel a sense of community, that is, of common fate and common prospect.

We have large and growing cleavages of class and background. In 1984, the wealthiest 20 percent of Americans had the largest share of national income (42.9 percent) and the poorest 20 percent the smallest share (4.7 percent) since the Census Bureau started keeping track in 1947.[1] The middle class is losing numbers to the richer and poorer, some children receive a fine education and others grow up illiterate, and young couples face long and painful struggles to find work and housing and get on with their lives. These are not gaps that increased national wealth or income will automatically solve. Our real gross national product has doubled in the past twenty-five years, so that, roughly speaking, the average person now has twice as much in goods and services; yet our sense of community is if anything more fragile.

The solutions offered in preceding chapters rest on identifying principles of our policies that will contribute to community and letting them shape the further developments of policies. These solutions represent an attempt to inform policy with a spirit that is egalitarian even while it is libertarian, that is integrationist even while pluralist, and that resists stigmatizing. Dealt with as abstractions, polemically, these goals can be made to seem impossible to achieve simultaneously. Egalitarianism and libertarianism are in tension, to be sure; every value must be balanced against another. Thus, the policy positions here may be read as an attempt to see whether a more egalitarian or more integrated society would exact a cost in freedom that should not be borne. Little can be found in these proposals or in what we might reasonably assume to be their long-term outcome to support such a view. On the other hand, these chapters take note of the cost to freedom of the extremes of inequality and racial and class separation to which we have come—alienation of citizens from the city and what a real city may offer, deterioration of public education, fear of personal violence and of the black in the night.

Mainstreaming may be simple and even persuasive in concept (chapter 2), but when cutbacks are required or some new money is available it often seems attractive to apply a test of means. One means test is added to another, and very soon our policies are heavily weighted toward means-testing. Against all intuition, scholars have lately concluded that means-tested programs are not cheaper or more efficient for poor people.[2] However, one must range broadly over the policy options and give considerable weight to their long-term development to understand that mainstreaming can be as efficient and effective as means-testing, provided that programs are carefully designed. The mainstream policy positions in prior chapters illustrate that conclusion.

The social objectives pursued here are not new, of course, though they are by no means universally approved. Some are in conflict with others, and all must accommodate themselves to constraints like reasonable cost, effectiveness, and ease of administration. I have tried in this book to arrive at optimum reconciliation of the five objectives—fair shares, mainstreaming, integration, full employment, and selective decentralization—and of the usual constraints on any policy. The reader will judge whether that has been achieved. Our political process openly attempts such reconciliations only episodically, partly because slogans and simplicities lend themselves to interest group activity and perhaps partly out of obtuseness. In F. Scott Fitzgerald's words, "The test of a first-rate intelligence is the ability to hold two opposed ideas in the mind at the same time and still retain the ability to function. One should, for example, be able to see that things are hopeless and yet be determined to make them otherwise." We have come upon times in which decency is not self-effectuating; a broader sense of responsibility, more concentrated application, and first-rate intelligence are all required of us.

It should perhaps be noted that there has been no call for a family policy here—no objective of family stability is added to the other five. This is because such an objective lays a gloss of agreement on a subject about which there is much disagreement. For example, President Carter set out to stage a White House Conference on the Family, renamed it a White House Conference on Families, and in the end split it into three conferences so that citizens might not notice the banalities and shrillness that were engendered. That was a product of conflicting ideologies but also of the limitations of genuine knowledge about the use of policy to influence family relationships. Having himself called for a national family policy in 1965, Senator Daniel Patrick Moynihan said recently, "It is neither possible nor desirable to attempt to construct a family policy on the basis of presumed social science knowledge. Far too little is known or, perhaps, knowable."[3]

Here, I have abstained from speculation about the effects

of welfare on teenage pregnancy, of Social Security on filial relations,[4] or even more fanciful connections between government programming and family life. Still, perhaps it is fair to say that the policies recommended here can only tend to ameliorate family disorder. They would provide margin for social capital (see chapter 4), improve health, education, and housing for those for whom these are most inadequate, and reduce means-testing—which in turn means that fewer people would face lost benefits if they increase their earnings. And the policies recommended here would tend to build community. We do know that a sense of belonging enhances family stability.

Much that has been offered in prior chapters is incremental—that is, it builds on existing institutions and structures. Usually, although not always, increments are easier to bring off. In two chapters a genuine departure is recommended. One is the proposal of a Refundable Tax Credit (chapter 4). This is offered because the situation of many families with children is difficult and that of poor families and single-parent families is desperate. Yet no economic developments are in sight that promise serious improvement for them, and no existing program provides a sound base for assisting them. The other departure is the proposal that politicians and experts explore the merits of national health insurance and a national health service, with a view to moving to one or the other institutional reform in the next several years. This is offered because ample evidence makes clear that each new incremental effort in health care delivery distorts the system in unacceptable ways even as it creates practices and vested interests that make true reform increasingly difficult (chapter 6). For the rest, changes would readily be encompassed within existing programs. That does not necessarily make them easy to achieve. At stake are income shares, which occasion as much struggle between groups as the competition for turf causes between nations.[5] The discussion in this book does not create a distributive issue, of course, but merely reveals it.

In the case of Aid to Families with Dependent Children, policy is not the problem so much as chaotic administration. The problem of administration arises out of destructive treatment of the program (chapter 4) and will not be resolved by reorganization, in-service training, or any other familiar device of consultants. Policy recommendations are offered elsewhere (chapters 3 and 4, in particular) that would relieve pressure on the program, providing space and time for administrative reconstruction, but the administrative task would then have to be undertaken with the utmost seriousness. Thus one sees what may in any case be obvious, that the chapters are interrelated. Apart from supporting one another, they offer alternative solutions. For example, the Refundable Tax Credit would obviate the need for dependency benefits in Unemployment Insurance and for altering the maximum family benefit in Social Security. The RTC is preferable for a variety of reasons that have been indicated; in its absence, one would pursue the narrower solutions. Measures that promote or retard integrated residential patterns simplify or compound the development of integrated schools. Tax policy turns up everywhere, in housing, in Social Security, in health care. It is the government's negative budget, so to speak, and it touches all social programming.

During the 1960s and 1970s, it was popular to seek packaged solutions that would achieve major domestic goals: a negative income tax to replace welfare and wipe out poverty, an employment strategy to interrupt the cycle of poverty, and so forth. An advantage of the approach taken here is that it applies itself to our political system as it actually works, seeking deep reorganization only when the case for it is compelling and permitting progress here while we mark time there, testing an approach in one place before trying it in another. The basic message is not the specific proposals so much as the feasibility of an approach to embodying our principles and search for community in the quotidian tasks of government.

We take note in the chapter on education that public school integration in the absence of economic and other integration is difficult, at best, and may have little real effect. Creating an environment or culture in which a formal change in one institution will be meaningful, that is, will not be undone in a thousand informal ways, is a classic problem of social change.

Yet cultural change is itself made up of a series of institutional changes. One need not precede the other. For example, there was not a true concept of retirement before there was Social Security. It has, indeed, been argued that Social Security *created* the idea of retirement.[6] So too integrated education will contribute to integrated economic and political power which, feeding back, will shape the climate for integrated education. This may be one way to state the argument of this book: if we shape our institutions to reflect a decent society, we are likely in the process to develop the culture of a decent society.

Policies and programs have been worked out as nearly as possible at level cost. The notion that policies that reflect community are costly has been costly in its own way. It is a true irony that we seem to have concluded that generosity is feasible when we are most prosperous and least feasible when need is greatest. Spirit or principles are the heart of our policies, not cost. Obviously, increased resources make the task easier, but they are not essential. To try to make that evident, these chapters have generally accepted no increased cost as a constraint. Nevertheless, the combined effect of the measures considered here would transform living arrangements and heal relationships between groups of people. For example, poverty would be reduced by half or more. That is because the measures here deal with the issue of shares—the unacknowledged core of our definition of poverty (see chapter 2) and an issue generally avoided even during the years of the official war against poverty.

Domestic policy is in disarray. Many people are disadvantaged; yet there is a large degree of pessimism about our capacity to relieve disadvantage and moderate conflict through the deliberate use of policy. There are reasons for pessimism. On the other hand, a broad band of middle-income people were for many years served by national policies in housing and health that are now operating seriously counter to their interests (see chapters 5 and 6). Complexity and ideology will mask this circumstance only so long, and then the middle classes may be expected to react politically. The nation is wealthy, moreover, and in large measure made up of people with a good deal of fellow feeling that may be called forth. If we will express decency through policy as well as in personal relationships, if we will understand that in the modern world one affects us as deeply as the other, and if we will call on the skill and sophistication that are widely available, we may yet build a society that is just and fraternal.

Notes

Chapter 1. Struggle and Transition

1. Commencement Address, Howard University, Washington D.C., June 4, 1965.

2. Joseph A. Pechman, *Who Paid the Taxes, 1966–85*, Washington D.C., Brookings Institution, 1985, p. 10.

3. Fred Hirsch, *Social Limits to Growth*, London, Routledge & Kegan Paul, 1977.

4. Ibid., p. 1.

5. Richard P. Nathan, "The Reagan Presidency in Domestic Affairs," prepared for a conference on "The Reagan Presidency at Mid-Term" at Princeton University, November 19–20, 1982.

6. Terms found in, e.g., Executive Office of the President, Office of Management and Budget, *Major Themes and Additional Budget Details, FY 1983*, Washington, D.C., chap. 3, "Reforming Entitlement Programs."

7. George Gilder, *Wealth and Poverty*, New York, Basic Books, 1981, p. 111.

8. *Major Themes.*

9. Lester M. Salamon and Alan J. Abramson, "The Federal Government and the Nonprofit Sector: Implications of the Reagan Budget Proposals," Washington D.C., Urban Institute, 1981.

10. Tamar Lewin, "Corporate Giving Fails to Offset Cuts by U.S.," *The New York Times*, February 15, 1985; and Lester M. Salamon, "Charities Are Surviving Aid Cuts," Letter to *The New York Times*, October 6, 1984.

11. Kathleen Teltsch, "Nonprofit Groups Facing Big Reductions in Federal Aid, Study Says," *The New York Times*, April 21, 1985.

12. Joel Havemann, "Sharing the Wealth: The Gap between Rich and Poor Grows Wider," *National Journal*, vol. 14, no. 43, October 23, 1982.

13. "Facts and Figures for the President," *The New York Times*, July 31, 1984, editorial page. For census report of shift from 1980 to 1984, see "Children Poor and Getting Poorer," *The New York Times*, September 7, 1985, editorial page.

14. Kevin P. Phillips, "Post-Conservative America," *The New York Review of Books*, May 13, 1982.

15. Kevin P. Phillips, *Staying on Top*, New York, Random House, 1984.

16. Garden City, New York, Doubleday, Doran, 1935.

Chapter 2. Five Principles for Community

1. Norman Mackenzie, ed., *Conviction*, MacGibbon & Kee, London, 1958.

2. W. G. Runciman, *Relative Deprivation and Social Justice*, London, Routledge & Kegan Paul, 1966.

3. National Commission on the Causes and Prevention of Violence, quoted in *The Washington Post*, November 29, 1969, editorial page.

4. Bertrand de Jouvenel, *The Ethics of Redistribution*, Cambridge, Cambridge University Press, 1951; I. McLeod and J. E. Powell, *The Social Services: Needs and Means*, n.p., 1949.

5. Harold L. Wilensky, Introduction to Harold L. Wilensky and Charles N. Lebeaux, *Industrial Society and Social Welfare*, 2d ed., New York, Free Press, 1965.

6. Irving Kristol, "Equity as an Ideal," *International Encyclopedia of the Social Sciences*, New York, Macmillan, 1968, p. 108.

7. John Rawls, *A Theory of Justice*, Cambridge, Harvard University Press, 1971, p. 62.

8. Harold M. Hochman and George E. Peterson, eds., *Redistribution through Public Choice*, New York, Columbia University Press, 1974. See also Walter Korpi, "Economic Growth and the Welfare State: Leaky Bucket or Irrigation System," Paper prepared for the World Congress of Political Science, Paris, July 15–20, 1985. Stockholm University, typescript.

9. S. Anna Kondratas, "What Shall We Do about America's Poor?" *The Washington Post*, February 3, 1985.

10. Victor Fuchs, "Redefining Poverty," *The Public Interest*, no. 8, Summer 1967, p. 89.

11. Robert Hunter, *Poverty*, New York, 1904.

12. Harold W. Watts, "Special Panel Suggests Changes in BLS Family Budget Program," *Monthly Labor Review*, December 1980.

13. Alvin L. Schorr, ed., *Jubilee for Our Times*, New York, Columbia University Press, 1977.

14. Joel Havemann, "Sharing the Wealth: The Gap between Rich and Poor Grows Wider," *National Journal*, vol. 14, no. 43, October 23, 1982.

15. McLeod and Powell, *Social Services*.

16. Wilbur J. Cohen, Michigan News Service, May 12, 1960.

17. For example, Joseph A. Pechman, Henry J. Aaron, and Michael K. Taussig, *Social Security: Perspectives for Reform*, Washington, D.C., Brookings Institution, 1968.

18. Benjamin Bridges, Jr., "Redistributive Effects of Transfer Payments among Age and Economic Status Groups," Washington, D.C., U.S. Department of Health, Education, and Welfare, Social Security Administration, Office of Research and Statistics, staff paper no. 10; and U.S. Congress, Congressional Budget Office, *Poverty Status of Families under Alternative Definitions of Income*, Background Paper no. 17, Rev., Washington, D.C., 1977.

19. U.S. Congress, Joint Economic Committee, Subcommittee on Fiscal Policy, *Handbook of Public Income Transfer Payments, 1975*, Washington, D.C., 1974.

20. President's Commission on Income Maintenance Programs, *Poverty amid Plenty: The American Parodox*, Washington, D.C., Government Printing Office, 1969, table 5–5, p. 62.

21. See David Betson, David Greenberg, and Richard Kasten, "A Simulation Analysis of the Economic Efficiency and Distributional Effects of Alternative Program Structures: The Negative Income Tax versus the Credit Income Tax," in Irwin Garfinkel, ed., *Income-Tested Transfer Programs, The Case For and Against*, New York, Academic Press, 1982.

22. Robert Theobald, *Free Men and Free Markets*, New York, Clarkson, N. Potter, 1963.

23. Sar A. Levitan and William B. Johnston, *Work Is Here to Stay, Alas*, Salt Lake City, Olympus, 1973; and a revision of that book, Sar A. Levitan and Clifford M. Johnson, *Second Thoughts on Work*, Kalamazoo, Mich., W. W. Upjohn Institute, 1982.

24. Robert B. Hill, "The Widening Economic Gap," National Urban League, New York, 1978.

25. Kim B. Clark and Lawrence H. Summers, a Study for the National Bureau of Economic Research, cited in *The New York Times*, November 29, 1978.

26. Marie Jahoda, *Employment and Unemployment*, Cambridge, Cambridge University Press, 1982, p. 39.

27. M. Harvey Brenner, *Estimating the Effects of Economic Change on National Health and Social Well-Being*, a Study for U.S. Congress, Joint Economic Committee, Washington, D.C., Government Printing Office, 1984.

28. Jahoda, *Employment*, p. 27.

29. G. Stokes, "Unemployment Among School-Leavers," University of Birmingham, 1981, mimeographed.

30. "London Melee Not a Race Riot, Study Says," *The New York Times*, November 26, 1981.

31. Association of Community Organizations for Reform Now, Campaign for Human Development, and People United to Serve Humanity, respectively.

32. Peter L. Berger and Richard Neuhaus, *To Empower People: The Role of*

Mediating Structures in Public Policy, American Enterprise Institute for Public Policy Research, Washington, D.C., 1977.

33. Mary Ann Test and Leonard I. Stein, "Community Treatment of the Chronic Patient: Research Overview," *Schizophrenia: A Bulletin,* vol. 4, no. 3, 1978.

34. Committee for Economic Development, *Reshaping Government in Metropolitan Areas,* New York, 1970.

35. Books that have attempted to explore the relationship of citizen action to government policy include Hans B. C. Spiegel, ed., *Citizen Participation in Urban Development,* Washington, D.C., National Education Association, 1968; John B. Turner, ed., *Neighborhood Organization for Community Action,* New York, National Association of Social Workers, 1968; David E. Biegel and Arthur J. Naparstek, eds., *Community Support Systems and Mental Health,* New York, Springer, 1982, esp. the chapter by Naparstek and Biegel; and Diane L. Pancoast, Paul Parker, and Charles Froland, *Rediscovering Self-Help,* Beverly Hills, Sage, 1983, esp. chap. 9, "Voluntary Action in the Welfare State," and succeeding chapters about Great Britain and Quebec.

36. Kenneth B. Clark, "Desegregation: The Role of the Social Sciences," *Teachers College Record,* vol. 62, no. 1, October 1960.

37. Edward A. Suchman, John P. Dean, Robin M. Williams, Jr., with the assistance of Morris Rosenberg, Lois Dean, and Robert Johnson, *Desegregation: Some Propositions and Research Suggestions,* New York, Anti-Defamation League of B'nai B'rith, 1958, p. 15.

38. Griffin v. Prince Edward School Board, 377 U.S. 218, 1964.

39. Albert P. Blaustein and Robert L. Zangrando, eds., *Civil Rights and the American Negro,* New York, Trident Press, 1968.

40. Milton M. Gordon, *Assimilation in American Life,* New York, Oxford University Press, 1964, p. 249.

41. Barry Sussman, "In Attitudes, at Least, White Resistance to Integration Has Eased," *The Washington Post National Weekly Edition,* January 14, 1985, p. 38. The quotation is attributed to Garth Taylor.

42. W. E. B. DuBois, "The Immediate Program of the American Negro," *The Crisis,* vol. 9, April 1915, pp. 310–12.

43. William L. Taylor, "Affirmative Action in the United States," paper prepared for the International Conference on Affirmative Action, Bellagio, Italy, August 16–20, 1982.

44. Report of the U.S. Commission on Civil Rights, Washington, D.C., Government Printing Office, 1961.

45. A survey by *The Dallas Morning News,* February 10–18, 1985, reported in *The New York Times,* February 11, 1985.

46. U.S. Commission on Civil Rights, *Twenty Years after Brown,* Washington, D.C., Government Printing Office, 1974.

47. Richard P. Nathan, *Jobs and Civil Rights,* United States Commission on Civil Rights, Washington, D.C., Government Printing Office, 1969.

48. Gunnar Myrdal with the assistance of Richard Sterner and Arnold Rose, *An American Dilemma,* Harper & Brothers, 1944, pp. 1022–23.

49. Report of the U.S. Commission on Civil Rights, Government Printing Office, 1977.

Chapter 3. Income Security: The Social Insurances

1. The 1979 Advisory Council on Social Security, *Social Security Financing and Benefits*, Washington, D.C., U.S. Department of Health, Education, and Welfare, 1979, p. 22.

2. *Report of the National Commission on Social Security Reform*, Washington, D.C., Government Printing Office, 1983, p. 2–2.

3. Bruno Stein, *Social Security and Pensions in Transition*, New York, Free Press, 1980.

4. Bill Keller, "Another Stab at Pension Reform," *The New York Times*, July 15, 1984.

5. U.S. Congress, Joint Economic Committee, *Social Security and Pension: Programs of Equity and Security*, Washington, D.C., 1980, p. 31. (Emphasis supplied.) See also President's Commission on Pension Policy, *Coming of Age: Toward a National Retirement Policy*, Washington, D.C., 1981. For a complex proposal to make Social Security optional, see Peter J. Ferrara, "Expand IRAs to Social Security," *The Wall Street Journal*, December 7, 1984. Also see Stuart M. Butler, "For Serious Action on Privatization," *Journal of the Institute for Socioeconomic Studies*, vol. 10, no. 2, Summer 1985.

6. Gayle Thompson Rogers, "Vesting of Private Pension Benefits in 1979 and Change from 1972," *Social Security Bulletin*, vol. 44, no. 7, July 1981, table 5.

7. Joint Economic Committee, *Social Security and Pension*.

8. Alicia H. Munnell, *The Economics of Private Pensions*, Washington, D.C., Brookings Institution, 1982, table 3–2. See also the 1983 study of the Employee Benefit Research Institute, reported by Deborah Rankin, "Employee Benefit Plans under Fire," *The New York Times*, December 16, 1984.

9. Melinda Opp, "Relative Importance of Various Income Sources of the Aged, 1980," *Social Security Bulletin*, vol. 46, no. 1, January 1983.

10. Baruch Brody, director of the Center for Ethics, Medicine, and Public Issues, Baylor School of Medicine, Houston, quoted in *The New York Times*, July 7, 1983.

11. Robert M. Ball, *Social Security: Today and Tomorrow*, New York, Columbia University Press, 1978, p. 461.

12. Lea Achdut and Yossi Tamir, "Retirement and Well-Being among the Elderly," Discussion Paper 34 for Luxembourg Income Study, National Insurance Institute, Jerusalem, 1986. Mimeograph.

13. "Social Security: Young vs. Old," *The Socioeconomic Newsletter*, vol. 7, no. 4, June–July 1982; and Martha N. Ozawa, *Social Security: Toward a More Equitable and Rational System*, Center for the Study of American Business, Washington University, St. Louis, October 1982, table 1.

14. Advisory Council, *Social Security Financing and Benefits*.

15. Malcolm H. Morrison, "The Aging of the U.S. Population: Human

Resource Implications," *Monthly Labor Review*, vol. 106, no. 5, May 1983, p. 13.

16. See, for example, Eric R. Kingston, "The Health of Very Early Retirees," and Robert J. Myers, "Why Do People Retire from Work Early?" *Social Security Bulletin*, vol. 45, no. 9, September 1982; and Philip L. Rones, "The Labor Market Problems of Older Workers," *Monthly Labor Review*, vol. 106, no. 5, May 1983.

17. Karen Schwab, "Early Labor Force Withdrawal of Men: Participants and Non-Participants Aged 58–63," in Lola M. Irelan, Dena K. Motley, Karen Schwab, Sally R. Sherman, and Janet Murray, *Almost 65: Baseline Data from the Retirement History Study*, Research Report no. 49, U.S. Social Security Administration, Office of Research and Statistics, Washington, D.C., 1976.

18. For an analysis of the absence of any sizable return to work in years when the exempt amount for purposes of the retirement test moved sharply upward, see Wayne Vroman, "Some Economic Effects of the Social Security Retirement Test," Washington, D.C., The Urban Institute, 1984.

19. For the data and studies on which material in this section is based, see Alvin L. Schorr, "... *Thy Father and Thy Mother* ...": *A Second Look at Filial Responsibility and Family Policy*, U.S. Social Security Administration, Office of Research and Statistics, Washington, D.C., Government Printing Office, 1980.

20. See Ball, *Social Security*. See also Advisory Council, *Social Security Financing and Benefits*, p. 192.

21. Bruce D. Schobel and Steven F. McKay, "Characteristics of Newly Awarded Recipients of the Social Security Regular Minimum Benefit," *Social Security Bulletin*, vol. 45, no. 6, June 1982.

22. Advisory Council, *Social Security Financing and Benefits*, pp. 76–78.

23. Ibid.

24. Deanne Bonner, "Women, Poverty, and Policy: A World Wide Challenge," *Journal of International and Comparative Social Welfare*, vol. 1, no. 2, Spring 1985.

25. National Commission on Unemployment Compensation, *Unemployment Compensation: Final Report*, Washington, D.C., Government Printing Office, 1980.

26. Ibid.

27. Calculation based on table 1 in Wayne Vroman, "Taxing Unemployment Compensation," in Commission on Unemployment, *Unemployment Compensation, Studies and Research*, vol. 1.

28. Commission on Unemployment, *Unemployment Compensation*, p. 38.

29. Walter Corson, et al., *A Study of Federal Supplemental Benefits and Special Unemployment Assistance*, Princeton, Mathematics Policy Research, 1977.

30. Walter Corson and Walter Nicholson, "Extending Benefits During Recessions: Lessons from the FSB Experience," in Commission on Unemployment, *Studies and Research*, vol. 1, tables 6, 8.

31. Apart from Social Security program statistics, see James R. Storey, "Overlap of UI Benefits and Other Income Transfer Payments," and Ida C.

Merriam, "Unemployment Insurance and Other Income Maintenance Benefits," in Commission on Unemployment, *Studies and Research,* vol. 3.

32. Saul J. Blaustein, "Proposal for a New Job Security System with Three Tiers of Unemployment Insurance," Commission on Unemployment, *Studies and Research,* vol. 1. See also Stuart E. Eizenstat and William Spring, "Let's Give the Unemployed New Skills, Not Just Handouts," *The Washington Post National Weekly Edition,* December 3, 1984.

33. Daniel N. Price, "Workers' Compensation Programs in the 1970s," *Social Security Bulletin,* vol. 42, no. 5, May 1979. See also Daniel N. Price, "Workers' Compensation: Coverage, Benefits, and Costs, 1982," *Social Security Bulletin,* vol. 47, no. 12, December 1984.

34. For full development of the issues, see *The Report of the National Commission on State Workmen's Compensation Laws,* Washington, D.C., Government Printing Office, 1972; Edward Berkowitz and Monroe Berkowitz, "The Survival of Workers' Compensation," *Social Service Review,* vol. 58, no. 2, June 1984; and Daniel N. Price, "Workers' Compensation, 1976–80, Benchmark Revisions," *Social Security Bulletin,* vol. 47, no. 7, July 1984.

35. Daniel N. Price, "Workers' Compensation in the '70s."

36. Daniel N. Price, "Cash Benefits for Short-Term Sickness, 1948–1981," *Social Security Bulletin,* vol. 47, no. 8, August 1984.

37. Ibid. See also Daniel N. Price, "Income Protection During Sickness, 1948–78," *Social Security Bulletin,* vol. 44, no. 5, May 1981.

Chapter 4. Women and Children Last

1. Alice M. Rivlin, *The New York Times,* January 29, 1983.

2. For example, Diana Pearce, "The Feminization of Poverty: Women, Work, and Welfare," *Urban and Social Change Review,* February 1978; and National Advisory Council on Economic Opportunity, *The American Promise: Equal Justice and Economic Opportunity,* Final Report, Washington, D.C., Government Printing Office, September 1981, pp. 7 ff.

3. Marilyn E. Manser and Myles Maxell, Jr., *Targeting CETA and Single Headed Families,* Washington, D.C., Mathematica Policy Research, April 30, 1979.

4. Lisa Belkin, "Delivery of Child Support Money Shows Slight National Rise," *The New York Times,* July 12, 1985.

5. Allyson Sherman Grossman, "More Than Half of All Children Have Working Mothers," *Monthly Labor Review,* vol. 105, no. 2, February 1982; U.S. Department of Commerce, Bureau of the Census, *Money Income of Families and Persons in the United States, 1977,* Consumer Reports, ser. P–60, no. 118, Washington, D.C.

6. Paul H. Douglas, *Wages and the Family,* Chicago, University of Chicago Press, 1927.

7. Howard Hayghe, "Husbands and Wives as Earners: An Analysis of Family Data," *Monthly Labor Review,* vol. 104, no. 2, February 1981.

8. National Commission on Unemployment Compensation, *Unemployment*

Compensation: Final Report, Washington, D.C., Government Printing Office, 1980, p. 38.

9. U.S. Department of Commerce, Bureau of the Census, *Characteristics of the Population below the Poverty Level, 1981,* ser. P–60, no. 138, Washington, D.C., March 1983.

10. See, for example, Alvin L. Schorr, *Poor Kids,* New York, Basic Books, 1966; Valerie Kincade Oppenheimer, *Work and Family, A Study in Social Demography,* New York, Academic Press, 1982; and Arthur J. Norton, "Family Life Cycle: 1980," and Sandra L. Hanson, "A Family Life-Cycle Approach to the Socioeconomic Attainment of Working Women," *Journal of Marriage and the Family,* vol. 45, no. 2, May 1983.

11. Harold L. Wilensky's term for the phenomenon was "life cycle squeeze." See "The Moonlighter: A Product of Relative Deprivation," *Industrial Relations,* vol. 3, no. 1, October 1963.

12. W. W. Rostow, *The Stages of Economic Growth,* Cambridge, Cambridge University Press, 1960.

13. Thomas J. Espenshade, Gloria Kamenske, and Boone A. Turchi, "Family Size and Economic Welfare," *Family Planning Perspectives,* vol. 15, no. 6, November–December 1983, p. 290.

14. Stephen J. Rose, "Social Stratification in the United States," Johns Hopkins University, Baltimore, Maryland, 1983; and Michael Harrington, "U.S.'s Next Economic Crisis," *The New York Times,* Op Ed, January 15, 1984. See also Lester C. Thurow, "The Disappearance of the Middle Class," *The New York Times,* February 5, 1984.

15. But now and then, someone suggests that it should. See "Fatherless Child Insurance," in Schorr, *Poor Kids;* "The Idea of Divorce Insurance," *International Herald Tribune,* January 17, 1973; and Letty Cottin Pogrebin, *Family Politics,* New York, McGraw Hill, 1983.

16. Sheila B. Kamerman, "Child Care and Family Benefits: Policies of Six Industrialized Countries," *Monthly Labor Review,* vol. 103, no. 11, November 1980.

17. Sheila B. Kamerman and Alfred J. Kahn, "Income Transfers, Work and the Economic Well-Being of Families with Children: A Comparative Study," *International Social Security Review,* March 1982.

18. *Rapport,* Presente par le Gouvernement au Parlement, en application de l'article 15 de la loi du 12 Juillet 1977, Imprimerie Nationale, Paris; United Kingdom, *Family Expenditure Survey,* Her Majesty's Stationery Office, 1977; U.S. Department of Commerce, Bureau of the Census, *Money Income of Families and Persons in the United States, 1977,* Consumer Reports, ser. P–60, no. 118, Washington, D.C., March 1979. See also Alfred J. Kahn and Sheila B. Kamerman, *Income Transfers for Families with Children,* Philadelphia, Temple University Press, 1983; and "Single Parent Families," Working Party no. 6 on "The Role of Women in the Economy," Organization for Economic Cooperation and Development, Paris, February 27, 1984.

19. For example, see chapter by Martha N. Ozawa in Alvin L. Schorr, ed., *Jubilee for Our Times,* New York, Columbia University Press, 1977.

20. Susan Grad, *Income of the Population 55 and Over, 1980,* U.S. Social Security Administration, Office of Research and Statistics, Washington, D.C., Government Printing Office, January 1983.

21. Women's Research and Education Institute, *Older Women: The Economics of Aging,* Washington, D.C., 1984.

22. Grad, *Income, 55 and Over.*

23. Alvin L. Schorr, ". . . *Thy Father and Thy Mother . . .*": *A Second Look at Filial Responsibility and Family Policy,* U.S. Social Security Administration, Office of Research and Statistics, Washington, D.C., Government Printing Office, 1980, pp. 13–14.

24. Daniel Patrick Moynihan, "Family and Nation," the Godkin Lectures, Harvard University, April 8–9, 1985. Moynihan attributes the calculation to Eugene Steuerle.

25. Derived from Arthur L. Kahn with Theodosia P. Rasberry, *Program and Demographic Characteristics of Supplemental Security Income Beneficiaries,* U.S. Department of Health and Human Services, Social Security Administration, Washington, D.C., December 1980, rev. May 1982. Tables C, D.

26. U.S. Department of Labor, Bureau of Labor Statistics, *Consumer Expenditure Survey: Interview Study, 1972–73,* vol. 1, bulletin 1997, Washington, D.C., 1978, table 5. See also statement of Joseph Scully, hearing before the Select Committee on Children, Youth, and Families, House of Representatives, July 18, 1983. Washington, D.C., Government Printing Office, 1983.

27. Regarding the merits of a tax credit with respect to simplification and equity, see Murray L. Weidenbaum, "Shifting from Income Tax Deductions to Credits," *Taxes,* vol. 51, no. 8, August 1973; Thomas F. Pogue, "Deductions versus Credits: A Comment," *National Tax Journal,* vol. 27, no. 4, December 1974; Peter Gottschalk, "Deductions versus Credits Revised," *National Tax Journal,* vol. 29, no. 2, June 1976; Emil M. Sunley, "The Choice between Deductions and Credits," *National Tax Journal,* vol. 30, no. 3, September 1977. On the other hand, see Gerard M. Brannon and Elliott R. Morse, "The Tax Allowance for Dependents; Deductions versus Credits," *National Tax Journal,* vol. 26, no. 4, December 1973; and Reka Potgeiter Hoff, "An Appropriate Role for Tax Credits in an Income Tax System," *Tax Lawyer,* vol. 35, no. 2, Winter 1982.

28. "The Battle to Solve the Problem of Child Abuse in New York City Goes On," *The New York Times,* May 22, 1984.

29. Marc Bendick, Jr., Abe Levine, and Toby H. Campbell, *Anatomy of AFDC Errors,* Washington, D.C., The Urban Institute, 1978; Community Service Society of New York, *Applying for Public Assistance in New York City: A Study of Families at an Income Maintenance Center,* 1976; E. L. Green, *The Hidden Agenda: Content and Nature of the Income Maintenance (IM) Worker's Job,* Washington, D.C., Social Security Administration, 1980; Joel F. Handler and E. J. Hollingsworth, *The Deserving Poor: A Study of Welfare Administration,* Chicago, Markham, 1971; U.S. Department of Health, Education, and Welfare, Social Security Administration, *Final Report: Improving Interviewing in the AFDC Program,* Washington, D.C., Office of Research and Statistics, 1979; "Denial of

Welfare Payments by New York City Criticized," *The New York Times*, May 18, 1984; and Marie Vesely with Sheila McEntee and Alvin L. Schorr, *Fair Play: A Report of a Study of the Administration of Aid to Families with Dependent Children in Several Midwestern States*, School of Applied Social Sciences, Case Western Reserve University, Cleveland, 1982.

30. Intelligible statistics are not available.

31. National Analysts, *Report of Study for Department of Health, Education, and Welfare*, 4 vols., Philadelphia, 1970.

32. Vesely, *Fair Play;* see also "Denial of Welfare Payments."

33. Bendick, Levine, and Campbell, *Anatomy of AFDC Errors.*

34. Vesely, *Fair Play.*

35. Peter Jordan, with Alan Matthews, Barry Bluestone, Mario Fortuna, and Pam Megna, *Corrective Action and AFDC Dynamics: An Empirical Study in Six Jurisdictions*, Social Welfare Research Institute, Boston College, Boston, 1981.

36. David J. Rothman, *Conscience and Convenience: The Asylum and Its Alternatives in Progressive America*, Boston, Little Brown, 1980.

37. For example, Teknekron Research, *Improved Interviewing in the AFDC Programs*, Berkeley, 1979; and Bendick, Levine, and Campbell, *Anatomy of AFDC Errors.*

38. U.S. House of Representatives, Committee on Ways and Means, Subcommittee on Oversight and on Public Assistance and Unemployment Compensation, *Background Material on Poverty*, Washington, D.C., Government Printing Office, October 17, 1983.

39. Research Triangle Institute, *Final Report: Evaluation of the 1981 AFDC Amendments*, Durham, N.C., 1983.

40. John Trout and David R. Madson, "A 10-Year Review of the Supplemental Security Income Program," *Social Security Bulletin*, vol. 47, no. 1. See also William Farrell, Rene Parent, and Michael Tenney, "Administration and Service Delivery in the SSI Program: The First 10 Years," *Social Security Bulletin*, vol. 47, no. 8, August 1984.

41. Committee on Ways and Means, *Background on Poverty*, sec. 5, table 12.

42. Ibid., table 11.

43. Schorr, *Thy Father and Thy Mother*, pp. 30–32.

44. Ibid., pp. 28–30.

Chapter 5. Where Will Americans Live?

1. John L. Goodman, Jr., and Mary L. Streitwieser, "Explaining Racial Differences: A Study of City-to-Suburb Residential Mobility," *Urban Affairs Quarterly*, vol. 18, no. 3, March 1983, pp. 301–25.

2. In George Sternlieb, et al., *America's Housing: Prospects and Problems*, New Brunswick, Rutgers University Press, 1980, p. 436.

3. Katharine L. Bradbury, Anthony Downs, and Kenneth A. Small, *Urban Decline and the Future of American Cities*, Washington, D.C., Brookings Institution, 1982, p. 12; Paul E. Peterson, ed., *The New Urban Reality*, Washington, D.C., Brookings Institution, 1985; and Sternlieb, et al., *America's Housing.*

4. *Report of the President's Commission on Housing,* Washington, D.C., Government Printing Office, 1982, p. xx.

5. National Commission on Urban Problems, *Building the American City,* New York, Frederick A. Praeger, 1969; and the President's Committee on Urban Housing, *A Decent Home,* Washington, D.C., Government Printing Office, 1969.

6. Morton J. Schussheim, "Housing: An Overview," Statement submitted to the Hearing of the Select Committee on Children, Youth, and Families, House of Representatives, July 18, 1983. Washington, D.C., Government Printing Office.

7. George Sternlieb, Statement submitted to the Hearing of the Select Committee on Children, Youth, and Families, House of Representatives, July 18, 1983, Washington, D.C., Government Printing Office; and *Report of President's Commission on Housing,* p. 65.

8. Michael N. Danielson, *The Politics of Exclusion,* New York, Columbia University Press, 1976.

9. Sam Bass Warner, Jr., *The Private City: Philadelphia in Three Periods of Its Growth,* Philadelphia, University of Pennsylvania Press, 1968, quoted in Danielson, *Politics of Exclusion.* See also Todd Swanstrom, *The Crisis of Growth Politics: Cleveland, Kucinich, and the Challenge of Urban Populism,* Philadelphia, Temple University Press, 1985.

10. National Committee against Discrimination in Housing, *How the Federal Government Builds Ghettoes,* New York, 1967.

11. Quoted in Danielson, *Politics of Exclusion.*

12. National Commission on Neighborhoods, *People, Building Neighborhoods,* Washington, D.C., Government Printing Office, 1979; Henry B. Schechter, "Redlining and Fair Housing," AFL-CIO, Washington, D.C., April 18, 1977.

13. Norman Krumholz, "Recovery of Cities: An Alternate View," in Paul Porter and David Sweet, eds., *The Up-Beat Side of Cities,* New Brunswick, Rutgers University Press, 1984; and Bradbury, Downs, and Small, *Urban Decline.*

14. Henry J. Aaron, "Political Implications: A Progress Report," in Katharine L. Bradbury and Anthony Downs, eds., *Do Housing Allowances Work?,* Washington, D.C., Brookings Institution, 1981, p. 74.

15. Ibid., p. 92.

16. Krumholz, "Recovery of Cities."

17. Karl Taeuber, "Racial Residential Segregation, 1980," in *A Decent Home: A Report on the Continuing Failure of the Federal Government to Provide Equal Housing Opportunity,* New York, Citizens Committee on Civil Rights, 1983. See, however, John D. Kasarda, "Urban Change and Minority Opportunities," in Peterson, ed., *Urban Reality.*

18. Danielson, *Politics of Exclusion;* Sternlieb, et al., *America's Housing;* and Alvin L. Schorr, "The Duplex Society," *The New York Times,* June 4, 1972, Op Ed.

19. Nathaniel S. Keith, *Politics and the Housing Crisis Since 1930,* New York, Universe Books, 1973, p. 14.

20. Joann S. Lublin, "Shrinking Shelter," *The Wall Street Journal*, August 31, 1984.

21. General Accounting Office Report CED–80–59, June 6, 1980, cited in William Grigsby, Morton Baratz, and Duncan Maclennan, *Shelter Subsidies for Low Income Households*, Department of City and Regional Planning, University of Pennsylvania, Philadelphia, July 1983, p. 29.

22. See Tom Joe, Cheryl Rogers, Rick Weissbourd, "The Poor: Profiles of Families in Poverty," Center for the Study of Welfare Policy, University of Chicago, Washington, D.C., March 27, 1981.

23. Raymond J. Struyk, Neil Mayer, and John A. Tuccillo, *Federal Housing Policy at President Reagan's Midterm*, Washington, D.C., Urban Institute Press, 1983.

24. George Sternlieb, Statement, p. 142.

25. Frank Levy and Richard C. Michael, quoted in "Middle Class Shrinking as More Families Sink into Poverty, 2 Studies Find," *The New York Times*, December 12, 1983. See also "Smaller Slices of the Pie: The Growing Economic Vulnerability of Poor and Moderate Income Americans," Center on Budget and Policy Priorities, Washington, D.C., Nov. 1985.

26. U.S. Conference of Mayors, *Housing Needs and Conditions in America's Cities*, Washington, D.C., June 1984, table 5.

27. Alvin L. Schorr, *Slums and Social Security*, Washington, D.C., Government Printing Office, 1961; Jane G. Greene and Glenda P. Blake, *How Restrictive Practices Affect Families with Children*, U.S. Department of Housing and Urban Development, Washington, D.C., Government Printing Office, 1980; Marian Wright Edelman, *The New York Times*, November 24, 1983, Op Ed; and Grigsby, Baratz, and Maclennan, *Shelter Subsidies*.

28. Krumholz, "Recovery of Cities."

29. Schussheim, "Housing."

30. Craig Flournoy and George Rodrigue, "Separate and Unequal," *The Dallas Morning News*, February, 10, 1985.

31. Schussheim, "Housing."

32. Conference of Mayors, *Housing Needs*.

33. Henry, B. Schechter, "Closing the Gap Between Need and Provision," *Society*, vol. 21, March–April 1984.

34. George Sternlieb, Statement, p. 149; Martin Gottlieb, "New York Housing Agency Takes a Bow at 50," *The New York Times*, June 25, 1984; statement by Barry Zigas in John Herbers, "Housing Aid Debate Focuses on Questions of U.S. Duty to Poor," *The New York Times*, May 4, 1985.

35. Georgia L. McMurray, Statement to the House Select Committee on Children, Youth, and Families, House of Representatives, July 25, 1983. Washington, D.C., Government Printing Office.

36. U.S. Conference of Mayors, *Homelessness in America's Cities: Ten Case Studies*, Washington, D.C., June 1984; and Kim Hopper and Jill Hamberg, *The Making of America's Homeless: From Skid Row to New Poor, 1954–1984*, Community Service Society of New York, 1984.

37. Matthew L. Wald, "Owning a Home: A Dream Persists," *The New York Times,* February 28, 1985.

38. Aaron, "Political Implications," p. 71; and Frank Costigan, "Housing Must Be Tax-Subsidized," *The Plain Dealer,* February 20, 1985.

39. Cushing Dolbeare, Statement submitted to the Hearing of the Select Committee on Children, Youth, and Families, House of Representatives, July 18, 1983. Washington, D.C., Government Printing Office.

40. U.S. Bureau of the Census, cited in "Report Says Rents Take Larger Share of Income," *The New York Times,* July 10, 1985.

41. Henry B. Schechter, "Economic Squeeze Pinches the Future of Housing," *Journal of Housing,* vol. 37, no. 4, April 1980; and *Report of President's Commission on Housing.*

42. Dolbeare, Statement, chart D.

43. Thomas Ferguson and Mary G. Pettigrew, "A Study of 718 Slum Families Rehoused for Upwards of Ten Years," *Glasgow Medical Journal,* vol. 35, 1954.

44. See Schorr, *Slums and Social Insecurity.*

45. Schussheim, Statement, p. 188.

46. Michael Evans, "Slippage in Housing Starts?" quoted in *The New York Times,* August 14, 1983; and Leonard Silk, "The Warning from Volker," *The New York Times,* June 15, 1984.

47. Schechter, "Closing the Gap."

48. Schechter, "Economic Squeeze."

49. Joseph Scully, Statement submitted to the Hearing of the Select Committee on Children, Youth, and Families, House of Representatives, July 18, 1983, Washington, D.C., Government Printing Office.

50. *Report of President's Commission on Housing,* figure 5.6.

51. George Sternlieb, Statement, p. 149; and Hopper and Hamberg, *America's Homeless.*

52. Sternlieb, et al., *America's Housing,* p. 551.

53. *Report of President's Commission on Housing,* p. 69.

54. Patrick H. Hendershott and Kevin E. Villani, *Regulation and Reform of the Housing Finance System,* Washington, D.C., American Enterprise Institute for Public Policy Research, 1977, p. 80.

55. *Report of President's Commission on Housing,* p. xxi.

56. Henry B. Schechter, "Economic Squeeze," p. 47.

57. With regard to housing objectives, see United Nations, *World Housing Conditions and Estimated Requirements,* New York, 1965, and *World Housing Survey, 1974,* 1976. With respect to housing produced per thousand population, see United Nations, *Annual Bulletin of Housing and Building Statistics,* various years; *United Nations Statistical Yearbook,* various years, table on "Summary of Housing Conditions"; and *World Housing Survey, 1974,* table 50.

58. George Sternlieb, et al., *America's Housing,* p. 89.

59. See *United Nations Statistical Yearbook,* various years, and *Compendium of Housing Statistics,* 1972–1974, 1976; and Emily Paradise Achtenberg and

Peter Marcuse, "Towards the Decommodification of Housing: A Political Analysis and a Progressive Program," in Chester Hartman, ed., *America's Housing Crisis: What Is to Be Done?* Boston, Routledge & Kegan Paul, 1983. See also Keith, *Politics and the Housing Crisis,* p. 232.

60. Struyk, Mayer, and Tuccillo, *Federal Housing Policy,* table 18.

61. Cushing N. Dolbeare, "The Low Income Housing Crisis," in Hartman, ed., *America's Housing Crisis,* p. 69.

62. Herbers, "Housing Aid Debate," citing the Low Income Housing Information Service.

63. Ibid.; Rolf Goetze, "Federal Tax Expenditures Should Be Restructured to Aid Urban Housing," *Journal of Housing,* vol. 37, no. 90, October 1980. See also Bob Dole, "A Plan for a Tax Credit System," *The New York Times,* November 6, 1983.

64. Anthony Downs, *Rental Housing in the 1980s,* Washington, D.C., Brookings Institution, 1983, p. 11.

65. "Metropolitan Housing and the Income Tax," *The Urban Institute Policy and Research Report,* vol. 9, no. 2, Winter 1979.

66. Congressional Budget Office, *The Tax Treatment of Home Ownership: Issues and Options,* Washington, D.C., Government Printing Office, September 1981.

67. George Sternlieb, Statement, p. 147.

68. General Accounting Office, *The Costs and Benefits of Single Family Mortgage Revenue Bonds: A Preliminary Report,* Washington, D.C., April 18, 1983, p. 3.

69. Dole, "Tax Credit System."

70. Schechter, "Economic Squeeze."

71. Harrison G. Wehner, *Sections 235 and 236: An Economic Evaluation of HUD's Principal Housing Subsidy Programs,* Washington, D.C., American Enterprise Institute for Public Policy Research, 1973, pp. 37–38. See also Leonard F. Heumann, "Housing Needs and Housing Solutions: Changes in Perspectives from 1968 to 1978," in Gary A. Tobin, ed., *The Changing Structure of the City,* Beverly Hills, Sage, 1979, p. 234.

72. Aaron, "Political Implications," p. 90.

73. Wehner, *Sections 235 and 236.*

74. Percy Sutton, quoted in Danielson, *Politics of Exclusion,* p. 333.

75. For example, Hartman, ed., *America's Housing Crisis,* and Downs, *Rental Housing.*

76. Aaron, "Political Implications."

77. Wehner, *Sections 235 and 236;* and Grigsby, Baratz, and Maclennan, *Shelter Subsidies.* The study is General Accounting Office, *Rental Rehabilitation with Limited Federal Involvement: Who Is Doing It? With What Costs? Who Benefits?,* Washington, D.C., July 11, 1983.

78. Wehner, *Section 235 and 236,* p. 39.

79. Downs, *Rental Housing,* p. 10.

80. *Report of President's Commission on Housing;* and Downs, *Rental Housing.*

81. General Accounting Office, *Rental Rehabilitation.*

82. Schechter, "Closing the Gap."

83. Bradbury, Downs, and Small, *Urban Decline*, pp. 12, 17, 193ff. See also Krumholz, "Recovery of Cities"; and the Introduction by Paul E. Peterson in Peterson, ed., *Urban Reality.*

84. Bradbury, Downs, and Small, *Urban Decline*, p. 14; and Krumholz, "Recovery of Cities."

85. Herbert M. Franklin, David Falk, and Arthur J. Levin, *Zoning: A Guide for Policy Makers on Inclusionary Land-Use Programs*, Washington, D.C., Potomac Institute, 1974, quoted in Danielson, *Politics of Exclusion*, p. 334.

86. See the *Dallas Morning News* series on discrimination in federal housing policy, February 10–18, 1985.

87. National Committee against Discrimination in Housing, *Government Builds Ghettoes.*

88. For example, see Danielson, *Politics of Exclusion;* and the National Commission on Urban Problems, *Building the American City;* and Gary Orfield, "Ghettoization and Its Alternatives," in Peterson, ed., *Urban Reality.*

89. Danielson, *Politics of Exclusion*, p. 336.

90. For example, see "Quotas: Kenneth Clark vs. NAACP," *The Public Interest*, no. 75, Spring 1984; Joseph P. Fried, "U.S. Opposes Accord in Bias Suit on Housing Complex in Brooklyn," *The New York Times*, June 29, 1984; and "Integration Efforts Forcing U.S. Ruling on Quotas," *The New York Times*, March 18, 1985.

91. Krumholz, "Recovery of Cities," p. 28. See also Swanstrom, *Crisis of Growth Politics.*

92. Margaret Mead, Speech to the Annual Meeting of Family Service of Northern Virginia, Arlington, Virginia, 1958.

93. Heumann, "Housing Needs," p. 234. See also General Accounting Office, *Rental Rehabilitation.*

94. Patricia Schroeder and George Sternlieb, in Sternlieb, *Statement*, p. 148.

95. Anthony Downs, *Urban Problems and Prospects*, Chicago, Markham, 1970, p. 147

96. National Commission on Neighborhoods, *People, Building Neighborhoods*, pp. 27–35.

97. Florence Wagman Roisman, "Legal Strategies for Protecting Low-Income Housing," in Hartman, ed., *America's Housing Crisis.*

98. Lee Rainwater, *Behind Ghetto Walls: Black Family Life in a Federal Slum*, Chicago, Aldine, 1970.

99. *Report of President's Commission on Housing*, p. 35. See also "Most of Dispersed Housing Projects in 87 Cities Are Said to Be Succeeding," *The New York Times*, September 30, 1984, reporting study by James Hogan.

100. *Report of President's Commission on Housing*, p. 32.

101. Raymond J. Struyk, *A New System for Public Housing*, Washington, D.C., Urban Institute, 1980.

102. Raymond J. Struyk, "Public Housing Modernization Program: An

Analysis of Problems and Prospects," *Journal of Housing,* vol. 37, no. 90, October 1980.

103. Downs, *Rental Housing,* p. 17. The figures cited are based on an article by Duane T. McGough, "Housing Inventory Losses as a Requirement for New Construction," prepared for an Economic Commission for Europe seminar, Washington, D.C., January 1981.

104. George Sternlieb, et al., *America's Housing.*

105. Ibid., chapter by George Sternlieb and James W. Hughes, p. 177.

106. City of New York, *The In Rem Housing Program,* October 1982, 1983; Community Service Society of New York, *Saving Homes for the Poor: Low Income Tenants Can Own Their Own Apartments,* 1983; "Rebuilding Home, Tenants Take a New Lease on City Life," *City Limits,* April 1984; Matthew L. Wald, "Saving Aging Housing: A Costly City Takeover," *The New York Times,* November 27, 1983.

Chapter 6. The Public's Health

1. David Mechanic, *Future Issues in Health Care: Social Policy and the Rationing of Medical Services,* New York, Free Press, 1979, p. 7.

2. Vicente Navarro, *Medicine under Capitalism,* New York, Prodist, 1979, and *Health and Medical Care in the United States: A Critical Analysis,* Farmingdale, N. J., Baywood, 1977; and Victor W. Sidel and Ruth Sidel, eds., *Reforming Medicine,* New York, Pantheon, 1984.

3. Rashi Fein in Charles E. Lewis, Rashi Fein, and David Mechanic, *A Right to Health,* New York, John Wiley and Sons, 1976.

4. Karen Davis, "Reducing the Federal Deficit by Cutting Medicare and Medicaid: Impact on the Poor, Disabled, and Elderly," Testimony before the House of Representatives Budget Committee, February 24, 1983; and Robert Pear, "Many States Limit Medicaid Program," *The New York Times,* December 17, 1984.

5. Paul Starr, *The Social Transformation of American Medicine,* New York, Basic Books, 1982.

6. Ibid., p. 295.

7. Ibid., p. 310.

8. Quoted in David E. Rosenbaum, "One Thing Is Certain about Taxes: Disagreement," *The New York Times,* December 18, 1984.

9. Eli Ginzberg, *The Limits of Health Reform,* New York, Basic Books, 1977; and Peter A. Corning, *The Evolution of Medicare . . . From Idea to Law,* U.S. Department of Health, Education, and Welfare, Social Security Administration, Washington, D.C., 1969.

10. Starr, *Social Transformation,* p. 290.

11. Ibid., p. 327.

12. Irving J. Lewis and Cecil G. Sheps, *The Sick Citadel,* Cambridge, Mass., Oelgeschlager, Gunn & Hain, 1983.

13. Paul Atkinson, Robert Dingwall, and Ann Murcott, eds., *Prospects for*

the National Health, London, Croom Helm, 1979; Patrick Renshaw, "Keynesian Applications in the United States and Great Britain: Implications for the Welfare State," Paper delivered to a conference on the Future of the Welfare State, College of Urban and Public Affairs, University of Louisville, Louisville, Ken., November 29, 1984; Starr, *Social Transformation;* and Rosemary Stevens, "Comparisons in Health Care: Britain in Contrast to the United States," in David Mechanic, ed., *Handbook of Health, Health Care, and the Health Professions,* New York, Free Press, 1983.

14. Starr, *Social Transformation,* p. 367.

15. Mechanic, *Future Issues in Health Care,* p. 6.

16. Starr, *Social Transformation,* p. 375.

17. Arnold S. Relman, "The New Medical-Industrial Complex," *The New England Journal of Medicine,* vol. 303, 1980, p. 963.

18. Ibid.

19. Linda B. Miller, "For-Profit Hospitals: What about the Poor?" *The Washington Post National Weekly Edition,* February 11, 1985.

20. Stanley Wohl, *The Medical Industrial Complex,* New York, Harmony Books, 1984.

21. See Miller, "For-Profit Hospitals."

22. Alfred F. Connors, "Cost Battle Tramples Hospitals," *The Plain Dealer,* Cleveland, March 21, 1984; and Martin Tolchin, "As Companies Buy Hospitals, Treatment of Poor Is Debated," *The New York Times,* January 25, 1985.

23. Arnold S. Relman, "Who Will Pay for Medical Education in Our Teaching Hospitals?" *Science,* vol. 226, October 5, 1984; Paul Starr, "County Hospital, Public or Private?" Speech to the Consumers League of Cleveland, Ohio, October 19, 1984; Lester Thurow, "Learning to Say 'No,' " *The New England Journal of Medicine,* vol. 311, no. 24, December 13, 1984, and "Will the Urban Poor Get Hospital Care?" *Policy and Research Report,* vol. 13, no. 3, 1983, Washington, D.C., Urban Institute.

24. Pamela Doty, *Guided Change of the American Health System,* New York, Human Sciences Press, 1980.

25. Ibid., p. 24.

26. John K. Iglehart, "The Reagan Record on Health Care," *The New England Journal of Medicine,* vol. 308, no. 4, January 27, 1983.

27. Starr, *Social Transformation,* p. 444.

28. Stephen P. Strickland, *U.S. Health Care, What's Right and What's Wrong,* New York, Universe Books, 1972; and Robert E. Blendon and Drew E. Altman, "Public Attitudes about Health-Care Costs," *The New England Journal of Medicine,* vol. 211, no. 9, August 30, 1984.

29. Ginzberg, *Limits of Health Reform.*

30. Joel Brinkley, "In-Hospital Surgery to Be Reduced by Contracts to Save on Medicare," *The New York Times,* December 14, 1984.

31. Mechanic, *Future Issues in Health Care,* p. 5.

32. Starr, "County Hospital"; Victor R. Fuchs, *Who Shall Live?* New York, Basic Books, 1974, p. 68; Lewis and Sheps, *The Sick Citadel;* and Ginzberg, *Limits of Health Reform.*

33. Lewis, Fein, and Mechanic, *Right to Health*, p. 20.

34. Robert Pear, "15% of Americans Lacking Insurance," *The New York Times*, February 18, 1985.

35. Katherine Swartz, "Who Has Been without Health Insurance?" *Policy and Research Report*, vol. 14, no. 2, October 1984, Washington, D.C., Urban Institute.

36. Karen Davis, "Health Care's Soaring Costs," *The New York Times*, August 26, 1983.

37. Robert H. Brook, et al., "Does Free Care Improve Adults' Health?" *The New England Journal of Medicine*, vol. 309, no. 23, December 8, 1983.

38. Theodore R. Stent and Michael J. Taylor, "M.D. Distribution: Where the Doctors Aren't," Letter to *The New York Times*, January 7, 1984.

39. Lu Ann Aday, Ronald Andersen, and Gretchen V. Fleming, *Health Care in the United States: Equitable for Whom?*, Beverly Hills, Sage, 1980.

40. Donald O. Nutter, "Access to Care and the Evolution of Corporate, For-Profit Medicine," *The New England Journal of Medicine*, vol. 311, no. 14, October 4, 1984. Compare Pear, "Americans Lack Isurance."

41. Nutter, "Access to Care," p. 918.

42. Aday, Andersen, and Fleming, *Health Care in the U.S.*

43. Lisbeth Bamberger Schorr, C. Arden Miller, and Amy Fine, "The Social Policy Context for Families in the 1980s," Paper adapted from a presentation at the Harvard Medical School Conference on Stresses and Supports for Families in the 1980s, Cambridge, May 23, 1984, pp. 10, 11.

44. Fuchs, *Who Shall Live?* p. 148.

45. Henry J. Aaron and William B. Schwartz, "Severe Medical Choices," *The New York Times*, March 11, 1984.

46. Anne R. Somers, "Moderating the Rise in Health-Care Costs," *The New England Journal of Medicine*, vol. 307, no. 15, October 7, 1982; Blendon and Altman, "Public Attitudes."

47. Norman Macrae, "Health Care International," *The Economist*, April 28, 1984.

48. Lewis, Fein, and Mechanic, *Right to Health*.

49. Ibid., p. 250.

50. Fuchs, *Who Shall Live?*

51. Lewis, Fein, and Mechanic, *Right to Health*, pp. 75, 250.

52. Ibid.

53. Anne E. Crowley, "Summary Statistics on Graduate Medical Education in the United States," *Journal of the American Medical Association*, vol. 252, no. 12, September 28, 1984.

54. For an indication of the ideology that brought students into this specialty and the kind of practice that was intended, see John McPhee, "Heirs of General Practice," *The New Yorker*, July 23, 1984.

55. Roger A. Rosenblatt, et al., "Content of Family Practice: Current Status and Future Trends," *Journal of Family Practice*, vol. 15, no. 4, October 1982.

56. Sidel and Sidel, *Reforming Medicine*.

57. Lewis, Fein, and Mechanic, *Right to Health,* pp. 110, 250; also Mechanic, *Future Issues in Health Care.*

58. Fitzhugh Mullan, in "The National Health Service Corps and Health Personnel Innovations: Beyond Poorhouse Medicine," in Sidel and Sidel, eds., *Reforming Medicine,* chap. 8, p. 198.

59. Lewis, Fein, and Mechanic, *Right to Health.*

60. Lisbeth Bamberger Schorr and Joseph T. English, "Background, Context, and Significant Issues in Neighborhood Health Center Programs," *Milbank Memorial Fund Quarterly,* vol. 46, 1968, pp. 289–96.

61. Lewis, Fein, and Mechanic, *Right to Health,* p. 206.

62. Starr, *Social Transformation,* p. 372.

63. Ibid.

64. Section 1801 of the Medicare legislation.

65. Respectively, Davis, "Health Care's Soaring Costs"; Melvin A. Glasser, "Reverse Side of a Curb on Hospital Costs," Letter to *The New York Times,* September 11, 1984. Report of a speech by Henry Aaron, "No Easy Answers for Rising Health Costs," *NASW News,* July 1984. Thurow, "Learning to Say 'No.' "

66. Mark C. Hornbrook, "Allocative Medicine: Efficiency, Disease Severity, and the Payment Mechanism," in S. E. Berki, ed., *Health Care Policy in America, The Annals of the American Academy of Political and Social Sciences,* vol. 468, July 1983, p. 29.

67. Karen Davis and Cathy Schoen, *Health and the War on Poverty: A Ten-Year Appraisal,* Washington, D.C., Brookings Institution, 1978, p. 92; and Davis, "Health Care's Soaring Costs."

68. Linda H. Aiken and Karl D. Bays, "The Medicare Debate: Round One," *The New England Journal of Medicine,* vol. 211, no. 18, November 1, 1984, p. 1196.

69. Lewis, Fein, and Mechanic, *Right to Health;* Davis, "Cutting Medicare and Medicaid."

70. John K. Iglehart, "Report on the Duke University Medical Center Private Sector Conference," *The New England Journal of Medicine,* vol. 307, no. 1, July 1, 1982.

71. Henry J. Aaron and William B. Schwartz, *The Painful Prescription: Rationing Hospital Care,* Washington, D.C., Brookings Institution, 1984.

72. Doty, *Guided Change,* p. 31.

73. Margaret A. McManus and Stephen M. Davidson, *Medicaid and Children: A Policy Analysis,* American Academy of Pediatrics, Evanston, Ill., November 1982.

74. David E. Rogers, Robert Blendon, and Thomas W. Moloney, "Who Needs Medicaid?" *The New England Journal of Medicine,* vol. 307, no. 1, July 1, 1982.

75. E. Richard Brown, "Medicare and Medicaid: Bandaids for the Old and Poor," in Sidel and Sidel, eds., *Reforming Medicine,* chap. 3.

76. Rogers, Blendon, and Moloney, "Who Needs Medicaid?"

77. Davis, "Cutting Medicare and Medicaid."

78. Lewis, Fein and Mechanic, *Right to Health,* p. 185.

79. Ibid., p. 187.

80. Ibid., p. 185, quoting Roger O. Egeberg, assistant secretary of the U.S. Department of Health, Education, and Welfare.

81. Iglehart, "Reagan Record on Health Care"; Howard Kurtz, "States Seen Leading Attack on Health Care Costs," *The Washington Post,* August 2, 1983; "Many States Seeking to Cut Medicaid Costs," *The New York Times,* October 14, 1984.

82. Davis, "Cutting Medicare and Medicaid."

83. Lewis, Fein, and Mechanic, *Right to Health,* p. 187.

84. McManus and Davidson, *Medicaid and Children;* see also E. Richard Brown, "Medicare and Medicaid," p. 64.

85. Lewis, Fein, and Mechanic, *Right to Health,* p. 186.

86. Rogers, Blendon, and Moloney, "Who Needs Medicaid?"; McManus and Davidson, *Medicaid and Children.*

87. Doty, *Guided Change.*

88. U.S. Department of Health, Education, and Welfare, cited in ibid., p. 74.

89. Karen Davis, quoted in Iglehart, "Duke University Conference," p. 452.

90. Lawrence D. Brown, *Politics and Health Care Organization: HMOs as Federal Policy,* Washington, D.C., Brookings Institution, 1983; and Doty, *Guided Change.*

91. Doty, *Guided Change,* pp. 35–36.

92. John K. Iglehart, "Duke University Conference."

93. Milt Freudenheim, "Surge of Prepaid Health Plans," *The New York Times,* December 15, 1984.

94. Fuchs, *Who Shall Live?;* Lewis, Fein, and Mechanic, *Right to Health;* see also Nicole Lurie, et al., "Termination from Medi-Cal: Does It Affect Health?," *The New England Journal of Medicine,* vol. 311, no. 7, August 16, 1984.

95. Brown, *Politics and Health Care Organizations;* Mechanic, *Future Issues in Health Care,* p. 135.

96. Quoted in Doty, *Guided Change,* p. 85.

97. Freudenheim, "Surge of Prepaid Health Plans," and "HMO Growth Displays Vigor," *The New York Times,* April 16, 1985.

98. Doty, *Guided Change,* p. 103.

99. See Iglehart, "Reagan Record on Health Care."

100. Robert Lindsey, "Cost Rise and Corruption Charges Snag Model Health Care Program," *The New York Times,* January 6, 1984.

101. "Welfare HMOs—For Whose Benefit?" *The Plain Dealer,* Cleveland, December 1–3, 1985.

102. Robert Lindsey, "California Sees Innovations Cutting Medical Costs," *The New York Times,* November 20, 1983.

103. Starr, "County Hospital."

104. Lewis, Fein, and Mechanic, *Right to Health,* pp. 244–45.

105. Rashi Fein in ibid; see also Doty, *Guided Change.*

106. Thurow, "Learning to Say 'No,' " p. 1571.

107. Starr, *Social Transformation;* Brown, *Politics and Health Care Organizations;* Jack A. Meyer, American Enterprise Institute, quoted in Robert Pear, "Health Care Regulation: Bane, Balm, Accident?" *The New York Times,* January 15, 1985.

108. Mechanic, *Future Issues in Health Care,* p. 8.

109. Robert Pear, "Means Test for Medicare: Linking Benefits to an Elderly Person's Income," *The New York Times,* February 20, 1984.

110. Victor R. Fuchs, "The 'Rationing' of Medical Care," *The New England Journal of Medicine,* vol. 311, no. 23, December 13, 1984, p. 1573.

111. Aaron and Schwartz, *The Painful Prescription.*

112. Norman G. Levinsky, "The Doctor's Master," *The New England Journal of Medicine,* vol. 311, no. 24, December 13, 1984.

113. Sidel and Sidel, eds., *Reforming Medicine,* pp. 270–271.

114. Iglehart, "Duke University Conference," p. 68.

115. Doty, *Guided Change.*

116. Brown, *Politics and Health Care Organizations,* p. 532.

117. Starr, *Social Transformation,* p. 377.

118. Thomas McKeown, "Determinants of Health," in Philip R. Lee, Nancy Brown, and Ida Reed, eds., *The Nation's Health,* San Francisco, Boyd & Fraser, 1981.

119. For example, see Ginzberg, *Limits of Health Reform.*

120. Quoted in Lindsey, "Cost Rise and Corruption Charges."

121. Thurow, "Learning to Say 'No.' "

122. Blendon and Altman, "Public Attitudes," p. 614.

123. Ibid., p. 615.

124. Atkinson, Dingwall, and Murcott, eds., *Prospects for the National Health,* p. 21.

125. Starr, *Social Transformation,* p. 445.

126. Duncan Neuhauser and Florence A. Wilson, *Health Services in the United States,* Cambridge, Mass., Ballinger, 1982. See Starr, *Social Transformation,* p. 446.

127. *American Medical News,* vol. 27, no. 45, December 17, 1984, p. 19.

128. Monroe Lerner, *Health Programs in the United States, 1900–1960,* Chicago, University of Chicago Press, 1963, p. 224; and *Health U.S. 1982,* U.S. Department of Health and Human Services, Health Care Financing Administration, Washington, D.C., 1983, p. 114.

129. Swartz, "Without Health Insurance"; Pear, "Americans Lacking Insurance."

130. EPSDT *Does It Spell Health Care for Poor Children?* Children's Defense Fund of Washington Research Project, Washington, D.C., 1977.

131. Rosemary Stevens, "Comparison in Health Care."

132. Jack A. Meyer, quoted in Pear, "Health Care Regulation."

133. Stevens, "Comparisons in Health Care."

134. National Association for Public Health Policy, *A National Health Program for the United States*, South Burlington, Vt., 1985.

135. Nicky Hart, *Health and Inequality*, Department of Sociology, University of Essex (Eng.), March 1978.

Chapter 7. Education for Community

1. Theodore Lidz, *The Family and Human Adaptation*, New York, International Universities Press, 1963.

2. John A. Clausen, ed., *Socialization and Society*, Boston, Brown, 1968.

3. James P. Comer, *School Power*, New York, Free Press, 1980.

4. Arval A. Morris, *The Constitution and American Education*, 2d ed., St. Paul: West, 1980.

5. Saul K. Padover, ed., *Thomas Jefferson on Democracy*, New York, Appleton-Century-Crofts, 1946, pp. 89–90.

6. National Commission on Excellence in Education, *A Nation at Risk: The Imperative for Educational Reform*, Washington, D.C.: U.S. Department of Education, 1983.

7. Richard M. Jones, *Fantasy and Feeling in Education*, New York, Harper and Row, 1970.

8. H. Dean Evans, "We Must Begin Educational Reform 'Every Place at Once,' " *Phi Delta Kappan*, November 1983.

9. Fred L. Pincus, "From Equity to Excellence: The Rebirth of Educational Conservatism," *Social Policy*, Winter 1984.

10. M. Harvey Brenner, *Mental Illness and the Economy*, Cambridge, Harvard University Press, 1973.

11. James P. Comer, *School Power*, New York, Free Press, 1980.

12. Valerie Personick, "The Outlook for Industry Output and Employment through 1990," *Monthly Labor Review*, August 1981.

13. R. Freeman Butts and Lawrence A. Cremin, *A History of Education in American Culture*, New York, Holt, 1953.

14. Edgar Z. Friedenberg, "An Ideology of School Withdrawal," in D. Schreiber, ed., *Profile of the School Dropout*, New York, Random House, 1968.

15. Albert J. Solnit and Sally A. Provence, eds. *Modern Perspectives in Child Development*, New York, International Universities Press, 1963.

16. Safe School Study Report to Congress, vol. 1, *Violent Schools—Safe Schools*. Washington, D.C., U.S. Department of Health, Education and Welfare, National Institute of Education, January 1978.

17. James P. Comer, "Child Development and Social Change: Some Points of Controversy," *The Journal of Negro Education*, vol. 40, no. 3, Summer 1971.

18. David Blose and Caliver Ambrose, "Statistics of the Education of Negroes, 1929–30; 1931–32." U.S. Department of Interior, Office of Education, Bulletin no. 13, Washington, D.C., 1936, p. 16.

19. Commission on Excellence in Education. *A Nation at Risk;* Ian

McNett, *Charting a Course: A Guide to the Excellence Movement in Education*, Washington, D.C., Council for Basic Education, 1984; "Making the Grade," Report of the Twentieth Century Task Force on Federal Elementary and Secondary Education Policy, New York: Twentieth Century Fund, 1983.

20. Husen Torsten, "Are Standards in U.S. Schools Really Lagging Behind Those in Other Countries?" *Phi Delta Kappan*, March, 1983.

21. New World Foundation, *Choosing Equality: The Case for Democratic Schooling*, New York, 1985, p. 13.

22. Linda Darling-Hammond, *Beyond the Commission Reports: The Coming Crisis in Teaching*. California: Rand Corporation, July 1984.

23. New World Foundation, *Choosing Equality*, p. 14.

24. Michael Rutter, et al., *Fifteen Thousand Hours*, Cambridge, Harvard University Press, 1979.

25. "Action for Excellence: A Comprehensive Plan to Improve Our Nation's Schools," Report of the Task Force on Education for Economic Growth, Denver, Education Commission of the States, 1983; "America's Competitive Challenge: The Need for a National Response," Report of the Task Force of the Business-Higher Education Forum, Washington, D.C., Business-Higher Education Forum, 1983.

26. Glen E. Robinson, *Merit Pay for Teachers*, Arlington, Educational Research Service, 1979.

27. Arthur D. Efland, "Excellence in Education: The Role of the Arts," *Theory into Practice*, Autumn 1984.

28. Theodore R. Sizer, *Horace's Compromise: The Dilemma of the American High School*, Boston, Houghton Mifflin, 1984.

29. J. E. Brophy, "Stability of Teacher Effectiveness," *American Educational Research Journal*, vol. 10, 1973; "California School Effectiveness Study, 1974–75," Sacramento, State of California Department of Education, 1977.

30. James P. Comer, "Teachers' Merit Pay," *The New York Times*, Op Ed, July 1, 1983.

31. John I. Goodlad, *A Place Called School: Prospects for the Future*, New York, McGraw-Hill, 1983.

32. James P. Comer, *School Power*, New York, Free Press, 1980.

33. Jennifer L. Hochschild, *The New American Dilemma: Liberal Democracy and School Desegregation*, New Haven, Yale University Press, 1984.

34. Ronald Edmonds, "Effective Schools for the Urban Poor," *Educational Leadership*, October, 1979.

35. Westinghouse Learning Corporation, *The Impact of Head Start*, Springfield, Va., Clearinghouse for Federal Scientific and Technical Information, 1969; James Coleman, *Equality of Educational Opportunity*, Washington, D.C., Government Printing Office, 1966.

36. David Weikart, *Changed Lives*, Ypsilanti, Mich., High/Scope Press, 1984; Edward F. Zigler, *Project Head Start: A Legacy of the War on Poverty*, New York, Free Press, 1979.

37. LaMar P. Miller and Edmund W. Gordon, *Equality of Educational Opportunity*, New York, AMS Press, 1974.

38. James P. Comer, "Empowering Black Children's Educational Environments," in H. P. McAdoo and J. L. McAdoo, eds., *Black Children: Social, Educational and Parental Environments*, Beverly Hills, Sage, 1985.

Chapter 8. Policies for Decent People

1. "Smaller Slices of the Pie: The Growing Economic Vulnerability of Poor and Moderate Income Americans," Center on Budget and Policy Priorities, Washington, D.C., November 1985.

2. David Betson, David Greenberg, and Richard Kasten, "A Simulation Analysis of the Economic Efficiency and the Distributional Effects of Alternative Program Structures: The Negative Income Tax vs. the Credit Income Tax," in Irwin Garfinkel, ed., *Income-Tested Transfer Programs: The Case For and Against*, New York, Academic Press, 1982.

3. Daniel Patrick Moynihan, The Godkin Lectures, Harvard University, April 8–9, 1985.

4. However, I have struggled with this one elsewhere. See Alvin L. Schorr, ". . . *Thy Father and Thy Mother* . . .": *A Second Look at Filial Responsibility and Family Policy*, U.S. Social Security Administration, Office of Research and Statistics, Washington, D.C., Government Printing Office, 1980.

5. For example, see the proceedings of the conference on "Income Transfer Policies and the Economic Well-Being of the Poor," May 14–18, 1984, in the *Journal of Social Policy* (England), July 1985.

6. William Graebner, *A History of Retirement: The Meaning and Function of an American Institution, 1885–1978*, New Haven, Yale University Press, 1980.

Index